An Assessment of Quality in Graduate Education

A Study for

Commission on Plans and Objectives for Higher Education
American Council on Education

AN ASSESSMENT
OF QUALITY
IN GRADUATE EDUCATION

Allan M. Cartter

Vice-President, American Council on Education

American Council on Education · Washington, D.C.

© 1966 by the American Council on Education
1785 Massachusetts Avenue, N.W., Washington, D.C. 20036

Second impression, June 1966

Library of Congress Catalog Card No. 66-23292

Printed in the United States of America

Commission on Plans and Objectives for Higher Education

MEMBERSHIP 1964–66

Term ending December 31, 1964

Bernard Berelson, Vice-President, The Population Council

Robert D. Calkins, President, The Brookings Institution

Dale R. Corson, Provost, Cornell University

Winfred L. Godwin, Director, Southern Regional Education Board

Theodore M. Hesburgh, C.S.C., President, University of Notre Dame

Gordon N. Ray, President, John Simon Guggenheim Memorial Foundation

Term ending December 31, 1965

Victor L. Butterfield, President, Wesleyan University

†William C. Fels, President, Bennington College

L. D. Haskew, Vice-Chancellor, University of Texas

James W. Maucker, President, State College of Iowa (ex officio 1965–66)

T. R. McConnell, Chairman, Study for Higher Education, University of California, Berkeley

O. Meredith Wilson, President, University of Minnesota; *Chairman, 1963–65*

Term ending December 31, 1966

Sanford S. Atwood, President, Emory University

Elbert K. Fretwell, Jr., Dean of Academic Development, The City University of New York

Sterling M. McMurrin, Provost, University of Utah

Claus A. Moser, Director, Unit for Economic and Statistical Studies on Higher Education, The London School of Economics and Political Science

John F. Reed, President, Fort Lewis College

Frederick Rudolph, Professor of History, Williams College

Stephen J. Wright, President, Fisk University (ex officio 1965–66)

Term ending December 31, 1967

James I. Armstrong, President, Middlebury College

Gordon W. Blackwell, President, Furman University

Howard R. Bowen, President, University of Iowa; *Chairman, 1966–67*

Gerard J. Campbell, S.J., President, Georgetown University

Charles C. Cole, Jr., Dean of the College, Lafayette College

John K. Folger, Director, Commission on Human Resources and Advanced Education

Term ending December 31, 1968

James E. Allen, Jr., Commissioner of Education, New York State

Paul F. Sharp, President, Drake University

John S. Toll, President, State University of New York at Stony Brook

John C. Weaver, Vice-President, The Ohio State University; President-elect, University of Missouri

Board of Directors ex officio members

Robert K. Carr, President, Oberlin College (1964–66)

Oscar Edinger, Jr., President, Mount San Antonio College (1964–65)

W. Clarke Wescoe, Chancellor, University of Kansas (1964–65)

†Deceased.

Foreword

EXCELLENCE, by definition, is a state only the few rather than the many can attain. Striving for academic excellence, however, is a worthy ideal for colleges and universities, and it can be reasonably argued that every educational institution should meet minimum qualitative standards, and particularly if it offers graduate work. A present problem is the need for a better general understanding of what quality signifies. Allan Cartter's book *An Assessment of Quality in Graduate Education* is intended to further such an understanding.

Before this study was begun in the spring of 1964, serious deliberation was given to the question of American Council on Education sponsorship of an evaluation of selected graduate programs of major universities that comprise an important segment of the Council's membership. There was never any question about the need for doing in a systematic and objective way what necessarily goes on continually in any event, though usually in a piecemeal and more impressionistic way. Our Commission on Plans and Objectives for Higher Education, and other leading educators consulted, concluded that a thoroughgoing study should be made and that the Council's aegis was a suitable one.

As the text mentions, this inquiry has three broad purposes: (1) to bring up to date the information yielded by earlier studies; (2) to widen and improve the assessment of certain graduate programs in all major universities in the United States; and (3) to examine critically the available techniques of evaluation.

Although this study is the most comprehensive ever undertaken, it is neither the first of its kind nor the first to be issued by the American Council on Education. Raymond Hughes made the first published appraisal in 1924, and then another, sponsored by the Council, in 1934. A third evaluation was made by Hayward Keniston in 1957, limited to major institutions with membership in the A.A.U.

The present survey is in some respects comparable to the earlier studies, and it is therefore interesting to note variations in departmental repute at different time intervals covering a period of more than forty years. Dr. Cartter's investigation differs from the others, however, in some important respects. It includes a larger number of institutions, respondents, and fields. Nearly 900 department chairmen, 1,700 outstanding senior scholars and scientists, and 1,400 younger academicians made the assessments; they represent a wide geographic distribution. Their judgments are subjected to a more involved analysis, and their opinions are checked against other factors more extensively, than was the case in previous inquiries.

Several respondents, as the author points out, expressed initial objections to a study of this kind. One thought it would tend to "fix a pecking order" among graduate departments and schools. Others felt that the inclusion of respondents from over a hundred institutions would "water down" the results. I believe that Dr. Cartter has countered these criticisms forthrightly and successfully. This volume does not claim to be more than it is—a survey and analysis of *informed* opinion. To any who would discount the value of such an approach to the assessment of quality in graduate education, it should be added that in the final analysis the national reputation of a department or an institution is nothing more than an aggregation of individual opinions.

Library holdings, faculty publications and honors, student scores on standardized tests, per-capita expenditures, and other desiderata (Dr. Cartter also takes such factors into account) are sometimes regarded as more valid and reliable bases of program appraisal. None of these items, however, has any more significance than informed opinion attaches to it. Lacking agreed-upon units for precise measurement, we can at present only approximate an elusive entity through a rank ordering of cumulative judgments.

I predict that Allan Cartter's book will provoke a great deal of comment and discussion. The findings themselves will please some and displease others. In any such discussions it will be recognized, I trust, that this inquiry was not undertaken either to soothe or disturb academic egos. This inquiry was not intended merely to supply a conversation piece in college and university circles but, rather, to be an aid to those departments and institutions, not to mention other educational agencies, which are seriously concerned about the improvement of graduate education. To effect improvement, a first step is to appraise existing strengths and weaknesses. *An Assessment of Quality in Graduate Education* should be a very useful book for all who engage in this complex and vital endeavor.

LOGAN WILSON, *President*
American Council on Education

Preface

SHORTLY AFTER the formation of the Commission on Plans and Objectives for Higher Education, and the author's appointment as its first director in 1963, it was decided that rather than undertake an over-all review of higher education following the pattern of several earlier national commissions we would attempt to study in depth selected critical areas. This is the first book-length study, reflecting the concentration of the Commission's attention on graduate education during 1964 and 1965.

Thirty-two years ago the American Council on Education published the report of its Committee on Graduate Education, a rating of graduate schools in the United States undertaken by President Raymond Hughes of Iowa State College. The academic scene has altered greatly since then. In the 1930's there were only 45 universities which granted as many as ten Ph.D.'s a year, as contrasted with 106 who met this criterion for inclusion in the present study. In 1934 only 2,800 doctorates were awarded in the United States; today the figure is 16,000—and rising rapidly. In the 1930's Federal aid to graduate education was for all practical purposes nonexistent; in fiscal year 1967 the Federal budget allots $329 million in financial support for graduate students alone. By whatever measuring rod one chooses, the expansion of graduate education has been and continues to be dramatic, matched only by the rapidly expanding demand for teachers, researchers, and qualified specialists in private industry, government, and the professions who have attained highest educational levels. If, as Whitehead once noted, the future indeed lies with the nation which values and fosters education at the highest creative levels, this is reason enough for a study attempting to assess the strengths of present-day American graduate schools.

A generation after Hughes' A.C.E. report, the Council has now undertaken a second, and more detailed, study. It was initiated in the spring of 1964 with financial support from the National Science Foundation, the National Institutes of Health, and the U.S. Office of Education. As so frequently happens with major research studies, some costs were incurred in the initial pre-grant development of the project, and the completion of this book ran far beyond the grant period. We are indebted to several foundations for general support grants which provide sufficient flexibility to the Council that such projects can continue uninterrupted. To each of these supporting agencies, public and private, both for their support and their patience, the author makes grateful acknowledgment.

One of the pleasantest aspects of the study was the occasional meetings of the special advisory committee appointed for the survey. The members—among the busiest members of the academic community—gave unbegrudgingly of their time. More importantly, their advice and counsel in the early design stages of the study, their editorial suggestions near the end, and their enthusiastic support throughout the two years made this an enjoyable and rewarding venture for the author. Members of the Commission were also most helpful in discussions of the project at various stages, and I particularly value the close and warm relationship I was fortunate to have with O. Meredith Wilson, president of the University of Minnesota and chairman of the Commission (1963–65). Service on Council commissions is a labor of love, and the educational community can be grateful for these contributions by many of the nation's distinguished educators.

I would also like to express appreciation for the cooperation of all the graduate deans in the selection of faculty participants, and to acknowledge my indebtedness to the several thousand scholars who took time to complete the questionnaire. In a very literal sense, this is their book, for it is their judgments which are here reported.

A study such as this requires many man months of painstaking conscientious work on the minutiae of questionnaire details. I was fortunate to have a worthy and tireless lieutenant, Charles J. Andersen, to whom I could delegate much of the data analysis. With technical assistance from Richard A. Bain, he labored uncomplainingly from the inception of the study through the last page proof. At various stages of the project others have also made valuable contributions—Donald A. Sears on the special analysis of English, Robert Farrell and Penelope West on some of the tabular materials, and editorial assistance by Jane Graham and Olive Mills. My colleague, Alexander W. Astin, was also kind enough to contribute a brief statistical appendix. Others among the A.C.E. staff contributed in unsung ways, most particularly my secretary, Maybelle Frashure. As both study director and taskmaster, however, I must take responsibility for any deficiencies in the study.

In the initial planning of this project, the Advisory Committee agreed that it should be repeated within five years to avoid "fixing" reputations when in fact the academic scene is changing constantly. I believe such follow-up surveys can be done in much simpler and speedier fashion than the present study. We felt our way slowly in the analysis accompanying the tables by academic field, making several reruns of the data for new-found purposes; the ratings themselves could have been published within nine months of the original questionnaire mailing. We went to considerable pains to weigh our findings against those provided by other sorts of indices reflecting quality to determine insofar as possible the validity of such evaluation procedures. Another study could omit these efforts. I now believe—and I hope that the open-minded reader will also find sufficient evidence to convince him—that the type of assessment reported in this volume is both valuable and as fair as a single index can be. The educational community has been accused of fostering "a conspiracy of silence" concerning qualitative aspects of higher education; perhaps this study and its possible successors will help to belie that view.

ALLAN M. CARTTER

April 11, 1966

Contents

List of Tables

List of Figures

I · An Overview

THE COMMISSION ON PLANS and Objectives for Higher Education was created in 1963 by the American Council on Education as a continuing body to study important long-range problems facing the nation's colleges and universities and, where appropriate, to make policy recommendations for the consideration of the educational leadership. It is not surprising that one of the first problems studied dealt with the adequacy of the future supply of college teachers. Two questions were posed: first, what has happened, and is likely to happen, to the quality of the teacher supply in light of the present and projected expansion of higher education; and, second, what are the present strengths and weaknesses of our graduate schools in providing well-trained scholars for both teaching and research? [1] This book is a report on the basic studies undertaken in the attempt to answer the second of these questions. The perspective for this report may be made clearer, however, by a brief review of the answers we have found to the first question, for they may be important in interpreting the measures of quality in graduate education.

The supply of college teachers

The last decade has seen a steady improvement in the level of academic salaries, both absolute and relative to other professions. Rising relative salaries are usually an indication of a continuing shortage in qualified manpower, and most observers have interpreted this phenomenon as evidence of the inadequacy of doctoral output. It has commonly been believed that the quality of present college and university faculties, as measured by formal degree preparation for scholarly careers, has deteriorated steadily over the last decade. This view of the recent past has led many educators to the conviction that our graduate schools are un-

likely in the future to turn out a sufficient number of persons trained at the highest level to maintain the quality of existing college faculties and to meet the rapid expansion in total enrollments expected over the coming decade.[2]

Recent studies by the Commission and by the United States Office of Education now indicate that our suppositions about trends over the last decade were incorrect. As summarized in Table 1, the percentage of college and university faculty who possess the doctorate has risen since the early 1950's, and has risen for each category of institution. Such an improvement, when most educational observers believed that the reverse was occurring, raises serious questions about the validity of the many dire predictions for the coming decade.

Errors in judging the recent past have arisen from two sources: (1) insufficient data have been available to assess properly the year-by-year changes in the supply and demand for college faculty, and (2) models projecting future needs have commonly been constructed on assumptions that proved to be in error. The model used by the National Education Association [3] and by the Office of

---

[1] A third question might logically have been posed: What is the nation's supply of intellectual talent, and how well does the educational system work in advancing those with intellectual promise into appropriate educational and career paths? The American Council on Education is one of four sponsoring agencies for the newly formed Commission on Human Resources and Advanced Education, chaired by Dael Wolfle and directed by John Folger. Many of the relevant problems of educational and occupational choice will be dealt with by this commission over the next several years.

[2] For a sample of views over the last ten years by knowledgeable educators, see: President's Committee on Education Beyond the High School, *Second Report to the President* (Washington: Government Printing Office, 1957), p. 30; Committee of Fifteen, *The Graduate School Today and Tomorrow: Reflections for the Profession's Consideration* (New York: Fund for the Advancement of Education, December 1955), p. 7; Earl J. McGrath, *The Graduate School and the Decline of Liberal Education*, A Publication of the Institute of Higher Education (New York: Teachers College Press, Columbia University, 1959), pp. 26–27; *Teachers for Tomorrow* (New York: Fund for the Advancement of Education, 1955), p. 25; Oliver C. Carmichael, *Graduate Education: A Critique and a Program* (New York: Harper & Bros., 1961), pp. 132–33; *The Flight from Teaching* (New York: Carnegie Foundation for the Advancement of Teaching, 1964), p. 4.

About the only contrary view, now proved more correct, to the surprise of his critics, was that of Bernard Berelson in *Graduate Education in the United States* (New York: McGraw-Hill Book Co., 1960), pp. 79–80.

[3] Developed by Ray C. Maul in *Teacher Supply and Demand in Universities, Colleges, and Junior Colleges, 1957–58 and 1958–59*, NEA Research Report 1959-R10 (Washington: National Education Association, 1959), pp. 50–54. The model was used again in the next biennial report, 1961-R12, but omitted from the two most recent reports in the series.

Education [4] has been built on several crucial assumptions. One concerns the predicted future student-staff ratio, by means of which the demand for faculty to staff the expansion in total enrollment is derived; another concerns the assumed replacement rate for college teachers dying, retiring, and leaving teaching for other occupations. Judging by the experience of the last decade, the current Office of Education model appears to overstate the expansion demand for new faculty by about 10 percent and overstates the net replacement demand for doctorates by a factor of three.[5] Thus the conclusion that American higher education will experience a "deficit" of some 120,000 Ph.D.'s by 1973–74 turns out to be a most dubious one; a more appropriate conclusion, in view of what we now know about the recent past, is that we will be able to raise the percentage of college faculty with the

---

[4] *Projections of Educational Statistics to 1973–74*, OE-10030 (1964), p. 26. This model was also incorporated in memoranda on "Estimates of Demand for and Supply of Higher Education Staff," by Higher Education Personnel Staff, Office of Education, Oct. 26, 1964, and Jan. 4, 1965.

[5] The N.E.A. assumption on student-staff ratios has been approximately correct for the 1958–59—1963–64 period but the 6 percent faculty replacement rate has proved much too high for teachers with the doctorate.

doctorate by another few points over the coming decade.[6]

It is frequently overlooked that the largest number of new faculty required each year is to meet the expansion of enrollment; thus the number of new teachers required varies directly with the absolute size of the annual increment in enrollment. The largest increments are likely to be in the years 1964–68, after which time total enrollment is expected to grow at a decreasing rate. Therefore, after 1968 the "expansion demand" for new faculty will shrink again, while there will be a steadily increasing number of doctoral degrees awarded each successive year. If the projections made by the Commission staff are approximately correct (these enrollment and degree projections differ only slightly from the estimates of the Office of Education and the National Science Foundation), then during the decade of the 1970's the nation can choose among a marked further improvement in the quality of teaching staff, a marked decline in the percentage of new Ph.D.'s entering teaching,

---

[6] For a detailed analysis of faculty growth models and a critique of past projections, see Allan M. Cartter, "A New Look at the Supply of College Teachers," *Educational Record*, Summer 1965, pp. 267–77, and "The Supply and Demand of College Teachers," *Proceedings*, American Statistical Association, September 1965, pp. 70–80.

TABLE 1: *Distribution of Faculty by Highest Degree, Private and Public Colleges and Universities,*[a] *1950–51—1962–63*

TYPE OF INSTITUTION	NUMBER	YEAR	PERCENTAGE DISTRIBUTION			
			Doctor's	Master's	Bachelor's	Professional
COLLEGES						
Private......	438	1962–63	35.4	47.0	12.0	5.6
		1958–59	33.7	46.9	13.0	6.4
		1954–55	32.5	47.5	14.8	5.2
		1950–51	29.7	49.0	19.2	2.1
Public.......	196	1962–63	33.5	52.5	9.3	4.7
		1958–59	32.0	53.4	10.8	3.8
		1954–55	30.1	58.4	9.9	1.6
		1950–51	23.2	63.7	12.4	0.7
Total........	634	1962–63	34.5	49.4	10.9	5.2
		1958–59	33.0	49.6	12.1	5.3
		1954–55	31.6	51.6	13.0	3.8
		1950–51	27.3	54.4	16.7	1.6
UNIVERSITIES						
Private......	67	1962–63	43.8	26.8	12.0	17.4
		1958–59	40.7	28.4	14.1	16.8
		1954–55	40.0	36.8	14.6	8.6
		1950–51	37.3	37.7	20.5	4.5
Public.......	80	1962–63	44.9	31.9	10.0	13.2
		1958–59	41.7	34.8	13.0	10.5
		1954–55	40.7	38.7	13.5	7.1
		1950–51	36.0	43.5	17.3	3.2
Total........	147	1962–63	44.5	29.9	10.8	14.8
		1958–59	41.3	32.4	13.4	12.9
		1954–55	40.4	37.9	13.9	7.8
		1950–51	36.6	41.0	18.7	3.7

[a] Excluding faculty in schools of medicine, dentistry, and veterinary medicine.

Source: Computed from data in *American Universities and Colleges* (Washington: American Council on Education, 1952, 1956, 1960, 1964).

or a decrease in the rate of expansion of graduate education. Each of these alternatives has implications for the future of the quality of education, the level of academic salaries, and the level of Federal support of graduate education. The more optimistic view of the future also raises important questions of public policy about the optimum number and distribution of major centers of graduate education. Just as each college or university faces the perennial problem of whether to strengthen weak academic areas or to build on present strengths, so for the educational system as a whole decisions of a similar nature are constantly arising which must be settled at the state, regional, or national level. Studies by the Commission on the adequacy of supply of future college teachers differ sharply from the view that we are facing a disastrous national shortage; in this light, the study in succeeding chapters of present strengths and weaknesses of graduate programs may contribute to better-informed decisions affecting the welfare of higher education.

Why try to assess quality?

The assessment of quality is a difficult task at all levels of education; it is perhaps both simpler and more complex at the level of the graduate school. It is simpler in that one can more easily assess the scholarly attributes of the most distinguished members of the academic community. It is more difficult in that the higher one goes on the ladder of formal learning, the more education becomes self-education and the more factors other than the quality of the faculty assume importance. A teacher is a true leader to the very young, an instructor to the youthful, a professor to the emerging adult, but a guide and fellow searcher after knowledge to the graduate student.

In the spring of 1964 the task of attempting to assess the quality of graduate programs in the arts and sciences was undertaken by the American Council on Education's Commission on Plans and Objectives for Higher Education. The task set for the study was threefold: (1) to bring earlier qualitative studies of graduate education up to date; (2) to widen the assessment to include all major universities in the United States, on the assumption that major expansion will not come from the 10–15 traditionally distinguished universities; and (3) to learn as much as possible about the vagaries and pitfalls of subjective assessments in the interest of improving such measurements for the future.

A number of reasons can be advanced for undertaking such a study. The diversity of the American system of higher education has properly been regarded by both the professional educator and the layman as a great source of strength, since it permits flexibility and adaptability and encourages experimentation and competing solutions to common problems. Yet diversity also poses problems. It has

frequently been noted that the poorest graduates of some selective colleges are better educated than the best students at some mediocre institutions. The typical baccalaureate winner at a few of the more prestigious liberal arts colleges is superior to the master's degree holder of some of the poorer universities. At the level of the Ph.D., great diversity in quality is known to exist among the approximately two hundred institutions granting this degree today.

Diversity can be a costly luxury if it is accompanied by ignorance. Our present system works fairly well because most students, parents, and prospective employers *know* that a bachelor's degree from Harvard, Stanford, Swarthmore, or Reed is ordinarily a better indication of ability and accomplishment than a bachelor's degree from Melrose A & M or Siwash College. Even if no formal studies were ever undertaken, there is always a grapevine at work to supply impressionistic evaluations. However, evaluation by rumor and word of mouth is far from satisfactory, particularly in advanced training for scholarship and the professions. In stating the case for studies of quality at the undergraduate level, David Riesman has argued:

> . . . the quality of a school changes faster than its clientele recognizes; and colleges that have developed a novel or more demanding program cannot get the students to match it, while other institutions that have decayed cannot keep away students who should no longer go there. While autos carry their advertising, so to speak, on their body shells, which speak as loudly as print or TV commercials, colleges can change inside their shells with hardly anyone's noticing. And the result can be tragic, not only for misled students, but for imaginative faculty and administrators who may not live long enough to be rewarded by the appearance of good students attracted by those changes.[7]

Just as consumer knowledge and honest advertising are requisite if a competitive economy is to work satisfactorily, so an improved knowledge of opportunities and of quality is desirable if a diverse educational system is to work effectively.

Evaluation of quality in education, at both the undergraduate and graduate levels, is important not only in determining the front-ranking institutions, but also in identifying lower-ranking colleges. Many prospective graduate students would not be suited to an education at Harvard, the Rockfeller Institute, or California Institute of Technology. Other institutions, in view of their educational offerings, level of work, and quality of students, would provide a happier and more productive experience. Universities, through their selection procedures, and students, through their natural proclivities, tend to sort themselves out into congenial environments. Anything that aids in this

[7] Riesman, *Constraint and Variety in American Education* (New York: Doubleday & Co., 1958), p. 5.

process—which is now accomplished rather haphazardly—may be useful in itself.

The assessment of quality in undergraduate colleges is a popular pastime today, as witnessed by the spate of books published in recent years for the general public, untold numbers of magazine articles and newspaper reports, and renewed interest in college "selector" services to help match students and colleges. Similar evaluations of education at the graduate level—although less publicized and less available to the general public—have been undertaken in the past and are being made today. Three major studies of quality in graduate education have been made during the last forty years, two by Raymond Hughes, in 1924 and 1934, and one by Hayward Keniston, in 1957. More recently, many agencies and organizations have been making their own evaluations. Most foundations continually make such assessments in an informal manner, and some (such as the Ford Foundation) that are engaged in major capital grants programs have developed formal and comprehensive procedures. The National Science Foundation, the National Institutes of Health, the Office of Education, and the National Aeronautics and Space Administration—to mention only the major Federal agencies supporting graduate education and research—all participate in evaluation studies of universities through the use of select panels, study teams, site visits, and the like.

In deciding to undertake an evaluation of quality in graduate education, the Commission took it as given that the public and its formal agencies will increasingly demand better information on graduate and professional education. It was known that the government agencies and private foundations engaged in making assessments frequently did so with limited information, and were basing major decisions on their findings. In the view of the Commission too much reliance was being placed upon earlier, and now outdated, studies, which had surveyed only a limited number of prestigious universities.

It was also felt that university presidents, deans, and department chairmen could benefit substantially from having such assessments made available periodically, even if the results were not always flattering. The last two purposes could have been served by confidential reports, but it was hoped that public discussion and criticism might be a means of improving future studies of quality.

The project was considered especially timely in view of the rapid expansion now occurring in graduate enrollments and in light of the impending marked increase in financial support for graduate education from governmental and private agencies. Since the current tendency in Federal aid is to increase the number of institutions which are strong centers of graduate education rather than to expand support for already outstanding institutions,

such an evaluation of present strengths may be viewed with greater objectivity. (At least one major university has spent considerable time recently trying to convince a Federal agency that it is *not* one of the top twenty universities in the country and thus is eligible for support as a "university of promise.")

Finally, the Commission felt that if an evaluation were to be made, it should be done as well as possible, it should be undertaken by an organization that is responsible to the institutions under review, and it should be subject to public criticism and correction if it should be in error.

Assessing quality

Quality is an elusive attribute, not easily subjected to measurement. No single index—be it size of endowment, number of books in the library, publication record of the faculty, level of faculty salaries, or numbers of Nobel laureates on the faculty, Guggenheim fellows, members of the National Academy of Sciences, National Merit scholars in the undergraduate college, or Woodrow Wilson fellows in the graduate school—nor any combination of measures is sufficient to estimate adequately the true worth of an educational institution. True, most of the universities esteemed as "distinguished" have rather more of each of the above than do institutions that are not held in as high regard by the academic community. But Berkeley has relatively little endowment, Cal. Tech. has an extremely small library by university standards, Michigan and M.I.T. have no Nobel laureates on their faculties, and Rice, Rochester, and Minnesota have relatively few Woodrow Wilson fellows. Michigan State leads in National Merit scholars for 1964–65, and the American Association of University Professors list of institutions which lead in average faculty compensation shows Harvard first and Parsons College second in 1965.

The factors mentioned above are often referred to as "objective" measures of quality. On reflection, however, it is evident that they are for the most part "subjective" measures once removed. Distinguished fellows, Nobel laureates, and National Academy members are selected by peer groups on the basis of subjective assessments, faculty salaries are determined by someone's subjective appraisal, and endowments are the result of philanthropic judgments. Number of volumes in the library, though more readily quantifiable, is a factor of little value in measuring institutional resources unless one can make a qualitative judgment about the adequacy of the holdings.

In an operational sense, quality *is* someone's subjective assessment, for there is no way of objectively measuring what is in essence an attribute of value.

If there is a major difference between the type of subjective evaluation of academic departments undertaken in this study and the indices of faculty honors (Nobel laureates, Guggenheim fellows, National Academy members), it is that the latter are based on outstanding individuals rather than on groups of individuals organized into departmental units. Faculty and student honors and awards are also qualitative judgments; therefore, summing such information does not create an "objective" measure, but another type of subjective measure once removed. Another limitation of using distinguished honors and awards as a basis for rating departments is that a faculty group of perhaps thirty or forty professors is judged on the basis of its several luminaries rather than on its total strength.

In chapter 5 comparisons are made between the subjective assessments provided by the more than four thousand scholars participating in the Commission's study and a number of other indices. It is concluded that the leading institutions could be equally well identified using either approach, for the two kinds of data corroborate each other. However, below the top 10–15 departments or institutions, the broad departmental assessment undertaken in the present study appears to provide a much fairer treatment for the good but not outstanding institutions. The distribution of Woodrow Wilson and NSF fellows, Guggenheim awards, Nobel Prize winners, and other such awards is heavily skewed in favor of a few institutions and tends to exaggerate differences in quality or effectiveness.

As noted above, three major subjective qualitative assessments of graduate education have been undertaken in the last forty years. In 1924 Raymond Hughes, then president of Miami University in Ohio, concerned about the guidance of Miami undergraduates, set out to devise a means of evaluating the quality of graduate instruction in 38 of the 65 universities then offering the Ph.D. He requested his faculty at Miami to draw up a list of distinguished national scholars in each of 20 fields of study and then sent questionnaires to each of these selected scholars. In 1925 the findings were incorporated into a report to the annual meeting of the Association of American Colleges, and this first national ranking of graduate schools was subsequently published.

Hughes' initial study stirred up considerable interest, and no little criticism; its results, reprinted in the first edition of *American Universities and Colleges,*[8] presumably had an impact on that student generation. A second study by Hughes, made in 1934 for a Committee on Graduate Education of the American Council on Education, classified graduate departments into two categories: adequate or distinguished.[9]

In 1957 a third major evaluation study was undertaken by Hayward Keniston at the Univer-

sity of Pennsylvania. Since its purpose was to determine Pennsylvania's position relative to similar senior universities, only 25 of the institutions belonging to the Association of American Universities were reviewed. Keniston, after consulting department chairmen at the 25 institutions, reported his findings in an appendix to a study of graduate education at the University of Pennsylvania.[10] These results, like those of the Hughes study a generation earlier, were widely read and debated.

Although the present study shares with the earlier studies the general limitation of being essentially subjective, it was designed to avoid some of their shortcomings. It elicited responses similar in nature to those asked for by Hughes and Keniston and thus partially duplicates their studies. But at the same time it was constructed to provide broader coverage of both respondents and institutions: over four thousand scholars at more than one hundred universities participated. The nature of the sample is discussed more fully in chapter 2.

Pains have been taken to ensure that the study reported in the succeeding chapters be as objective as an opinion study can be, and that it represent fairly the large and the small, the public and the private, the nationally recognized and the regionally oriented graduate schools. Also the study was designed to elicit more information about evaluation techniques than has previously been known, and the results obtained have been compared with other measures which reflect institutional quality.

Some common criticisms of subjective evaluations

An impressionistic survey of quality has both strengths and weaknesses. It may be useful to review at the outset the criticisms made of the Hughes and Keniston surveys (most of which had to do with doubts about the expertise and representativeness of the judges) and the efforts made in the 1964 study to avoid these shortcomings or to test the validity of these criticisms.

Hughes in 1924 used small panels of experts selected by his faculty at Miami University; Keniston used only department chairmen at 25 leading universities. Expert panels are a useful device provided the groups are large enough and sufficiently representative of regions, types of universities, and subject specialties within a particular field.

The panels for the Hughes studies, which ranged from 20 to 60 members, generally met these criteria. However, experience with the 1964 study has indicated that panels should be carefully balanced to provide broad experience and knowledge, and should be composed of at least 40–50 specialists. In 1924 the great majority of distinguished scholars in almost every field were both trained and employed in the Northeast. Strong biases in

[8] Published quadrennially since 1928 by the American Council on Education as a definitive guide to all accredited four-year colleges and universities.
[9] *Educational Record,* April 1934, pp. 192–234.

[10] Keniston, *Graduate Study in the Arts and Sciences at the University of Pennsylvania* (Philadelphia: University of Pennsylvania Press, 1959).

favor of region, alma mater, and current institution are evident in the 1964 ratings (these are discussed in chapter 4), and presumably these prejudices were reflected in the Hughes study.

Some critics of the Keniston study held that department chairmen are not the best judges of quality. Among the arguments they advanced were: (*a*) chairmen are frequently not the most distinguished scholars in their departments; (*b*) the average age of chairmen is considerably above that of their faculties, and thus a time lag may be built into the sample; and (*c*) chairmen tend to be traditionalists in hiring, overly favoring the few major universities that have turned out the largest number of distinguished Ph.D.'s in the past. The 1964 study included nearly nine hundred department chairmen (along with seventeen hundred distinguished senior scholars and fourteen hundred carefully selected junior scholars), and a comparison of the responses of these three subgroups partially—although not entirely—dispels these criticisms. The chairmen generally rated departments as the other scholars did, although there is some evidence that the chairmen are more likely to be traditionalists in that as a group they tended to rate the high-ranking departments slightly higher, and the low-ranking departments slightly lower, than did non-chairmen. Their average age, however, is nearly the same as that of the distinguished senior scholars, and their publications records are similar (at least in quantity) to those of the senior scholars. In short, if we had used *only* department chairmen as participants in the study, the over-all results would differ little from those reported in chapter 3.

To explore further the use of expert panels, we chose, with the advice of the appropriate professional associations, small panels of experts from four academic fields and asked them to rate the top departments in their fields. The ratings provided by these small panels differed somewhat from those of the main body of respondents, but a careful review suggests that the disparities are more the result of the small number of responses (12–15 on each panel) than of any positive difference in the pattern of judgments.

Critics of both the Hughes and Keniston studies questioned the representativeness of the judges in relation to geographical areas, institutions of own highest degree, specialties within a subject field, age and rank, size and eminence of present universities, and knowledge of the general academic scene. Each of these factors deserves a brief comment.

The Hughes judges tended to be concentrated geographically in the Northeast and Midwest simply because, in 1925, most of the distinguished universities were in those areas. Keniston was limited by his choice of the 25 universities to be surveyed. Table 2 gives a percentage distribution of invited participants by broad regional classification for the Keniston study and the 1964 A.C.E. Commission survey. The definition of universities used in the 1964 study (see chapter 2) tended to give somewhat greater weight to states or regions with small graduate programs, most notably those in the South.

Chapter 4 indicates that region of residence has a moderately important influence on ratings, particularly those given to institutions other than the 10–15 universities with highest national reputations.

The Keniston study did not give information about the institutions from which his respondents had received their highest degrees, but data from the 1964 study suggest a high degree of concentration from institutions in the Northeast. For example, the department chairmen at the 25 highest-ranked English departments all received their highest degrees from one of these same 25 institutions; 17 received their degrees from universities in the Northeast, five from universities in the Midwest, two from the South, and only one from the Far West. Harvard and Yale accounted for ten of the 25. There is more inbreeding in English chairmanships than is true of most academic fields (ten of the 25 chairmen received their highest degrees from the universities at which they now serve as chairman); however, this field serves to indicate that, in educational background, department chairmen may not be typical of scholars in a discipline. As our intensive study of four disciplines (described in chapter 4) indicates, most respondents have a marked predisposition to judge their Ph.D. alma mater generously; the Keniston study undoubtedly reflected this factor.

TABLE 2: *Regional Percentage Distribution of Respondents, by Area of Current Employment, 1957 and 1964 Studies*

REGION	RESPONDENTS (%)		DEGREES AND ENROLLMENTS (%)	
	Keniston (1957)	A.C.E. (1964)	Ph.D.'s Awarded, 1960–62	Institutional Enrollments, 1964
Northeast.........	36	33	36	27
Midwest..........	36	31	35	28
South............	12	20	13	24
Far West.........	16	16	16	21
Total.........	100	100	100	100

The 1964 study, using chairmen, senior scholars, and junior scholars in 106 universities, is much less vulnerable to the charge of institutional and regional concentration. Of the approximately four thousand scholars returning usable questionnaires, 39 percent received their highest degrees in the Northeast, 36 percent in the Midwest, 13 percent in the Far West, and 7 percent in the South (5 percent held degrees from foreign universities). In no field of study did more than 15 percent of the respondents get their degrees from a single institution.

In many academic disciplines, department chairmen traditionally tend to come from one or two specialized subject areas within the field. For example, of the nearly two hundred respondents to the 1964 survey in the field of English, 80 percent of the department chairmen and 79 percent of the senior and junior scholars in English were specialists in British literature. Of the chairmen, half or more had as their primary special field Renaissance literature or eighteenth-century literature. Another example is history, in which department chairmen are commonly European specialists. Presumably, these respondents may tend to underrate departments strong in specialties other than their own.

It is difficult to correct for a possible over- or underrepresentation of special fields within a discipline (although the problem of specialty bias is not as pronounced in the case of respondents selected for scholarly achievement as it seems to be for those chosen for general administrative responsibility). In the 1964 study, we tried to control for representativeness by requesting those deans (and department chairmen) who were asked to submit two or more names to recommend respondents with different specializations. For one discipline, English, we attempted to classify responses by the special fields of the participants and to review the differences in the ratings of the various subgroups. Although we discovered several notable differences, we were pleasantly surprised to find them no greater than they were. (See pp. 90–92 for a fuller discussion of this point.) In general, our

conclusion is that a broad sample that includes scholars of various age and rank categories is much less subject to possible distortion on this count than a sample of department chairmen only would be.

Some reviewers charged that the Keniston study, because it was limited to department chairmen, presented only the views of faculty members who were full professors and generally senior in age. Implicit in this criticism was the belief that if the sample had been a cross section of ages and ranks, quite different ratings would have resulted. On the other hand, a number of respondents to the 1964 study questioned our inclusion of junior scholars, suggesting that they were too young and inexperienced to provide mature judgments.

The rankings for the top departments in each of the fields studied were tabulated separately for department chairmen, senior scholars, and junior scholars (see chapter 3). A review of the data indicates that neither criticism has great validity: there is little to distinguish the ratings of the chairmen or of the junior scholars from those of the senior scholars. In judging the top departments, the junior scholars appear to be a little less impressed by the traditional eminence of an institution, and perhaps a little more impressed by departments that are active in the development of new specialized fields. As one moves down the list past the 15–20 highest-rated departments, one finds that the junior scholars more frequently disagree with their senior colleagues, particularly in their evaluations of smaller institutions which do not have outstanding national reputations. However, in most cases where there was marked disagreement, the senior scholars were in the middle between the chairmen and junior scholars. Thus the slight biases of both chairmen and junior scholars as groups tend to cancel each other out.

Table 3 summarizes the extent of agreement concerning the high-ranking departments.

Of the three groups, the chairmen differed most from the over-all judgment of the total sample of respondents, and the senior scholars differed least.

TABLE 3: *Mean Difference between Over-all Scores and Rater Subgroup Scores for High-ranking Departments in Ten Fields*

Department	Chairmen	Senior Scholars	Junior Scholars	Average
English	.077	.049	.044	.057
Philosophy	.088	.093	.076	.086
History	.088	.041	.072	.067
Economics	.134	.071	.047	.084
Botany	.107	.093	.100	.100
Zoology	.092	.091	.080	.088
Chemistry	.085	.048	.096	.076
Physics	.068	.045	.079	.064
Electrical engineering	.120	.085	.099	.101
Mechanical engineering	.117	.072	.111	.100
Average of means for ten fields	±.098	±.069	±.080	±.082

There are also interesting differences by field: English, physics, and history exhibit the greatest degree of consensus; the engineering fields and botany reveal the most marked differences of opinion. The senior scholars appear to be the most reliable predictors of the over-all scores and the chairmen the least reliable, although the differences are not very great.

It is often contended that faculty members in the large and distinguished universities have a different view of the relative strengths of other institutions from that of people who teach in universities less well endowed (financially and intellectually). As far as can be discerned from the 1964 study this difference in outlook exists, but does not have a significant effect on the relative over-all standing of departments. For several fields, the responses of raters currently employed in the institutions with the highest-ranked departments were compared with the responses of raters teaching in departments judged as being of lower quality (see chapter 4). Although there was almost no difference in the rank order of departments, there was a noticeable difference in the shape of the rating curve. The raters currently teaching in the top departments were harder on the mediocre departments, and somewhat easier on themselves, than were those teaching in the less distinguished departments. One might say that each group had its own grading scale, the respondents in the best departments grading from A to F, and those in the poorer departments grading from B+ to D—.

In the 1964 survey a weighting factor was used so that the large departments, as measured by production of doctorates, would have greater representation than the small ones. The number of raters per institution in each field of study varied from one to four. The largest departments were commonly—though not invariably—the high-rated departments; thus the departments judged to be strongest are more heavily represented in our sample universe than the small, less reputed departments (see chapter 2).

Testing the reliability of a subjective survey

Several replies to the 1964 questionnaire were critical of the subjective method of the survey. Some persons in mediocre institutions accused us of designing still another study that would "fix the pecking order" and "boost the egos of the Ivy League universities." From some of the more distinguished institutions came accusations that we were watering down the results by including as respondents people and institutions which obviously did not know the meaning of quality. These criticisms probably cancel out: chapter 3 indicates that many reputable institutions made very poor showings in some fields while in other cases a generally weak institution showed up well in certain departments.

More to the point were comments that evaluation by experts is "a mere opinion survey"—or, as one disgruntled respondent, quoting Dr. Johnson, put it, "a compendium of gossip is still gossip." The present study is a survey of *informed* opinion. The opinions we have sought are what in a court of law would be called "the testimony of expert witnesses"—those persons in each field who are well qualified to judge, who by training are both knowledgeable and dispassionate, who through professional activities are competent to assess professional standards, and who by their scholarly participation within their chosen fields have earned the respect of their colleagues and peers. As is true for any panel of experts, there are evident differences of opinion and, indeed, some highly eccentric opinions (although only one respondent out of 4,000 judged his present department distinguished and rated all other departments—including those at Harvard, Berkeley, and M.I.T.—as inadequate to grant the Ph.D.).

One important factor in any opinion survey is the qualifications of the judges; a second is the assumption that the higher the degree of agreement among expert witnesses, the more likely it is that the opinion reflects a fact. One hundred or more individual judgments were obtained for most of the fields of study reviewed in chapter 3; this figure represents returns by slightly more than three-fourths of those queried. The findings for three subgroups—department chairmen, senior scholars, and junior scholars—within the total sample have been reported for the highest-ranked departments in each field. In addition, chapter 4 presents the rankings for four fields made by these subgroups, by respondents employed in four regions of the country, and by small panels of experts selected with the help of the appropriate professional associations. A high degree of consensus is evident among respondents grouped by age and rank. Among the regional groupings, where lack of firsthand knowledge and information were perhaps an obstacle to objectivity, the differences are somewhat greater, but in most cases still relatively minor. The greatest disparities are most common in ratings of institutions that are well known regionally but do not yet have a wide national reputation—for example, Claremont, Clark, Emory, Oregon.

Another evidence of consensus is discussed in chapter 4, which compares the results for political science obtained in the present survey with those obtained by Somit and Tanenhaus in a similar study in 1963.[11] The latter survey used a much larger sample drawn at random from all members

[11] Albert Somit and Joseph Tanenhaus, *American Political Science: A Profile of a Discipline* (New York: Atherton Press, 1964).

of the American Political Science Association without regard to age, rank, or scholarly achievement. Some critics of this study argued that different results might have been obtained if the respondents had been selected more carefully for their expertise. However, the two surveys, based on very different methods, gave almost identical results for the leading departments; thus they tend to corroborate each other's findings.

Other means were used to test the accuracy of the subjective evaluations of quality. For three of the fields explored more fully in chapter 4, the departmental quality ratings were compared with the publications records of scholars in those same departments. These factors were rather closely correlated, as might be anticipated. In one field of study, where confidential information was available on faculty salaries in 45 leading departments, quality of the graduate faculty was found to be closely related to mean salaries of the top two academic ranks.

In chapter 5, estimates of over-all institutional quality are compared to the general level of faculty salaries, to educational and general income, to the distribution of national graduate fellowships, to library resources, and to other so-called objective measures.

We conclude from these various comparisons that a survey based on the opinions of well-informed scholars within the academic community is as reliable a guide as one can devise in attempting to measure the elusive attribute of quality. Undoubtedly there are some "halo effects" in individual department ratings, but such effects appear minimal. For example, by a clerical error, Harvard, Cornell, and Stanford, which do not have formal Ph.D. programs in geography, were inadvertently left on the list of departments for that field and they were each quite correctly voted as of insufficient quality to grant the doctorate. Examples at the other extreme are the departments of anthropology at the University of Arizona, philosophy at Pittsburgh, and chemical engineering at Delaware, each of which emerged as one of the leading centers in its field despite the poorer showing of other departments in the same universities.

Such a survey is no doubt subject to some time lag, for the opinions of respondents may be based on the standing of a department a few years earlier. However, the Department of German at the University of Texas, where several distinguished scholars have been appointed since 1962, was ranked fourth nationally. Other examples of recent changes in departmental fortunes show up in comparisons of the 1957 and 1964 surveys. The careful regional balance of the sample of respondents, plus the inclusion of a sizable number of junior scholars, seems to have minimized the problem of time lag in reputation.[12]

[12] Judging from the departments the author knows best, he would add the qualification that reputations do not

Because the results of a study such as this one tend to be "writ in stone," it has been planned from the beginning to do a follow-up *within the next five years*. Just as the Keniston study showed that many changes had occurred since the first Hughes survey, so the present study clearly indicates that there have been many changes since the Keniston study findings were published in 1959. To avoid "freezing" the reputations of various universities, the American Council on Education intends to repeat the study not later than 1970.

A final comment deserves inclusion in the introductory chapter since it concerns a point that caused some debate in the interpretation of the earlier studies. Both the Hughes and Keniston surveys asked participants to rate the strength of departments in selected universities. The scores given by respondents to these two surveys were probably partly an evaluation of the quality of the faculty and partly an estimate of the quality of education provided. To avoid the charge that the present study was just a popularity poll, we asked respondents in the 1964 survey to attempt to separate their assessment of the quality of the scholarly contributions of the faculty from their assessment of the quality of the educational program provided doctoral students. It is not surprising that the relative position of departments on these two questions does not differ greatly—although departments in the larger and somewhat more impersonal universities generally fared less well on the second question—but the strategy was to make the rater distinguish in his own mind between two very different types of evaluation. The reader is therefore warned to weigh the responses to both questions in forming any judgment of a department's quality. To some people, the quality of a department is the scholarly reputation of its faculty; to others, it is the educational experience provided to the apprentice scholar on his path to a doctorate. In answering the first question, the respondent was asked to cast himself in the role of a potential faculty colleague; to answer the second, he was asked to cast himself in the role of the doctoral candidate. Even though somewhat more attention is given in succeeding chapters to the former role, each of these views is important and deserves equal attention.

seem to lag greatly for departments where a number of distinguished professors have either been added to, or have departed from, the faculty. On the other hand, departments which have been changing more gradually by adding or subtracting promising younger men may experience a lag in reputation. However, all evidence points to much more accurate and more rapid communication of information concerning graduate schools than is the case with undergraduate colleges. Riesman's complaint that it may take forty years for the reputation of a liberal arts college to catch up with actuality does not seem appropriate in the case of graduate education.

II · *The Sample and the Questionnaire*

IN DESIGNING THE 1964 SURVEY, the Commission initially posed four questions. First, what academic disciplines should be included? Second, how many of the institutions with doctoral programs should be covered? Third, how many and what types of persons should be asked to participate? And, finally, what questions should be asked to elicit the most meaningful responses? How each of these questions was answered affects the interpretation one should give to the results, and the reader should acquaint himself with the procedures before drawing conclusions from the data presented in chapter 3.

Academic disciplines

Thirty academic fields were selected for study. Their selection was based on two criteria: (*a*) to provide as great as possible overlap with the earlier Hughes and Keniston surveys, and (*b*) to give broad coverage through inclusion of most of the major disciplines in the arts and sciences.

Table 4 lists the fields reviewed by the four major studies of quality of graduate education. Nineteen fields were covered by all surveys, and provide an interesting comparison over a forty-year period.

Four fields in the humanities reviewed by Keniston were omitted from the 1964 survey—fine arts, linguistics, music, and Oriental studies. The number of departments giving doctorates in these disciplines was quite limited, and the total number of degrees awarded relatively small. Also, except for music, these are fields that are difficult to define clearly and in which the orientation of various departments differs markedly. For example, degrees reported as fine arts include special concentrations in art history, art criticism, aesthetics, drama, painting, sculpture, musicology, and the dance and various other performing arts. Similarly, Oriental studies appears to cover a multitude of fields, variously organized into departments, schools, or special programs. Doctorates in linguistics are occasionally awarded by independent departments, frequently by language or literature departments, and on occasion by special committees drawn from faculty in English, anthropology, philosophy, and other areas in the humanities. The Keniston study and the 1934 Hughes study queried Romance language specialists, whereas for the 1924 Hughes

and 1964 A.C.E. surveys the field was divided into French and Spanish.

In the social sciences and physical sciences, the 1964 survey included all of the fields reviewed by the 1934 Hughes study and the Keniston survey.

In the biological sciences, the first Hughes study and the 1957 Keniston survey examined only zoology, botany, and psychology. The 1934 Hughes study sought opinions on a wider range of fields. The 1964 study includes the fields of bacteriology-microbiology and entomology added by Hughes, and further adds biochemistry, pharmacology, and physiology, but excludes the 1934 categories of genetics, human nutrition, plant pathology, and plant physiology.

Both the Keniston and A.C.E. surveys omitted the fields of agriculture and education, which Hughes had studied. The 1964 study, however, includes the four major traditional fields of engineering, which were included only in the Hughes 1934 survey. A majority of the universities in our survey offer the doctorate in engineering, and each of the institutes of technology awards the Ph.D. in some arts and sciences fields. It was felt that the inclusion of the core engineering fields would provide a broader basis for comparison of these two types of institutions.

The fields covered by the 1964 study account for three-fourths of all Ph.D.'s awarded during the most recent decade; thus, numerically, the survey includes the bulk of doctoral programs. The findings for 29 of the 30 fields surveyed are reported in chapter 3. Because of difficulties in identifying degrees and degree programs in Russian, it was later omitted from the study (see Appendix B).

Institutions

The 1964 survey covers doctoral work at 106 institutions. Keniston had limited himself to 25 major universities. The Hughes 1924 study covered 38 institutions and the 1934 review, 59. Slightly more than two hundred universities grant the doctorate today, but the largest 100 account for more than 95 percent of all earned doctorates and nearly 98 percent of doctorates in arts and sciences. In view of the decision to survey the major graduate schools, the simplest device was to include the institutions which formed the Council

TABLE 4: *Fields of Study Reviewed by Four Surveys, and Ten-Year Doctorate Production, 1953–62*

Field of Study	Hughes (1924)	Hughes (1934)	Keniston (1957)	A.C.E. (1964)	Number of Doctorates, 1953–62
ALL FIELDS..............	20	35	24	30	56,579[a]
HUMANITIES............	6	6	10	7	6,387
Classics.............	★	★	★	★	290
English.............	★	★	★	★	3,746
Oriental studies......	..	..	★	..	NA[b]
Fine arts............	..	★	★	..	323[c]
French.............	★	..	..	★	506
German............	★	★	★	★	334
Linguistics..........	..	..	★	..	NA
Music..............	..	..	★	..	911[c]
Philosophy..........	★	★	★	★	1,069
Romance languages..	..	★	★	..	NA
Russian.............	..	..	★ [d]	★	80
Spanish.............	★	..	..	★	362
EDUCATION.............	★	★	..	..	15,926[c]
SOCIAL SCIENCES........	5	6	6	6	10,724
Anthropology.......	..	★	★	★	528
Economics..........	★	★	★	★	2,979
Geography..........	★	★	★	★	514
History............	★	★	★	★	3,216
Political science......	★	★	★	★	1,850
Sociology..........	★	★	★	★	1,637
BIOLOGICAL SCIENCES.....	3	9	3	8	14,813
Bacteriology-microbiology......	..	★	..	★	1,422
Biochemistry........	..	..	..	★	1,526
Botany.............	★	★	★	★	1,800
Entomology.........	..	★	..	★	756
Genetics...........	..	★	..	..	NA
Human nutrition.....	..	★	..	..	NA
Pharmacology.......	..	..	..	★	391[e]
Physiology..........	..	..	..	★	725
Plant pathology.....	..	★	..	..	NA
Plant physiology.....	..	★	..	..	NA
Psychology..........	★	★	★	★	6,406
Zoology.............	★	★	★	★	1,787
PHYSICAL SCIENCES.......	5	5	5	5	19,812
Astronomy..........	★	★	★	★	169
Chemistry..........	★	★	★	★	10,247
Geology............	★	★	★	★	1,561
Mathematics........	★	★	★	★	2,774
Physics.............	★	★	★	★	5,061
ENGINEERING...........	..	6	..	4	4,843
Aeronautical........	..	★	..	..	335[c]
Chemical...........	..	★	..	★	1,537
Civil...............	..	★	..	★	681
Electrical...........	..	★	..	★	1,731
Mechanical.........	..	★	..	★	894
Mining and metallurgical......	..	★	..	..	169[c]
AGRICULTURE...........	..	2	..	..	3,930[c]
Animal nutrition.....	..	★	..	..	NA
Soil science.........	..	★	..	..	NA

[a] This total, composed only of those fields suggested for the A.C.E. survey, represents approximately 60 percent of all the earned doctorates reported by the U.S. Office of Education for the ten-year period 1953–62 and 82 percent of all doctorates excluding those in education.

[b] NA signifies ten-year totals not available for this field.

[c] Not included in totals since field is not included in A.C.E. 1964 survey.

[d] Keniston's term was "Slavic studies."

[e] Estimated total for ten-year period. The U.S. Office of Education began reporting pharmacology as a separate field in its 1955–56 publication. Degree production for the previous three years is estimated at 30 doctorates per year.

of Graduate Schools in the United States in 1961. To this group of 100, we added six universities which had granted 100 or more doctorates (spread over three or more fields) in the preceding decade. Thus, the 106 institutions include every university which averaged ten doctorates a year in the 1953–62 period.[1]

Participating scholars

Early in the design of the 1964 study it was decided to make the sample of participating scholars quite heterogeneous, representing informed opinions of persons in various age and rank levels. Three major groups were selected: (1) department chairmen; (2) distinguished senior scholars; and (3) knowledgeable junior scholars who had completed their formal training not more than ten years earlier.

It was decided to weight the sample by size of department as measured in doctorates awarded during the last decade. Four participants were invited from departments that had awarded more than 2 percent of the doctorates in a particular field of study, three from departments that had awarded 0.5–1.9 percent of the doctorates, two from departments that had awarded less than 0.5 percent and one from departments that offered graduate credit courses but had not awarded a doctorate in the preceding decade. For each department falling in the first category, the chairman, two senior scholars, and one junior scholar were sent questionnaires. For departments in the second category, one person from each of these groups was mailed a questionnaire. In categories three and four, the requests were randomized so as to provide an approximately equal number of junior and senior scholars. For each field reported in chapter 3, a table labeled "Profile of Respondents" gives the number in each rank-group participating.

A letter was sent to the deans of the 106 graduate schools, requesting the names of the chairmen and of senior and junior professors. The deans were asked to provide names of persons in residence during the spring semester of 1964, to confer with department chairmen in selecting suitable participants in fields where their own acquaintance might be limited, and to attempt to ensure that those nominated from a single department represented diverse specialized fields. It was most gratifying that within four weeks all but one dean had provided the necessary names;[2] the faculty

of the Rockefeller Institute is not organized into traditional academic fields, and because of the difficulty in designating the appropriate persons, it was decided to omit them as respondents but to leave the Institute on the rating sheets.

The questionnaire

The questionnaire (which is reproduced in Appendix D) asked two basic questions:

A. Which of the terms below best describes your judgment of the *quality of the graduate faculty* in your field at each of the institutions listed? Consider only the scholarly competence and achievements of the present faculty.

  1. Distinguished
  2. Strong
  3. Good
  4. Adequate
  5. Marginal
  6. Not sufficient to provide acceptable doctoral training
  7. Insufficient information

B. How would you rate the institutions below if you were selecting a graduate school to work for a doctorate in your field today? Take into account the accessibility of faculty and their scholarly competence, curricula, educational and research facilities, the quality of graduate students and other factors which contribute to the *effectiveness of the doctoral program*.

  1. Extremely attractive
  2. Attractive
  3. Acceptable
  4. Not attractive
  5. Insufficient information

There followed a list of each of the universities among the 106 in the survey that had awarded one or more doctorates in the particular field of study within the preceding decade.

A third question was added in an attempt to see if the likely direction of change in the quality of graduate programs could be discerned.

C. What *changes in relative positions* of departments in your field do you anticipate in the next 5–10 years? Base your judgments on administrative leadership, quality of younger staff, and the general environment at each institution. Assume continuation of present trends in financial support.

  1. Relative improvement
  2. Same relative position
  3. Relative decline
  4. Insufficient information

---

[1] Claremont Graduate School, Brandeis University, the Rockefeller Institute, the University of North Dakota, and West Virginia University awarded fewer than 100 doctorates in 1953–62, but were among the charter institutions in the Council of Graduate Schools.

[2] One member of the Advisory Committee, when he received a copy of initial request for names sent to the graduate deans, telephoned the Director of the study with the dire prediction that it would take a year to get their

replies. Much to his surprise, and to our pleasure, three-quarters of the deans replied within ten days of the initial request. Only two dozen follow-up letters, and two final telephone calls, were necessary to get 100 percent response. This is good evidence that, contrary to reputation, graduate deans are frequently on their own campuses and invariably answer their mail.

The answers to this question were carefully reviewed for a number of fields. However, these responses appeared less meaningful when aggregated, for the expectation of change is directly related to one's current perception of departmental strengths and weaknesses. An example of this is the ratings given to an economics department that had recently lost a number of distinguished professors. Nearly a third of the outside observers rated this department as still strong but likely to decline over the next five to ten years. Another third rated the department quite low, but indicated that it would probably improve. It seemed both groups thought the department would end up at about the same place but some were more distressed by the recent defections than others. In a majority of fields the respondents thought that most departments would remain in about the same relative position.

The questionnaire for each field of study included only the names of institutions which reported to the U.S. Office of Education the award of one or more doctorates in that subject in the 1953–62 period. Thus some new Ph.D. programs in established universities which granted their first doctorate in 1963 or later were omitted. In determining which departments had granted doctoral degrees, the following sources were used: the *Earned Degrees* reports [3] of the Office of Education; the 1964 edition of *American Universities and Colleges,* Appendix IV, "Tables of Earned Doctorates Conferred by American Universities and Colleges, 1861–1962"; [4] and doctoral programs reported in *A Guide to Graduate Study: Programs Leading to the Ph.D. Degree,* second edition.[5] Because of inconsistencies in the reporting of degrees in Romance languages, the initial questionnaires mailed out for French and Spanish omitted several departments. Western Reserve University, the University of Cincinnati, and the University of Pennsylvania were inadvertently omitted from the list in French; George Washington University, Cornell University, Fordham University, and University of Pennsylvania, from the list in Spanish. A supplementary questionnaire listing these institutions was sent to recipients of the original questionnaire. In processing the data for these two fields, only the information from respondents returning both questionnaires was included.

The questionnaire also asked for some basic biographical information about the respondents. This information is summarized in the tables of "Profile of Respondents" in chapter 3.

Questionnaires were mailed on April 1, 1964

[3] *Earned Degrees Conferred: Bachelor's and Higher Degrees* (Washington: Government Printing Office, annually).
[4] 9th ed.; Washington: American Council on Education. Pp. 1260–78.
[5] Washington: American Council on Education, 1960.

(a purely fortuitous date) to the 5,367 faculty members designated by the graduate deans. Follow-up letters were sent to non-respondents in mid-May, and postcard reminders, again in mid-June. Table 5 indicates, by field, the number of mailings and the number of replies received as of July 15, when the data processing began. An additional 50–75 replies were received after that date, but were not included in the study.

Approximately 80 percent of the questionnaires (4,256) were returned by July 15. Among them were 4,008 usable replies. Nearly 250 returns were discarded because only portions of the questionnaires were filled in. Any return that included answers to both Questions A and B was included; excluded were those containing replies to only parts of these questions.

A modest number of questionnaires were returned marked "deceased" or "not known at this address." One late response was received from a faculty member who had been gone for three years from the institution where we had addressed him, and in one instance a widow wrote that her husband had been dead for two years. In neither case did the study staff embarrass the graduate dean with the information.

An approximately equal percentage of returns was received from each of the three age-and-rank groups, the junior scholars being slightly above the average and the senior scholars slightly below. In only two instances where three or four faculty members of a department had received questionnaires was no response received; in one of these cases it was later learned that they had mutually agreed not to reply.

Those familiar with questionnaire surveys will recognize that an 80 percent response (75 percent usable) is a creditable record in an opinion survey of this nature. In his first survey Hughes received approximately a 50 percent response, and 71 percent in 1934. Keniston reported "about 80 percent" return. Somit and Tanenhaus received 68 percent. The Commission had hoped for at least 65 percent, and doubted that it would achieve higher than 75 percent. It was particularly pleasing that the response rate was almost uniformly high for all fields; in only one (Russian, which was later omitted for other reasons) were fewer than 70 percent returned, and only three language areas and three biological science fields fell below 70 percent in usable replies.

When the questionnaires were returned, the information was coded and then key-punched for automatic data processing. The data were then printed out, and many tedious hours were spent checking the punched data against the original questionnaires. One-half of all returns were checked in this fashion, and every observed error corrected. In fields where one-half of one percent of the data items were in error, all returns were completely checked. Thus the final tabulations should be correct within approximately one-quarter of one percent. Even allowing for the exaggeration of errors through the various weights assigned to different response categories, the maximum error in reporting average scores would not exceed one percent.

TABLE 5: *Questionnaire Response Rate for the 1964 Graduate Education Study, by Field of Study*

Field of Study	Number of Questionnaires Sent	Number of Responses Received, July 15, 1964	Number of Usable Responses	Usable Responses as a Percent of Questionnaires Sent
GRAND TOTAL	5,367	4,256	4,008	75
HUMANITIES	1,082	865	800	74
Classics	132	112	108	82
English	226	192	185	82
French	164	123	108	66
German	160	141	124	78
Philosophy	184	142	137	74
Russian	71	46	44	62
Spanish	145	109	94	66
SOCIAL SCIENCES	1,093	871	850	78
Anthropology	122	95	91	75
Economics	219	177	173	79
Geography	100	85	84	84
History	229	186	180	79
Political science	215	168	165	77
Sociology	208	160	157	75
BIOLOGICAL SCIENCES	1,456	1,122	1,043	72
Bacteriology-microbiology	218	168	156	72
Biochemistry	211	161	152	72
Botany	186	140	130	70
Entomology	116	98	90	78
Pharmacology	109	80	74	68
Physiology	177	133	117	66
Psychology	252	208	198	79
Zoology	187	134	126	67
PHYSICAL SCIENCES	1,038	842	806	78
Astronomy	74	66	62	84
Chemistry	268	230	218	81
Geology	191	166	158	83
Mathematics	255	184	178	70
Physics	250	196	190	76
ENGINEERING	698	556	509	73
Chemical engineering	192	156	144	75
Civil engineering	157	124	118	75
Electrical engineering	182	145	128	70
Mechanical engineering	167	131	119	71

III · *The Findings*

THE RESULTS OBTAINED for each of the 29 fields of study included in the 1964 survey are reported in this chapter. A brief introduction explains the format and the choice of data for reporting.

Each field of study is treated on two facing pages, which contain five tables. The left-hand page shows the leading departments in the field as they were rated on the quality of their graduate faculty (Question A on the questionnaire). Below that are tables summarizing the biographical information provided by respondents. The right-hand page gives the leading departments in the field as they were rated on the effectiveness of their doctoral programs (Question B on the questionnaire). Below this is a table showing the highest-ranked departments in the field in the 1964 survey, the 1957 Keniston survey, and the 1924 Hughes survey (not all fields have this fifth table since not all fields covered in 1964 were included in earlier studies). The fields of study are arranged alphabetically within divisions in the following order: humanities, social sciences, biological sciences, physical sciences (including mathematics), and engineering.

Quality groupings

In the two large tables reporting the ratings, the groupings were determined on a numerical basis, with the group titles approximating the categories in the questionnaire.

For the ratings provided in answer to Question A, quality of graduate faculty, groupings are on the following basis:

Questionnaire Category	Numerical Weight
Distinguished	5
Strong	4
Good	3
Adequate	2
Marginal	1
Not sufficient to provide adequate doctoral training	0

Rating Categories	Numerical Range
Distinguished	4.01–5.00
Strong	3.01–4.00
Good	2.51–3.00
Adequate plus	2.00–2.50
(Not grouped)	Below 2.00

The dividing lines between groups were arbitrary selections; in most fields there were no major gaps in the distribution below the first few departments that would provide more reasonable boundaries. Figure 1, for example, arrays the overall scores on the first question for the 96 departments in chemistry. Near the top of the distribution there are some noticeable gaps, but the lower end of the curve is smooth and unbroken. Any arbitrary division may separate two neighboring departments which differ in raw score by only a few hundredths of a point. The only alternative, however, would be to list all departments in rank order, and this seemed to be even less satisfactory. It may be possible to put the first few departments in any field in rank order with a fair degree of consensus, but in a subjective appraisal it is difficult to indicate fairly which department should be, say, seventy-third and which seventy-fourth. For departments in the "Distinguished" and "Strong" categories, both rank order and average scores are shown for the three major categories of respondents.

For the ratings provided in answer to Question B, the effectiveness of the doctoral program, the groupings were made on the following basis:

Questionnaire Category	Numerical Weight
Extremely attractive	3
Attractive	2
Acceptable	1
Not attractive	0

Rating Categories	Numerical Range
Very attractive	2.01–3.00
Attractive	1.51–2.00
Acceptable plus	.75–1.50
(Not grouped)	Below .75

These groupings are also rather arbitrary in definition, but include approximately the same number of departments as are shown in response to Question A.

Tables 6 and 7 summarize the over-all distribution of departments according to average score on each of these questions. The two columns at the right show the number of departments which were rated as "Marginal" or "Of insufficient quality" of faculty to provide acceptable doctoral training and as "Marginal" or "Not attractive" as judged on the effectiveness of the doctoral program. It is immediately apparent that, despite the

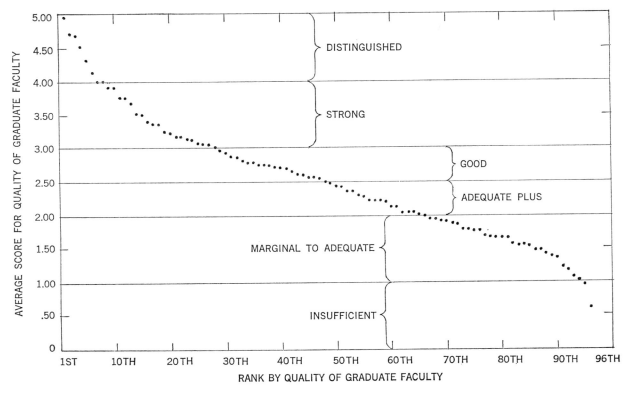

FIG. 1—Distribution of 96 chemistry departments, by quality of graduate faculty, spring 1964.

common terminology, respondents in various disciplines used somewhat different grading standards in judging their colleagues and their departments. The engineers, for example, appear to be relatively lenient raters, and it is likely that they assumed that any department which had passed muster with the Engineers' Council for Professional Development, the professional accrediting body, was of sufficient quality to provide an adequate doctoral program. The fact that only two engineering departments out of approximately 200 received the lowest rating on either question suggests that the responding engineers left the identification of inadequate programs to their professional association.

The hardest graders were in economics, mathematics, physics, and sociology. Economics is the only field in which approximately half of the departments reviewed appear in the two lowest groupings. In some fields two-thirds or more of the departments were rated "Good" or better, but in the four fields named above and in history, political science, psychology, and geology, less than 45 percent were in this category. It is not clear whether there is in fact a more unequal distribution of academic talent in these fields, or whether the nature of the subject makes possible a clearer separation of the good from the mediocre talent. In any event, the reader is cautioned on this variance in standards before comparing different fields within an institution.

There are some interesting differences between the groupings under Questions A and B. In most cases where the quality of faculty was judged to be about equal, departments in smaller, private, and favorably located institutions fared better on Question B than those in institutions that were larger, public, and less favorably situated. Departments in the large urban institutions tended to fall on the "effectiveness" question, while departments in the smaller residential universities frequently improved their relative standing on this question.

Profile of respondents

The information summarized in the tables titled "Profile of Respondents" and "Respondents' Division of Time for Professional Activities" indicates the age and rank distribution of participants, and provides a rough index of their scholarly activities. In interpreting this information it should be emphasized that the respondents were all members of the *graduate* faculty, and were specially selected as scholars and administrators. Thus they are not necessarily typical or representative professors even at their own institutions. One can assume that members of our sample spend a larger proportion of their working day on writing and research than does the average professor and, in view of their scholarly distinction, spend a larger share of their teaching time with graduate than undergraduate students.

TABLE 6: *Departments Surveyed, by Field of Study and Classification of Average Score for Question A (Quality of Graduate Faculty)*

FIELD OF STUDY	TOTAL NUMBER OF DEPARTMENTS SURVEYED	NUMBER OF DEPARTMENTS WITH SCORES OF:					
		Distin-guished (4.01 +)	Strong (3.01– 4.00)	Good (2.51– 3.00)	Adequate Plus (2.00– 2.50)	Marginal (1.00– 1.99)	Not Sufficient (less than 1.00)
Anthropology.............	24	4	8	5	2	4	1
Astronomy...............	16	5	3	2	2	4	—
Bacteriology-microbiology..	75	6	21	17	18	13	—
Biochemistry.............	75	7	20	13	13	22	—
Botany..................	61	4	17	12	13	13	2
Chemistry...............	96	6	22	19	18	29	2
Classics.................	30	1	12	4	6	7	—
Economics...............	71	7	9	13	7	29	6
English.................	74	5	18	11	17	21	2
Engineering, chemical.....	56	7	8	11	15	15	—
Engineering, civil........	40	4	11	14	8	3	—
Engineering, electrical.....	54	4	18	9	13	10	—
Engineering, mechanical...	47	3	14	10	11	9	—
Entomology..............	31	1	9	6	8	7	—
French..................	48	3	13	8	10	14	—
Geography..............	30	3	7	9	4	7	—
Geology.................	55	4	15	3	15	17	1
German.................	39	4	15	3	5	9	3
History.................	75	8	12	13	17	19	6
Mathematics.............	81	9	16	7	14	27	8
Pharmacology............	52	4	16	8	12	12	—
Philosophy..............	48	4	12	7	10	14	1
Physics.................	86	9	12	17	11	34	3
Physiology..............	71	2	25	15	14	13	2
Political science..........	64	6	12	10	9	26	1
Psychology..............	88	6	17	14	23	23	5
Sociology...............	64	5	12	7	10	24	6
Spanish.................	48	4	12	10	9	11	2
Zoology................	64	5	19	11	14	15	—
Total.................	1,663	140	405	288	328	451	51

TABLE 7: *Departments Surveyed, by Field of Study and Classification of Average Score for Question B (Effectiveness of Doctoral Program)*

FIELD OF STUDY	TOTAL NUMBER OF DEPARTMENTS SURVEYED	NUMBER OF DEPARTMENTS WITH SCORES OF:				
		Ex-tremely Attractive (2.01 +)	Attractive (1.51– 2.00)	Ac-ceptable Plus (.75– 1.50)	Marginal (.25– .74)	Not Attractive (less than .25)
Anthropology....................	24	3	8	7	3	3
Astronomy......................	16	3	4	5	3	1
Bacteriology-microbiology..........	75	7	15	35	17	1
Biochemistry....................	75	9	17	28	20	1
Botany.........................	61	9	10	26	14	2
Chemistry......................	96	9	14	37	30	6
Classics........................	30	4	9	9	8	—
Economics......................	71	7	8	15	30	11
English.........................	74	6	14	22	24	8
Engineering, chemical..............	56	8	7	22	17	2
Engineering, civil.................	40	5	6	24	5	—
Engineering, electrical.............	54	6	8	23	17	—
Engineering, mechanical...........	47	4	11	21	11	—
Entomology.....................	31	3	5	14	8	1
French.........................	48	6	9	18	14	1
Geography.....................	30	4	5	12	9	—
Geology........................	55	7	9	18	18	3
German........................	39	6	12	10	8	3
History........................	75	8	11	24	25	7
Mathematics....................	81	9	11	24	27	10
Pharmacology...................	52	4	14	26	7	1
Philosophy.....................	48	4	7	18	17	2
Physics........................	86	8	11	29	33	5
Physiology.....................	71	6	20	29	14	2
Political science.................	64	8	8	16	27	5
Psychology.....................	88	8	11	32	29	8
Sociology......................	64	5	9	15	27	8
Spanish........................	48	5	12	19	10	2
Zoology.......................	64	9	12	26	16	1
Total.......................	1,663	180	297	604	488	94

Comparison of high-ranking departments

Keniston sought to identify the top 15 departments in his survey in 1957. However, by restricting his study to only 25 multipurpose universities (similar in nature to the University of Pennsylvania), he omitted some institutions of considerable strength and reputation. In order to draw intertemporal comparisons, the leading twenty departments as rated by quality of graduate faculty in 1964 are shown with similar listings from the Hughes 1924 and Keniston 1957 surveys. The inclusion in the 1964 study of specialized institutions such as M.I.T., California Institute of Technology, Carnegie Tech., Purdue, and the Rockefeller Institute (all omitted by Keniston) results in some apparent "bumping" of departments even though their relative position may have remained unchanged since 1957. The listings in the scientific fields should be viewed with this factor in mind.

A note on the biological sciences

Special procedures were needed for obtaining and handling the data for six fields in the biological sciences because of the varied ways in which degrees are reported and graduate work is organized in that area. The method used for most fields to identify the institutions to be listed on the questionnaires was inadequate for the biological sciences. For example, a list composed of only those institutions reporting the award of doctorates in a specific field such as bacteriology or physiology would have omitted some institutions that report these degrees as doctorates in biology. In order to provide the survey participants with questionnaire lists as complete as possible, the roster of institutions reporting doctorates in the specific field was amplified to include: (1) institutions reporting at least ten doctorates in "biology" and indicating the availability of the specific field for graduate study and (2) in the pre-clinical fields, those institutions that had a medical school. Thus, Northwestern and Purdue, among others, were added to the zoology lists; Tufts and Yeshiva, among others, were added to the bacteriology/microbiology lists.

Subsequently, a number of the *added* institutions were dropped from the field of study statistics by reason of low scores or a high percentage of responses indicating "insufficient information." The number of *net* additions was two for biochemistry, three each for bacteriology/microbiology and botany, four for pharmacology, seven for physiology, and ten for zoology.

The variety in degree reporting, which prompted the modified procedures, reflects the diversity in departmental organization in the biological sciences. Whereas history and English are usually offered in departments so named, botany and zoology are frequently offered in biology departments; biochemistry, in chemistry, biology, or biological-chemistry departments, or in each; microbiology, in either the graduate school of arts and sciences or in the school of medicine, or in both. Although much of this organizational detail could have been put into the questionnaire, it would have delayed the study and confronted the participants with a longer, more complex questionnaire. Therefore, the decision was made to list only the institution's name and ask the respondents to rate the faculty and program in the *field,* not in a specific department or departments.

With few exceptions, the results are presented in the same manner. No attempt is made to indicate whether one, two, or all three of the departments offering biochemistry at Institution X earned its "Strong" rating. Nor does the "Adequate plus" for microbiology at Institution Y represent a rating of the department on the home campus or the one at its medical school. In the tables for the biological sciences, this simplification is shown by a double asterisk and is to be interpreted as (1) study is offered in a department other than the field named, and/or (2) study is offered by more than one department. *A Guide to Graduate Study,* third edition,[1] was used as the principal reference for this footnoting.

[1] Jane Graham, ed. (Washington: American Council on Education, 1965).

FIELDS OF STUDY

HUMANITIES

Classics	German
English	Philosophy
French	Spanish

SOCIAL SCIENCES

Anthropology	History
Economics	Political Science
Geography	Sociology

BIOLOGICAL SCIENCES

Bacteriology/ Microbiology	Pharmacology
Biochemistry	Physiology
Botany	Psychology
Entomology	Zoology

PHYSICAL SCIENCES

Astronomy	Mathematics
Chemistry	Physics
Geology	

ENGINEERING

Chemical Engineering	Electrical Engineering
Civil Engineering	Mechanical Engineering

CLASSICS

Leading Departments, by Rated Quality of Graduate Faculty

Institution†	All Respondents		Chairmen		Senior Scholars		Junior Scholars	
	Rank	Score	Rank	Score	Rank	Score	Rank	Score
"Distinguished"								
Harvard..............	1	4.63	1	4.63	1	4.76	1	4.40
"Strong"								
California, Berkeley.....	2	4.00	3*	3.90	4	3.98	2	4.10
Princeton.............	3	3.97	2	4.00	2	4.19	4	3.58
Bryn Mawr...........	4	3.88	5	3.78	3	4.02	3	3.68
Yale.................	5	3.71	3*	3.90	5	3.78	7*	3.43
Columbia.............	6*	3.60	7*	3.54	6	3.72	7*	3.43
Michigan.............	6*	3.60	6	3.68	7	3.64	6	3.46
Pennsylvania..........	8	3.46	9	3.45	11	3.41	5	3.53
Johns Hopkins.........	9	3.40	12	3.23	8	3.51	9	3.33
Cincinnati............	10	3.37	10	3.30	10	3.44	10	3.27
North Carolina........	11	3.30	7*	3.54	12	3.41	11	3.06
Chicago..............	12	3.22	16	2.86	9	3.48	12	3.03
Cornell..............	13	3.18	11	3.25	13	3.28	13	2.96

"Good" (4 departments arranged alphabetically):
Illinois	Texas	Wisconsin
N.Y.U.		

"Adequate plus" (6 departments arranged alphabetically):
Brown	Fordham	Northwestern
Catholic	Minnesota	Ohio State

† These tabulations and those for the effectiveness of the graduate program are based on ratings of the 30 institutions in the survey universe that reported the award of one or more doctorates in classics from July 1952 through June 1962.
* Rank and score shared with another department.

Profile of Respondents

Respondents	Number	Average Age	Average Number of Publications Since Highest Degree		Professional Meetings Attended in Last Four Years	
			Books	Articles	Regional	National
All respondents................	108	47.5	2.4	15	4.0	3.1
Chairmen....................	22	53.3	2.7	17	3.2	2.6
Senior scholars................	54	53.5	2.8	17	4.7	3.3
Junior scholars...............	32	35.7	1.4	9	3.6	3.3

Respondents' Division of Time for Professional Activities
(in percents)

Respondents	Instruction			Research and Writing	Administration	Other Professional	Other
	Under-graduate	Graduate	Total				
All respondents................	32	25	57	21	14	5	2
Chairmen....................	26	24	50	17	25	6	2
Senior scholars................	28	29	57	23	13	5	2
Junior scholars...............	43	21	64	20	8	5	3

CLASSICS

Leading Departments, by Rated Effectiveness of Graduate Program

Institution	All Respondents		Chairmen		Senior Scholars		Junior Scholars	
	Rank	Score	Rank	Score	Rank	Score	Rank	Score
"Extremely attractive"								
Harvard.............	1	2.67	1	2.61	1	2.62	1	2.81
Princeton............	2	2.29	2	2.33	2	2.40	3	2.07
California, Berkeley.....	3	2.14	5	1.94	3*	2.11	2	2.33
Bryn Mawr..........	4	2.05	3	2.12	3*	2.11	5*	1.88
"Attractive"								
Michigan............	5	1.92	4	2.06	7	1.89	5*	1.88
Yale................	6	1.88	13	1.59	5	2.00	8	1.85
Columbia............	7	1.83	12	1.61	8	1.87	4	1.93
Pennsylvania.........	8	1.82	7*	1.72	9	1.83	6	1.87
Cincinnati...........	9	1.78	11	1.63	6	1.90	11	1.68
North Carolina........	10	1.67	6	1.83	10	1.73	13	1.48
Johns Hopkins.........	11	1.66	9*	1.65	11	1.61	9	1.77
Cornell..............	12	1.63	9*	1.65	13	1.56	10	1.74
Chicago..............	13	1.55	15	1.33	12	1.57	12	1.65

"Acceptable plus" (9 departments arranged alphabetically):

Brown	Illinois	Northwestern
Catholic	Minnesota	Texas
Fordham	N.Y.U.	Wisconsin

* Rank and score shared with another department.

High-Ranking Graduate Departments: Hughes, Keniston, and A.C.E. Studies

Top 15 Departments, Hughes Study, 1925	Top 15 Departments, Keniston Study, 1957	Top 20† Departments, Rated Quality of Faculty, A.C.E. Study, 1964
1. Harvard	1. Harvard	1. Harvard
2. Princeton	2. Yale	2. California, Berkeley
3. Chicago	3. Princeton	3. Princeton
4. Johns Hopkins	4. California	4. Bryn Mawr
5. Pennsylvania	5. Columbia	5. Yale
6. Columbia	6. Cornell	6.* Columbia
7. Michigan	7. Chicago	6.* Michigan
8. Yale	8. Michigan	8. Pennsylvania
9. California	9. Johns Hopkins	9. Johns Hopkins
10. Illinois	10. Illinois	10. Cincinnati
11. Wisconsin	11. North Carolina	11. North Carolina
12. Bryn Mawr	12. Bryn Mawr	12. Chicago
13. Cornell	13. Pennsylvania	13. Cornell
14. Northwestern	14. N.Y.U.	14. Wisconsin
15. Iowa (Iowa City)	15. Stanford	15. Illinois
		16. Texas
		17. N.Y.U.
		18. Northwestern
		19. Catholic
		20. Brown

* Rank shared with another department.
† These 20 departments represent 67 percent of the 30 departments for which ratings were calculated.

ENGLISH

Leading Departments, by Rated Quality of Graduate Faculty

Institution†	All Respondents		Chairmen		Senior Scholars		Junior Scholars	
	Rank	Score	Rank	Score	Rank	Score	Rank	Score
"Distinguished"								
Yale...................	1	4.87	1	4.97	1	4.84	1	4.84
Harvard..............	2	4.75	2	4.80	2	4.70	2	4.78
California, Berkeley.....	3	4.59	3	4.62	3	4.57	3	4.57
Princeton.............	4	4.21	5	4.12	4	4.24	4	4.21
Columbia.............	5	4.11	4	4.29	5	4.02	5	4.10
"Strong"								
Chicago..............	6	3.91	9	3.82	6	3.95	7	3.90
Stanford..............	7	3.86	6	4.00	11*	3.71	6	3.93
Cornell..............	8	3.83	8	3.85	7	3.83	8	3.81
Wisconsin............	9	3.78	7	3.87	10	3.74	9	3.75
Indiana...............	10	3.73	10*	3.75	9	3.76	11	3.66
Illinois................	11*	3.72	10*	3.75	8	3.80	13	3.60
Johns Hopkins..........	11*	3.72	12	3.70	11*	3.71	10	3.73
Michigan.............	13	3.63	13	3.53	13	3.67	12	3.63
U.C.L.A..............	14	3.48	15*	3.39	14	3.51	14	3.49
Minnesota............	15	3.42	17	3.34	17*	3.40	15	3.46
Northwestern..........	16	3.40	14	3.48	19	3.34	16	3.40
North Carolina........	17	3.36	18*	3.28	15	3.46	17*	3.28
Pennsylvania..........	18	3.33	18*	3.28	16	3.45	21	3.19
Washington (Seattle)....	19	3.30	21	3.20	17*	3.40	20	3.21
Duke.................	20	3.28	15*	3.39	20	3.26	19	3.22
N.Y.U...............	21	3.26	20	3.26	21	3.23	17*	3.28
Brown...............	22	3.06	24	2.94	22	3.08	22	3.10
Texas................	23	3.04	22	3.15	23	3.05	24*	2.95

"Good" (11 departments arranged alphabetically):

Brandeis	Ohio State	Tulane
Bryn Mawr	Rice	Virginia
Claremont	Rochester	Washington (St. Louis)
Iowa (Iowa City)	Rutgers	

"Adequate plus" (17 departments arranged alphabetically):

Connecticut	Nebraska	Southern California
Emory	Notre Dame	Syracuse
Florida	Oregon	Vanderbilt
Fordham	Penn State	Wayne State
Kansas	Pittsburgh	Western Reserve
Michigan State	St. Louis	

† These tabulations and those for the effectiveness of the graduate program are based on ratings of the 74 institutions in the survey universe that reported the award of one or more doctorates in English from July 1952 through June 1962.
* Rank and score shared with another department.

Profile of Respondents

Respondents	Number	Average Age	Average Number of Publications Since Highest Degree		Professional Meetings Attended in Last Four Years	
			Books	Articles	Regional	National
All respondents...............	185	47.8	2.7	16	3.5	3.7
Chairmen....................	41	53.0	3.6	22	4.3	5.3
Senior scholars...............	79	53.5	3.8	20	3.5	3.7
Junior scholars..............	65	36.9	.9	8	3.0	2.6

Respondents' Division of Time for Professional Activities
(in percents)

Respondents	Instruction			Research and Writing	Administration	Other Professional	Other
	Undergraduate	Graduate	Total				
All respondents...............	25	24	49	19	26	5	2
Chairmen....................	14	17	31	9	53	5	1
Senior scholars...............	21	28	49	23	21	5	3
Junior scholars..............	37	23	60	19	15	5	2

ENGLISH

Leading Departments, by Rated Effectiveness of Graduate Program

Institution	All Respondents		Chairmen		Senior Scholars		Junior Scholars	
	Rank	Score	Rank	Score	Rank	Score	Rank	Score
"Extremely attractive"								
Harvard...............	1*	2.77	2	2.78	2	2.75	1	2.80
Yale.................	1*	2.77	1	2.81	1	2.76	2	2.76
California, Berkeley.....	3	2.44	3	2.50	4	2.32	3	2.53
Princeton.............	4	2.41	4	2.31	3	2.45	4	2.44
Stanford.............	5	2.08	5	2.19	5	2.00	5	2.10
Cornell...............	6	2.04	6	2.17	7	1.96	6	2.05
"Attractive"								
Chicago...............	7	1.95	10	1.92	6	1.97	8	1.95
Indiana..............	8*	1.89	8	1.95	8	1.94	10*	1.79
Johns Hopkins..........	8*	1.89	11	1.83	9	1.86	7	1.96
Columbia.............	10	1.85	7	2.00	10	1.83	10*	1.79
Wisconsin..............	11	1.82	9	1.94	13*	1.74	9	1.84
Michigan..............	12	1.76	13	1.71	11	1.80	12	1.75
Illinois.................	13	1.74	12	1.81	12	1.77	14	1.65
North Carolina........	14	1.66	14	1.70	13*	1.74	18	1.53
Northwestern..........	15*	1.62	15	1.65	17	1.59	15	1.62
U.C.L.A..............	15*	1.62	18	1.60	15	1.66	16	1.59
Duke................	17	1.58	16*	1.61	16	1.61	19	1.52
Minnesota............	18	1.56	16*	1.61	20	1.52	17	1.57
Pennsylvania..........	19	1.52	20	1.47	18	1.55	20	1.51
Washington (Seattle)....	20	1.51	19	1.52	19	1.53	21	1.48

"Acceptable plus" (22 departments arranged alphabetically):

Brandeis	N.Y.U.	Rutgers
Brown	Nebraska	Syracuse
Bryn Mawr	Ohio State	Texas
Claremont	Oregon	Tulane
Connecticut	Penn State	Vanderbilt
Emory	Rice	Virginia
Iowa (Iowa City)	Rochester	Washington (St. Louis)
Michigan State		

* Rank and score shared with another department.

High-Ranking Graduate Departments: Hughes, Keniston, and A.C.E. Studies

Top 16 Departments, Hughes Study, 1925	Top 16 Departments, Keniston Study, 1957	Top 20† Departments, Rated Quality of Faculty, A.C.E. Study, 1964
1. Harvard	1. Harvard	1. Yale
2. Columbia	2. Yale	2. Harvard
3. Yale	3. Columbia	3. California, Berkeley
4. Chicago	4. California	4. Princeton
5. Princeton	5. Princeton	5. Columbia
6. Cornell	6. Wisconsin	6. Chicago
7. Bryn Mawr	7. Michigan	7. Stanford
8. Johns Hopkins	8. Chicago	8. Cornell
9. Pennsylvania	9.* Cornell	9. Wisconsin
10.* Illinois	9.* Johns Hopkins	10. Indiana
10.* North Carolina	11. Illinois	11.* Illinois
12. Stanford	12. Pennsylvania	11.* Johns Hopkins
13. Wisconsin	13. Indiana	13. Michigan
14. California	14. U.C.L.A.	14. U.C.L.A.
15. Michigan	15. Stanford	15. Minnesota
16. Iowa	16. Minnesota	16. Northwestern
		17. North Carolina
		18. Pennsylvania
		19. Washington (Seattle)
		20. Duke

* Rank shared with another department.
† These 20 departments represent 27 percent of the 74 departments for which ratings were calculated.

FRENCH

Leading Departments, by Rated Quality of Graduate Faculty

Institution†	All Respondents		Chairmen		Senior Scholars		Junior Scholars	
	Rank	Score	Rank	Score	Rank	Score	Rank	Score
"Distinguished"								
Yale**................	1	4.70	2	4.71	1	4.65	1	4.73
Columbia**...........	2	4.43	1	4.76	2	4.44	2	4.27
Harvard**............	3	4.15	3	4.23	4	4.08	3	4.16
"Strong"								
California, Berkeley.....	4	3.98	8	3.57	3	4.13	4	4.04
Princeton**...........	5	3.85	4	4.00	7	3.75	5	3.85
Johns Hopkins**.......	6	3.82	5*	3.80	5	3.80	6	3.82
Wisconsin**...........	7	3.76	5*	3.80	8*	3.69	7	3.79
Chicago**.............	8	3.63	7	3.61	6	3.77	9	3.50
Pennsylvania**........	9	3.56	9	3.50	8*	3.69	10*	3.46
Michigan**............	10	3.48	10	3.47	12	3.45	8	3.51
U.C.L.A.**.............	11	3.44	13*	3.15	10	3.59	10*	3.46
Stanford**............	12	3.40	13*	3.15	11	3.50	12	3.45
Cornell**.............	13	3.26	12	3.23	14	3.25	14	3.27
North Carolina**.......	14	3.24	15	3.10	16	3.17	13	3.35
Indiana**.............	15	3.23	11	3.45	15	3.24	17	3.11
Illinois...............	16	3.19	16	2.95	13	3.28	15	3.21

"Good" (8 departments arranged alphabetically):

Brown	Minnesota**	Texas**
Bryn Mawr	N.Y.U.**	Washington (Seattle)**
Duke**	Ohio State**	

"Adequate plus" (10 departments arranged alphabetically):

Catholic**	Pittsburgh**	Tulane**
Colorado	Rice	Washington (St. Louis)**
Fordham	Syracuse**	Western Reserve**
Northwestern**		

† These tabulations and those for the effectiveness of the graduate program are based on ratings of the 48 institutions in the survey universe that reported the award of one or more doctorates in French and/or Romance languages from July 1952 through June 1962. Although most institutions offer doctoral study in French in departments of Romance languages, respondents were requested to provide their judgments on the faculties and programs in French specifically, not in Romance languages.
* Rank and score are shared with another department.
** Doctoral study is offered in a department other than a department of French, i.e., department of Romance languages, modern languages, etc.

Profile of Respondents

Respondents	Number	Average Age	Average Number of Publications Since Highest Degree		Professional Meetings Attended in Last Four Years	
			Books	Articles	Regional	National
All respondents...............	108	45.2	2.0	14	4.5	3.1
Chairmen....................	21	54.8	3.2	30	4.7	4.0
Senior scholars...............	39	49.2	2.9	18	4.3	3.5
Junior scholars...............	48	36.6	.8	4	4.7	2.4

Respondents' Division of Time for Professional Activities
(in percents)

Respondents	Instruction			Research and Writing	Administration	Other Professional	Other
	Undergraduate	Graduate	Total				
All respondents	27	25	52	19	22	5	1
Chairmen....................	11	26	37	12	46	5	—
Senior scholars...............	25	28	53	23	17	6	1
Junior scholars	36	23	59	19	15	4	2

FRENCH

Leading Departments, by Rated Effectiveness of Graduate Program

Institution	All Respondents		Chairmen		Senior Scholars		Junior Scholars	
	Rank	Score	Rank	Score	Rank	Score	Rank	Score
"Extremely attractive"								
Yale.................	1	2.68	1	2.61	1	2.70	1	2.69
Columbia.............	2	2.35	2	2.22	2	2.38	2	2.38
Harvard..............	3	2.17	3	2.06	3	2.20	5	2.19
Princeton............	4	2.12	5	1.88	5	2.13	3*	2.20
California, Berkeley.....	5	2.06	12	1.56	4	2.16	3*	2.20
Johns Hopkins.........	6	2.03	4	1.94	6*	2.11	7	2.02
"Attractive"								
Wisconsin.............	7	1.99	6*	1.78	9	1.89	6	2.15
Pennsylvania..........	8	1.88	8	1.72	8	2.04	9	1.84
Chicago..............	9	1.86	6*	1.78	6*	2.11	12	1.72
Stanford..............	10	1.80	10	1.63	10	1.81	8	1.87
Michigan.............	11	1.72	11	1.59	11	1.74	11	1.77
North Carolina........	12	1.69	13	1.53	15*	1.58	10	1.83
Cornell..............	13	1.66	14	1.50	13	1.70	13	1.71
Indiana..............	14	1.64	9	1.65	15*	1.58	14	1.68
U.C.L.A..............	15	1.58	15	1.44	12	1.73	15*	1.53

"Acceptable plus" (18 departments arranged alphabetically):

Brown	Illinois	Syracuse
Bryn Mawr	Minnesota	Texas
Catholic	N.Y.U.	Tulane
Colorado	Northwestern	Washington (St. Louis)
Duke	Ohio State	Washington (Seattle)
Fordham	Rice	Western Reserve

* Rank and score shared with another department.

(ROMANCE LANGUAGES [1])

High-Ranking Graduate Departments: Hughes, Keniston, and A.C.E. Studies

Top 15 Departments, Hughes Study, 1925	Top 15 Departments, Keniston Study, 1957	Top 20 Departments, Rated Quality of Faculty, A.C.E. Study, 1964[1]
1. Chicago	1. California	1. California, Berkeley
2. Harvard	2. Columbia	2. Harvard
3. Columbia	3. Harvard	3. Yale
4. Princeton	4. Pennsylvania	4. Wisconsin
5. California	5. Michigan	5. Columbia
6. Johns Hopkins	6. Yale	6. Princeton
7. Pennsylvania	7. Wisconsin	7. Michigan
8. Yale	8. North Carolina	8. U.C.L.A.
9. Illinois	9. Princeton	9. Pennsylvania
10. Michigan	10. Ohio State	10. Chicago
11. Cornell	11. Illinois	11. Illinois
12. Wisconsin	12. N.Y.U.	12. Johns Hopkins
13. Stanford	13. Johns Hopkins	13. North Carolina
14. Minnesota	14. Indiana	14. Stanford
15. Ohio State	15. Chicago	15. Texas
		16. Brown
		17. Indiana
		18. N.Y.U.
		19. Ohio State
		20. Cornell

[1] The A.C.E. study obtained separate ratings for French and for Spanish. This ranking is based on the sum of the average scores for the two fields.

GERMAN

Leading Departments, by Rated Quality of Graduate Faculty

Institution†	All Respondents		Chairmen		Senior Scholars		Junior Scholars	
	Rank	Score	Rank	Score	Rank	Score	Rank	Score
"Distinguished"								
California, Berkeley	1	4.39	2	4.51	1	4.29	1	4.46
Harvard.............	2	4.31	4	4.33	2	4.23	2	4.41
Yale................	3	4.30	3	4.42	3	4.21	3	4.35
Texas..............	4	4.16	1	4.53	4	4.08	4	3.96
"Strong"								
Pennsylvania........	5	3.84	5	4.00	5	3.72	5	3.90
Princeton...........	6	3.65	8	3.74	7	3.50	6	3.83
Indiana.............	7	3.63	6	3.88	6	3.55	8	3.53
Cornell.............	8	3.58	7	3.77	8	3.42	7	3.68
Ohio State..........	9	3.38	13	3.29	9	3.41	11	3.40
Columbia...........	10	3.35	14*	3.23	11	3.33	9*	3.50
Michigan...........	11	3.30	11	3.34	10	3.34	18	3.15
Chicago............	12	3.27	9	3.40	16	3.18	16	3.27
Illinois.............	13	3.24	14*	3.23	12*	3.20	14	3.31
Wisconsin..........	14	3.23	18	3.03	14*	3.19	9*	3.50
Stanford............	15	3.22	17	3.11	14*	3.19	12	3.37
Northwestern.......	16	3.21	12	3.30	17	3.08	13	3.36
Brown..............	17	3.20	16	3.12	12*	3.20	15	3.28
Washington (Seattle)....	18	3.08	10	3.38	20	2.95	20	3.00
Johns Hopkins.......	19	3.04	19*	3.00	18	3.01	19	3.10

"Good" (3 departments arranged alphabetically):
North Carolina   U.C.L.A.   Washington (St. Louis)

"Adequate plus" (5 departments arranged alphabetically):
Cincinnati   Minnesota   Southern California
Colorado   N.Y.U.

† These tabulations and those for the effectiveness of the graduate program are based on ratings of the 39 institutions in the survey universe that reported the award of one or more doctorates in German from July 1952 through June 1962.
* Rank and score shared with another department.

Profile of Respondents

Respondents	Number	Average Age	Average Number of Publications Since Highest Degree		Professional Meetings Attended in Last Four Years	
			Books	Articles	Regional	National
All respondents...............	124	46.8	2.6	15	4.4	3.8
Chairmen...................	27	52.3	3.2	21	3.7	4.4
Senior scholars................	63	49.7	3.2	18	5.2	4.1
Junior scholars...............	34	36.9	.9	5	3.4	2.8

Respondents' Division of Time for Professional Activities
(in percents)

Respondents	Instruction			Research and Writing	Adminis- tration	Other Profes- sional	Other
	Under- graduate	Graduate	Total				
All respondents...............	25	27	52	20	21	5	2
Chairmen...................	14	25	39	22	35	5	—
Senior scholars................	24	29	53	19	19	6	2
Junior scholars...............	35	25	60	21	15	3	1

GERMAN

Leading Departments, by Rated Effectiveness of Graduate Program

Institution	All Respondents		Chairmen		Senior Scholars		Junior Scholars	
	Rank	Score	Rank	Score	Rank	Score	Rank	Score
"Extremely attractive"								
Harvard..............	1	2.51	1	2.52	1	2.52	1	2.46
Yale.................	2	2.43	2	2.50	2	2.46	2	2.31
California, Berkeley.....	3	2.26	8	2.13	3	2.35	3	2.21
Texas................	4	2.11	3	2.46	4	2.20	14	1.62
Pennsylvania..........	5	2.05	7	2.16	5	2.04	5*	1.96
Cornell..............	6	2.02	4	2.24	8	1.92	4	2.00
"Attractive"								
Indiana..............	7	1.99	5	2.22	6	1.96	7*	1.83
Princeton.............	8	1.97	6	2.20	9*	1.85	5*	1.96
Michigan.............	9	1.84	9	1.96	9*	1.85	11	1.71
Columbia.............	10	1.81	18	1.54	7	1.94	7*	1.83
Chicago..............	11	1.72	11	1.92	14	1.63	12	1.70
Wisconsin............	12	1.71	20	1.36	11	1.82	10	1.79
Stanford.............	13	1.69	16	1.63	13	1.67	9	1.81
Northwestern..........	14*	1.68	10	1.95	16	1.55	13	1.68
Ohio State............	14*	1.68	13	1.71	12	1.74	17	1.52
Illinois...............	16	1.60	14	1.70	15	1.62	19	1.48
Johns Hopkins.........	17	1.58	15	1.67	17	1.53	15	1.59
Washington (Seattle)....	18	1.57	12	1.75	19	1.49	18	1.50

"Acceptable plus" (10 departments arranged alphabetically):

Brown	Minnesota	Southern California
Bryn Mawr	N.Y.U.	U.C.L.A.
Cincinnati	North Carolina	Washington (St. Louis)
Colorado		

* Rank and score shared with another department.

High-Ranking Graduate Departments:
Hughes, Keniston, and A.C.E. Studies

Top 15 Departments, Hughes Study, 1925	Top 15 Departments, Keniston Study, 1957	Top 21† Departments, Rated Quality of Faculty, A.C.E. Study, 1964
1. Wisconsin	1. California	1. California, Berkeley
2. Harvard	2. Yale	2. Harvard
3. Columbia	3. Harvard	3. Yale
4. Johns Hopkins	4. Columbia	4. Texas
5. Chicago	5. Michigan	5. Pennsylvania
6. Illinois	6. Wisconsin	6. Princeton
7. Yale	7. Pennsylvania	7. Indiana
8. Michigan	8. Illinois	8. Cornell
9. Northwestern	9. Texas	9. Ohio State
10.* Bryn Mawr	10. Indiana	10. Columbia
10.* Cornell	11. Chicago	11. Michigan
12. Princeton	12. Cornell	12. Chicago
13. California	13. U.C.L.A.	13. Illinois
14. Pennsylvania	14. Northwestern	14. Wisconsin
15. Ohio State	15. Ohio State	15. Stanford
		16. Northwestern
		17. Brown
		18. Washington (Seattle)
		19. Johns Hopkins
		20.* North Carolina
		20.* U.C.L.A.

* Rank shared with another department.
† These 21 departments represent 54 percent of the 39 departments for which ratings were calculated.

PHILOSOPHY

Leading Departments, by Rated Quality of Graduate Faculty

Institution†	All Respondents		Chairmen		Senior Scholars		Junior Scholars	
	Rank	Score	Rank	Score	Rank	Score	Rank	Score
"Distinguished"								
Harvard..............	1	4.27	1	4.41	3	4.12	1	4.34
Michigan.............	2	4.14	3	4.06	2	4.20	2	4.10
Yale.................	3	4.12	4	4.03	1	4.34	5	3.94
Princeton............	4	4.11	2	4.40	4	4.00	3	4.06
"Strong"								
Cornell..............	5	3.88	5*	3.82	7	3.82	4	3.97
California, Berkeley.....	6	3.87	5*	3.82	5	3.96	7	3.78
Columbia.............	7	3.83	7	3.80	6	3.90	8	3.76
Pittsburgh............	8	3.63	9	3.55	9	3.44	6	3.86
Chicago..............	9	3.57	8	3.56	8	3.51	9	3.63
Stanford.............	10	3.42	10	3.51	10	3.38	10*	3.39
U.C.L.A.............	11	3.30	11	3.30	11	3.28	12	3.31
Brown...............	12	3.23	12	3.27	14	3.06	10*	3.39
Wisconsin............	13	3.11	13	3.25	13	3.12	17	3.00
Minnesota............	14	3.08	18	2.96	12	3.16	13*	3.04
Indiana..............	15	3.05	14	3.24	16	2.96	16	3.02
Johns Hopkins.........	16	3.02	16	3.06	15	2.98	13*	3.04

"Good" (7 departments arranged alphabetically):

Duke	N.Y.U.	Texas
Illinois	Pennsylvania	Washington (Seattle)
Iowa (Iowa City)		

"Adequate plus" (10 departments arranged alphabetically):

Bryn Mawr	Northwestern	Rochester
Fordham	Notre Dame	St. Louis
Michigan State	Ohio State	Washington (St. Louis)
North Carolina		

† These tabulations and those for the effectiveness of the graduate program are based on ratings of the 48 institutions in the survey universe that reported the award of one or more doctorates in philosophy from July 1952 through June 1962.
* Rank and score shared with another department.

Profile of Respondents

Respondents	Number	Average Age	Average Number of Publications Since Highest Degree		Professional Meetings Attended in Last Four Years	
			Books	Articles	Regional	National
All respondents...............	137	45.2	2.2	16	4.5	3.6
Chairmen....................	30	51.1	3.1	18	4.3	4.8
Senior scholars...............	55	52.5	3.2	26	5.0	4.2
Junior scholars...............	52	34.2	.5	5	4.1	2.2

Respondents' Division of Time for Professional Activities
(in percents)

Respondents	Instruction			Research and Writing	Administration	Other Professional	Other
	Under-graduate	Graduate	Total				
All respondents...............	28	25	53	24	16	6	2
Chairmen....................	19	25	44	18	31	6	1
Senior scholars...............	25	25	50	28	13	7	1
Junior scholars...............	36	25	61	22	12	4	2

PHILOSOPHY

Leading Departments, by Rated Effectiveness of Graduate Program

Institution	All Respondents		Chairmen		Senior Scholars		Junior Scholars	
	Rank	Score	Rank	Score	Rank	Score	Rank	Score
"Extremely attractive"								
Princeton	1	2.27	1	2.31	1	2.29	1	2.22
Michigan	2	2.13	2	2.30	3	2.10	2	2.07
Yale	3	2.09	3	2.22	2	2.17	6	1.94
Harvard	4	2.03	4	2.14	4	2.02	4*	1.98
"Attractive"								
Cornell	5	1.85	7	1.88	8	1.70	4*	1.98
California, Berkeley	6*	1.82	5	2.04	5	1.85	9	1.66
Pittsburgh	6*	1.82	8	1.77	11	1.62	3	2.05
Brown	8	1.73	12	1.60	7	1.78	7	1.77
Chicago	9	1.72	6	1.89	9	1.67	8	1.67
Stanford	10	1.66	10	1.72	6	1.82	13	1.44
Columbia	11	1.62	9	1.75	10	1.63	11	1.53

"Acceptable plus" (18 departments arranged alphabetically):

Bryn Mawr	Minnesota	Rochester
Duke	N.Y.U.	Texas
Illinois	North Carolina	U.C.L.A.
Indiana	Northwestern	Washington (St. Louis)
Iowa (Iowa City)	Ohio State	Washington (Seattle)
Johns Hopkins	Pennsylvania	Wisconsin

* Rank and score shared with another department.

High-Ranking Graduate Departments: Hughes, Keniston, and A.C.E. Studies

Top 15 Departments, Hughes Study, 1925	Top 15 Departments, Keniston Study, 1957	Top 20† Departments, Rated Quality of Faculty, A.C.E. Study, 1964
1. Harvard	1. Harvard	1. Harvard
2. Columbia	2. Yale	2. Michigan
3. Chicago	3. Michigan	3. Yale
4. Cornell	4. Columbia	4. Princeton
5. Yale	5. Cornell	5. Cornell
6. Princeton	6. Princeton	6. California, Berkeley
7. California	7. Chicago	7. Columbia
8. Johns Hopkins	8. California	8. Pittsburgh
9. Michigan	9. Minnesota	9. Chicago
10. Pennsylvania	10.* Illinois	10. Stanford
11. Wisconsin	10.* U.C.L.A.	11. U.C.L.A.
12. Ohio State	12. Pennsylvania	12. Brown
13. Bryn Mawr	13. Wisconsin	13. Wisconsin
14. Minnesota	14. Washington (Seattle)	14. Minnesota
15. Northwestern	15. Iowa (Iowa City)	15. Indiana
		16. Johns Hopkins
		17. Pennsylvania
		18. Texas
		19. Illinois
		20. Washington (Seattle)

* Rank shared with another department.
† These 20 departments represent 42 percent of the 48 departments for which ratings were calculated.

SPANISH

Leading Departments, by Rated Quality of Graduate Faculty

Institution†	All Respondents		Chairmen		Senior Scholars		Junior Scholars	
	Rank	Score	Rank	Score	Rank	Score	Rank	Score
"Distinguished"								
California, Berkeley**...	1	4.78	1	4.82	1	4.67	1	4.90
Wisconsin**............	2	4.13	4	3.94	2	4.14	4	4.22
Harvard**............	3	4.10	2	4.05	3	4.00	2	4.25
Michigan**...........	4	4.02	3	4.00	5	3.87	3	4.23
"Strong"								
U.C.L.A.**...........	5	3.85	6*	3.76	4	3.89	6*	3.82
Illinois**............	6*	3.69	6*	3.76	8	3.55	6*	3.82
Princeton**...........	6*	3.69	9	3.50	7	3.60	5	3.92
Pennsylvania**........	8	3.64	5	3.93	10	3.47	8	3.71
Texas**..............	9	3.56	8	3.56	9	3.52	11*	3.61
North Carolina**......	10	3.53	12	3.29	6	3.63	13	3.51
Columbia**...........	11	3.43	10	3.47	11	3.42	15	3.41
Chicago**............	12	3.34	15	3.11	13*	3.20	9*	3.67
Brown**.............	13	3.33	11	3.46	13*	3.20	14	3.44
Yale**..............	14	3.31	19	2.93	12	3.21	9*	3.67
N.Y.U.**............	15	3.13	14	3.12	16	2.94	16	3.37
Johns Hopkins**.......	16	3.01	13	3.13	23	2.55	11*	3.61

"Good" (10 departments arranged alphabetically):

Bryn Mawr	Minnesota**	Ohio State**
Catholic**	New Mexico**	Stanford**
Duke**	Northwestern**	Tulane**
Indiana**		

"Adequate plus" (9 departments arranged alphabetically):

Colorado**	Iowa (Iowa City)**	Southern California**
Cornell**	Kansas**	Syracuse**
George Washington**	Pittsburgh**	Washington (Seattle)**

† These tabulations and those for the effectiveness of the graduate program are based on ratings of 48 institutions in the survey universe that reported the award of one or more doctorates in Spanish and/or Romance languages from July 1952 through June 1962. One other institution was reported as having awarded the doctorate during this period. However, its graduate dean indicates that doctoral study is not offered, and data pertaining to it have been eliminated from all calculations. Although most institutions offer doctoral study in Spanish in departments of Romance languages, respondents were requested to provide their judgments of the faculties and programs in Spanish specifically, not in Romance languages.

* Rank and score shared with another department.

** Doctoral study is offered in a department other than a department of Spanish, i.e., department of Romance languages, modern languages, etc.

Profile of Respondents

Respondents	Number	Average Age	Average Number of Publications Since Highest Degree		Professional Meetings Attended in Last Four Years	
			Books	Articles	Regional	National
All respondents...............	94	47.6	2.7	19	3.8	3.7
Chairmen....................	17	51.3	4.4	15	4.5	4.5
Senior scholars...............	45	51.7	3.3	29	3.2	3.4
Junior scholars...............	32	38.4	.9	6	4.2	3.7

Respondents' Division of Time for Professional Activities
(in percents)

Respondents	Instruction			Research and Writing	Administration	Other Professional	Other
	Undergraduate	Graduate	Total				
All respondents...............	27	28	55	21	17	5	1
Chairmen....................	16	26	42	16	36	5	1
Senior scholars...............	24	32	56	23	15	5	2
Junior scholars...............	38	25	63	20	11	6	—

SPANISH

Leading Departments, by Rated Effectiveness of Graduate Program

Institution	All Respondents		Chairmen		Senior Scholars		Junior Scholars	
	Rank	Score	Rank	Score	Rank	Score	Rank	Score
"Extremely attractive"								
California, Berkeley.....	1	2.73	1	2.60	1	2.72	1	2.80
Harvard..............	2	2.35	2	2.40	2	2.24	2*	2.46
Wisconsin............	3	2.29	3	2.27	3	2.17	2*	2.46
Michigan.............	4	2.18	4	2.20	4	2.08	4	2.31
U.C.L.A..............	5	2.05	5	2.07	5	2.06	7	2.04
"Attractive"								
Princeton............	6	1.91	12	1.73	8	1.84	5	2.12
Illinois...............	7	1.90	6*	2.00	10	1.79	8	2.00
North Carolina........	8	1.84	9	1.87	6	1.91	12	1.74
Yale.................	9	1.81	18*	1.50	11	1.74	6	2.08
Pennsylvania..........	10	1.80	8	1.92	12	1.71	10	1.86
Columbia.............	11	1.79	10	1.80	7	1.87	14	1.69
Texas................	12	1.78	6*	2.00	9	1.82	16	1.62
Brown................	13	1.65	11	1.77	15	1.53	13	1.73
Stanford..............	14	1.64	15*	1.60	13	1.68	17	1.60
Chicago..............	15	1.62	20*	1.47	16*	1.49	9	1.92
Johns Hopkins.........	16	1.57	15*	1.60	18	1.41	11	1.78
New Mexico...........	17	1.56	14	1.64	14	1.59	20*	1.46

"Acceptable plus" (19 departments arranged alphabetically):

Bryn Mawr	Iowa (Iowa City)	Ohio State
Catholic	Kansas	Pittsburgh
Colorado	Minnesota	Southern California
Cornell	Missouri	Syracuse
Duke	N.Y.U.	Tulane
George Washington	Northwestern	Washington (Seattle)
Indiana		

* Rank and score shared with another department.

(ROMANCE LANGUAGES [1])

High-Ranking Graduate Departments: Hughes, Keniston, and A.C.E. Studies

Top 15 Departments, Hughes Study, 1925	Top 15 Departments, Keniston Study, 1957	Top 20 Departments, Rated Quality of Faculty, A.C.E. Study, 1964[1]
1. Chicago	1. California	1. California, Berkeley
2. Harvard	2. Columbia	2. Harvard
3. Columbia	3. Harvard	3. Yale
4. Princeton	4. Pennsylvania	4. Wisconsin
5. California	5. Michigan	5. Columbia
6. Johns Hopkins	6. Yale	6. Princeton
7. Pennsylvania	7. Wisconsin	7. Michigan
8. Yale	8. North Carolina	8. U.C.L.A.
9. Illinois	9. Princeton	9. Pennsylvania
10. Michigan	10. Ohio State	10. Chicago
11. Cornell	11. Illinois	11. Illinois
12. Wisconsin	12. N.Y.U.	12. Johns Hopkins
13. Stanford	13. Johns Hopkins	13. North Carolina
14. Minnesota	14. Indiana	14. Stanford
15. Ohio State	15. Chicago	15. Texas
		16. Brown
		17. Indiana
		18. N.Y.U.
		19. Ohio State
		20. Cornell

[1] The A.C.E. study obtained separate ratings for French and for Spanish. This ranking is based on the sum of the average scores for the two fields.

ANTHROPOLOGY

Leading Departments, by Rated Quality of Graduate Faculty

Institution†	All Respondents		Chairmen		Senior Scholars		Junior Scholars	
	Rank	Score	Rank	Score	Rank	Score	Rank	Score
"Distinguished"								
Chicago................	1	4.57	1	4.56	1	4.53	1	4.61
Harvard................	2	4.34	2	4.33	3	4.43	2	4.22
California, Berkeley.....	3	4.31	3	4.18	2	4.45	3	4.16
Michigan..............	4	4.04	5	3.93	4	4.13	5	3.96
"Strong"								
Pennsylvania...........	5	3.94	8	3.68	5	3.90	4	4.13
Yale...................	6	3.81	4	4.00	6	3.86	9	3.63
Columbia..............	7*	3.76	7	3.75	9	3.67	6	3.90
U.C.L.A...............	7*	3.76	6	3.87	8	3.76	8	3.70
Cornell...............	9	3.74	9	3.37	7	3.80	7	3.83
Stanford..............	10	3.32	10	3.31	11	3.23	10	3.45
Wisconsin.............	11	3.29	11	3.21	10	3.35	11	3.24
Arizona...............	12	3.01	12	3.00	12	3.02	14	3.00

"Good" (5 departments arranged alphabetically):

Indiana	Northwestern	Washington (Seattle)
Minnesota	Oregon	

"Adequate plus" (2 departments arranged alphabetically):

New Mexico   North Carolina

† These tabulations and those for the effectiveness of the graduate program are based on ratings of 24 institutions in the survey universe that reported the award of one or more doctorates in anthropology from July 1952 through June 1962. Two other institutions were reported as having awarded doctorates in the field during the ten-year period. However, their graduate deans indicate that doctoral study is not offered, and data pertaining to them has been eliminated from all calculations.

* Rank and score shared with another department.

Profile of Respondents

Respondents	Number	Average Age	Average Number of Publications Since Highest Degree		Professional Meetings Attended in Last Four Years	
			Books	Articles	Regional	National
All respondents...............	91	44.9	2.5	23	2.9	4.2
Chairmen...................	16	48.5	2.9	34	2.7	4.6
Senior scholars..............	44	48.9	3.3	30	2.9	4.3
Junior scholars..............	31	37.0	1.0	9	2.9	3.7

Respondents' Division of Time for Professional Activities
(in percents)

Respondents	Instruction			Research and Writing	Adminis-tration	Other Profes-sional	Other
	Under-graduate	Graduate	Total				
All respondents...............	29	24	53	21	17	6	3
Chairmen...................	17	24	41	15	37	7	1
Senior scholars..............	25	27	52	23	15	7	3
Junior scholars..............	40	21	61	21	9	5	4

ANTHROPOLOGY

Leading Departments, by Rated Effectiveness of Graduate Program

Institution	All Respondents		Chairmen		Senior Scholars		Junior Scholars	
	Rank	Score	Rank	Score	Rank	Score	Rank	Score
"Extremely attractive"								
Chicago	1	2.27	1	2.47	2	2.10	1	2.38
Harvard	2	2.12	2	2.21	1	2.13	3	2.07
Pennsylvania	3	2.06	4*	2.07	4	1.95	2	2.21
"Attractive"								
California, Berkeley	4	1.94	3	2.20	3	1.97	6	1.76
Michigan	5	1.89	7	1.87	6	1.78	4	2.04
Cornell	6	1.80	10	1.60	5	1.92	7*	1.74
U.C.L.A.	7	1.76	4*	2.07	7	1.66	7*	1.74
Yale	8	1.68	4*	2.07	8	1.64	12	1.52
Columbia	9	1.64	9	1.67	10*	1.53	5	1.78
Stanford	10	1.63	8	1.71	10*	1.53	9	1.71
Wisconsin	11	1.53	12	1.38	9	1.57	11	1.54

"Acceptable plus" (7 departments arranged alphabetically):

Arizona	North Carolina	Oregon
Indiana	Northwestern	Washington (Seattle)
Minnesota		

* Rank and score shared with another department.

High-Ranking Graduate Departments: Keniston and A.C.E. Studies

	Top 15 Departments, Keniston Study, 1957	Top 20† Departments, Rated Quality of Faculty, A.C.E. Study, 1964
	1. Chicago	1. Chicago
	2. Harvard	2. Harvard
	3. Columbia	3. California, Berkeley
	4. California	4. Michigan
	5. Yale	5. Pennsylvania
	6. Pennsylvania	6. Yale
	7. Michigan	7.* Columbia
	8. U.C.L.A.	7.* U.C.L.A.
	9. Cornell	9. Cornell
	10. Northwestern	10. Stanford
	11. Washington (Seattle)	11. Wisconsin
	12. Minnesota	12. Arizona
	13. Indiana	13. Washington (Seattle)
	14. Stanford	14. Oregon
	15. Wisconsin	15. Northwestern
		16. Minnesota
		17. Indiana
		18. North Carolina
		19. New Mexico
		20. Utah

* Rank shared with another department.
† These 20 departments represent 83 percent of the 24 departments for which ratings were calculated.

ECONOMICS

Leading Departments, by Rated Quality of Graduate Faculty

Institution†	All Respondents		Chairmen		Senior Scholars		Junior Scholars	
	Rank	Score	Rank	Score	Rank	Score	Rank	Score
"Distinguished"								
Harvard.............	1	4.82	1*	4.85	1	4.83	1*	4.77
M.I.T................	2	4.80	1*	4.85	2	4.77	1*	4.77
Chicago..............	3	4.57	5	4.45	3	4.60	3*	4.61
Yale.................	4	4.56	3	4.82	5	4.36	3*	4.61
California, Berkeley.....	5	4.50	7	4.41	4	4.55	5	4.50
Stanford.............	6	4.36	4	4.46	6	4.35	6	4.28
Princeton............	7	4.22	6	4.43	7	4.15	7	4.13
"Strong"								
Michigan.............	8	3.72	9*	3.78	9	3.60	8	3.79
Columbia.............	9	3.71	9*	3.78	8	3.67	9*	3.69
Wisconsin............	10	3.68	8	3.85	10	3.56	9*	3.69
Minnesota............	11	3.56	13	3.71	11	3.44	11	3.58
Northwestern..........	12	3.51	11	3.77	12	3.37	13	3.48
Carnegie Tech.........	13	3.48	12	3.73	14	3.29	12	3.51
Pennsylvania..........	14	3.33	14	3.42	13	3.32	15	3.26
Johns Hopkins.........	15	3.29	15	3.25	15	3.25	14	3.35
U.C.L.A.............	16	3.08	19	2.94	16	3.04	16	3.20

"Good" (13 departments arranged alphabetically):

Brown	Iowa State (Ames)	Rochester
Cornell	Michigan State	Vanderbilt
Duke	North Carolina	Virginia
Illinois	Purdue	Washington (Seattle)
Indiana		

"Adequate plus" (7 departments arranged alphabetically):

Claremont	Pittsburgh	Texas
Maryland	Syracuse	Washington (St. Louis)
N.Y.U.		

† These tabulations and those for the effectiveness of the graduate program are based on ratings of 71 institutions in the survey universe that reported the award of one or more doctorates in economics from July 1952 through June 1962. One other institution was reported as having awarded doctorates in the field during the period. However, its graduate dean indicates that doctoral study is not offered, and data pertaining to it have been eliminated from all calculations.
* Rank and score shared with another department.

Profile of Respondents

Respondents	Number	Average Age	Average Number of Publications Since Highest Degree		Professional Meetings Attended in Last Four Years	
			Books	Articles	Regional	National
All respondents................	173	45.2	2.1	15	2.6	3.7
Chairmen....................	41	48.6	2.9	18	2.8	4.1
Senior scholars...............	73	50.9	2.8	21	2.6	3.7
Junior scholars...............	59	35.5	.6	6	2.3	3.3

Respondents' Division of Time for Professional Activities
(in percents)

Respondents	Instruction			Research and Writing	Administration	Other Professional	Other
	Under-graduate	Graduate	Total				
All respondents................	19	28	47	23	21	9	1
Chairmen....................	11	20	31	18	42	8	—
Senior scholars...............	18	30	48	23	19	9	2
Junior scholars...............	27	30	57	25	9	8	1

ECONOMICS

Leading Departments, by Rated Effectiveness of Graduate Program

Institution	All Respondents		Chairmen		Senior Scholars		Junior Scholars	
	Rank	Score	Rank	Score	Rank	Score	Rank	Score
"Extremely attractive"								
M.I.T..............	1	2.70	2	2.63	1	2.61	1	2.84
Harvard..............	2	2.60	4	2.51	2	2.60	3	2.66
Yale................	3	2.58	1	2.79	3	2.31	2	2.74
Stanford............	4	2.38	3	2.54	4	2.29	5	2.36
California, Berkeley.....	5	2.33	6	2.27	6	2.25	4	2.46
Princeton............	6	2.30	5	2.49	5	2.26	7	2.24
Chicago..............	7	2.21	7	2.14	7	2.15	6	2.33
"Attractive"								
Wisconsin............	8	1.91	9*	1.83	8	1.83	8	2.06
Michigan.............	9	1.78	9*	1.83	9	1.71	9	1.83
Northwestern.........	10	1.72	8	1.92	11	1.59	12	1.72
Carnegie Tech.........	11	1.66	12	1.69	12	1.57	10	1.75
Johns Hopkins........	12*	1.63	15	1.44	10	1.65	11	1.73
Minnesota............	12*	1.63	9*	1.83	14	1.53	13	1.63
Columbia.............	14	1.55	14	1.49	13	1.56	14	1.59
Pennsylvania.........	15	1.54	13	1.62	15	1.48	15	1.54

"Acceptable plus" (15 departments arranged alphabetically):

Brown	Indiana	Rochester
Claremont	Iowa State (Ames)	U.C.L.A.
Cornell	Michigan State	Vanderbilt
Duke	North Carolina	Virginia
Illinois	Purdue	Washington (Seattle)

* Rank and score shared with another department.

High-Ranking Graduate Departments: Hughes, Keniston, and A.C.E. Studies

Top 16 Departments, Hughes Study, 1925	Top 16 Departments,[a] Keniston Study, 1957	Top 20† Departments, Rated Quality of Faculty, A.C.E. Study, 1964
1. Harvard	1. Harvard	1. Harvard
2. Columbia	2. Chicago	2. M.I.T.
3. Chicago	3. Yale	3. Chicago
4. Wisconsin	4. Columbia	4. Yale
5. Yale	5.* California	5. California, Berkeley
6. Johns Hopkins	5.* Stanford	6. Stanford
7. Michigan	7. Princeton	7. Princeton
8. Pennsylvania	8. Johns Hopkins	8. Michigan
9. Illinois	9. Michigan	9. Columbia
10. Cornell	10. Minnesota	10. Wisconsin
11. Princeton	11. Northwestern	11. Minnesota
12. California	12. Duke	12. Northwestern
13. Minnesota	13. Wisconsin	13. Carnegie Tech.
14. Northwestern	14. Pennsylvania	14. Pennsylvania
15. Stanford	15. Cornell	15. Johns Hopkins
16. Ohio State	16. U.C.L.A.	16. U.C.L.A.
		17. Cornell
		18. Duke
		19. Purdue
		20. Michigan State

* Rank shared with another department.
† These 20 departments represent 28 percent of the 71 departments for which ratings were calculated.
[a] Technical and specialized institutions were omitted from the Keniston study.

GEOGRAPHY

Leading Departments, by Rated Quality of Graduate Faculty

Institution†	All Respondents		Chairmen		Senior Scholars		Junior Scholars	
	Rank	Score	Rank	Score	Rank	Score	Rank	Score
"Distinguished"								
Wisconsin..............	1	4.66	1	4.94	1	4.69	1	4.42
Chicago................	2	4.41	2	4.70	2	4.35	2	4.30
California, Berkeley.....	3	4.14	3	4.35	3	4.05	3	4.11
"Strong"								
Washington (Seattle)....	4	3.68	10	3.43	4	3.79	4	3.65
Syracuse...............	5	3.66	4	4.00	5	3.66	7	3.42
Northwestern..........	6	3.64	5	3.88	7	3.55	5	3.61
Minnesota.............	7	3.53	6	3.70	8	3.40	6	3.60
U.C.L.A...............	8	3.49	7	3.68	6	3.64	10	3.15
Michigan..............	9	3.33	8	3.47	9	3.21	8	3.40
Louisiana State........	10	3.17	11	3.35	10	3.08	9	3.19

"Good" (9 departments arranged alphabetically):

Clark	Iowa (Iowa City)	Michigan State
Illinois	Johns Hopkins	Ohio State
Indiana	Kansas	Penn State

"Adequate plus" (4 departments arranged alphabetically):

Columbia	Pittsburgh
Nebraska	Texas

† These tabulations and those for the effectiveness of the graduate program are based on ratings of 30 institutions in the survey universe that reported the award of one or more doctorates in geography from July 1952 through June 1962. Three additional institutions were reported as having awarded doctorates in the field during the ten-year period. However, their graduate deans indicate that doctoral study is not offered in the field, and data pertaining to them have been eliminated from all calculations.

Profile of Respondents

Respondents	Number	Average Age	Average Number of Publications Since Highest Degree		Professional Meetings Attended in Last Four Years	
			Books	Articles	Regional	National
All respondents...............	84	46.0	1.8	18	2.8	3.4
Chairmen....................	18	51.4	2.4	22	2.2	3.5
Senior scholars...............	40	47.7	2.2	21	3.1	3.4
Junior scholars...............	26	38.8	.6	10	2.7	3.2

Respondents' Division of Time for Professional Activities
(in percents)

Respondents	Instruction			Research and Writing	Administration	Other Professional	Other
	Under-graduate	Graduate	Total				
All respondents...............	29	24	53	22	16	7	1
Chairmen....................	18	25	43	16	34	7	—
Senior scholars...............	29	23	52	24	14	8	2
Junior scholars...............	36	24	60	24	8	7	1

GEOGRAPHY

Leading Departments, by Rated Effectiveness of Graduate Program

Institution	All Respondents		Chairmen		Senior Scholars		Junior Scholars	
	Rank	Score	Rank	Score	Rank	Score	Rank	Score
"Extremely attractive"								
Wisconsin.............	1	2.55	1*	2.65	1	2.61	2	2.39
Chicago..............	2	2.35	1*	2.65	3	2.16	1	2.44
California, Berkeley.....	3	2.25	3	2.29	2	2.19	3	2.29
Washington (Seattle)....	4	2.04	9	1.69	4	2.08	4	2.21
"Attractive"								
Minnesota............	5	1.88	6	1.88	6	1.91	6	1.83
Northwestern.........	6*	1.85	4*	2.00	8	1.73	5	1.92
Syracuse.............	6*	1.85	4*	2.00	5	1.92	8*	1.63
U.C.L.A.............	8	1.68	7*	1.71	7	1.79	11	1.50
Michigan............	9	1.61	7*	1.71	9*	1.51	7	1.70

"Acceptable plus" (12 departments arranged alphabetically):

Clark	Iowa (Iowa City)	Michigan State
Columbia	Johns Hopkins	Ohio State
Illinois	Kansas	Penn State
Indiana	Louisiana State	Pittsburgh

* Rank and score shared with another department.

High-Ranking Graduate Departments: Hughes, Keniston, and A.C.E. Studies

Top 8 Departments, Hughes Study, 1925	Top 15 Departments, Keniston Study, 1957	Top 20† Departments, Rated Quality of Faculty, A.C.E. Study, 1964
1. Chicago	1. Wisconsin	1. Wisconsin
2. Clark	2. Chicago	2. Chicago
3. Wisconsin	3. California	3. California, Berkeley
4. Columbia	4. Michigan	4. Washington (Seattle)
5. Harvard	5. Northwestern	5. Syracuse
6.* California	6. U.C.L.A.	6. Northwestern
6.* Michigan	7. Washington (Seattle)	7. Minnesota
8. Yale	8. Ohio State	8. U.C.L.A.
	9. Illinois	9. Michigan
	10. Minnesota	10. Louisiana State
	11.* Columbia	11. Penn State
	11.* Indiana	12. Indiana
	13. Iowa (Iowa City)	13. Iowa (Iowa City)
	14. Johns Hopkins	14. Johns Hopkins
	15. Yale	15. Kansas
		16. Michigan State
		17. Ohio State
		18. Illinois
		19. Clark
		20. Pittsburgh

* Rank shared with another department.
† These 20 departments represent 67 percent of the 30 departments for which ratings were calculated.

HISTORY

Leading Departments, by Rated Quality of Graduate Faculty

Institution†	All Respondents		Chairmen		Senior Scholars		Junior Scholars	
	Rank	Score	Rank	Score	Rank	Score	Rank	Score
"Distinguished"								
Harvard..............	1	4.89	1	4.92	1	4.89	1	4.87
California, Berkeley.....	2	4.64	2	4.57	2	4.64	2	4.66
Yale.................	3	4.50	3	4.48	3	4.53	3	4.46
Columbia.............	4	4.31	4	4.46	5	4.34	5	4.18
Wisconsin............	5	4.28	8	4.13	4	4.36	4	4.25
Princeton............	6	4.13	7	4.15	6	4.10	6	4.13
Chicago..............	7*	4.04	6	4.17	8	4.02	7	3.96
Stanford.............	7*	4.04	5	4.20	7	4.09	8	3.86
"Strong"								
Cornell..............	9	3.71	9*	3.65	9	3.75	9*	3.67
Michigan.............	10	3.67	9*	3.65	11	3.67	9*	3.67
Johns Hopkins.........	11	3.59	11	3.56	10	3.68	11	3.46
U.C.L.A.............	12	3.51	16	3.36	12	3.62	12	3.44
Pennsylvania..........	13	3.42	13	3.47	13	3.46	14	3.29
Northwestern..........	14	3.40	12	3.52	14	3.44	15*	3.25
Illinois...............	15	3.35	17	3.35	15	3.38	13	3.31
Minnesota............	16	3.29	19	3.21	16	3.35	15*	3.25
Duke................	17*	3.25	15	3.41	17	3.25	18	3.14
Indiana..............	17*	3.25	14	3.43	18	3.19	17	3.20
North Carolina........	19	3.17	18	3.31	20	3.16	19*	3.04
Washington (Seattle)....	20	3.14	20	3.18	19	3.17	19*	3.04

"Good" (13 departments arranged alphabetically):

Brandeis	Iowa (Iowa City)	Rutgers
Brown	N.Y.U.	Texas
Bryn Mawr	Ohio State	Virginia
Claremont	Rochester	Washington (St. Louis)
Emory		

"Adequate plus" (17 departments arranged alphabetically):

Colorado	Nebraska	Syracuse
Kansas	Notre Dame	Tulane
Kentucky	Oklahoma	Vanderbilt
Louisiana State	Oregon	Wayne State
Michigan State	Pittsburgh	Western Reserve
Missouri	Rice	

† These tabulations and those for the effectiveness of the graduate program are based on ratings of the 75 institutions in the survey universe that reported the award of one or more doctorates in history from July 1952 through June 1962.
* Rank and score shared with another department.

Profile of Respondents

Respondents	Number	Average Age	Average Number of Publications Since Highest Degree		Professional Meetings Attended in Last Four Years	
			Books	Articles	Regional	National
All respondents...............	180	45.7	2.7	13	3.9	4.7
Chairmen....................	39	49.5	3.7	15	5.2	5.6
Senior scholars...............	78	51.5	3.8	18	3.6	4.6
Junior scholars...............	63	36.6	.9	5	3.3	4.2

Respondents' Division of Time for Professional Activities
(in percents)

Respondents	Instruction			Research and Writing	Adminis- tration	Other Profes- sional	Other
	Under- graduate	Graduate	Total				
All respondents...............	28	24	52	22	19	5	2
Chairmen....................	17	21	38	19	37	5	1
Senior scholars...............	26	27	53	20	17	6	3
Junior scholars...............	37	22	59	25	12	4	1

HISTORY

Leading Departments, by Rated Effectiveness of Graduate Program

Institution	All Respondents		Chairmen		Senior Scholars		Junior Scholars	
	Rank	Score	Rank	Score	Rank	Score	Rank	Score
"Extremely attractive"								
Harvard.............	1	2.76	1	2.75	1	2.79	1	2.72
Yale.................	2	2.53	2	2.56	2	2.55	2	2.49
California, Berkeley.....	3	2.40	3	2.54	3	2.34	3	2.38
Princeton............	4	2.29	4	2.26	4	2.29	4	2.32
Wisconsin............	5	2.26	6	2.22	5	2.26	5	2.27
Stanford.............	6	2.23	5	2.25	6	2.21	6	2.24
Johns Hopkins.........	7	2.05	8	2.12	8	2.02	7	2.04
Chicago..............	8	2.04	7	2.19	7	2.06	8	1.91
"Attractive"								
Columbia............	9	1.93	9	2.08	9	1.97	10	1.78
Cornell..............	10	1.89	10	2.06	10	1.90	11	1.77
Michigan............	11	1.82	11	1.80	11	1.83	9	1.81
U.C.L.A.............	12	1.69	12*	1.71	12	1.74	14*	1.63
Pennsylvania.........	13	1.68	14	1.70	13	1.70	13	1.64
Northwestern.........	14	1.67	12*	1.71	14	1.67	14*	1.63
Duke................	15	1.61	16*	1.68	15	1.58	17	1.59
Indiana.............	16	1.60	15	1.69	17*	1.55	16	1.60
Washington (Seattle)....	17	1.57	16*	1.68	20	1.43	12	1.68
Illinois..............	18	1.55	20	1.57	17*	1.55	18	1.54
North Carolina........	19	1.54	18	1.60	19	1.54	19	1.50

"Acceptable plus" (24 departments arranged alphabetically):

Brandeis	Minnesota	Rutgers
Brown	Missouri	Syracuse
Bryn Mawr	N.Y.U.	Texas
Claremont	Ohio State	Tulane
Colorado	Oregon	Vanderbilt
Emory	Pittsburgh	Virginia
Iowa (Iowa City)	Rice	Washington (St. Louis)
Michigan State	Rochester	Western Reserve

* Rank and score shared with another department.

High-Ranking Graduate Departments: Hughes, Keniston, and A.C.E. Studies

Top 19 Departments, Hughes Study, 1925	Top 15 Departments, Keniston Study, 1957	Top 20† Departments, Rated Quality of Faculty, A.C.E. Study, 1964
1. Harvard	1. Harvard	1. Harvard
2. Columbia	2. Columbia	2. California, Berkeley
3. Chicago	3. Yale	3. Yale
4. Yale	4. California	4. Columbia
5. Cornell	5. Wisconsin	5. Wisconsin
6. Wisconsin	6. Princeton	6. Princeton
7.* Michigan	7. Chicago	7.* Chicago
7.* Pennsylvania	8. Cornell	7.* Stanford
9. California	9. Johns Hopkins	9. Cornell
10.* Illinois	10. Pennsylvania	10. Michigan
10.* Princeton	11. Northwestern	11. Johns Hopkins
12. Minnesota	12. Michigan	12. U.C.L.A.
13. Johns Hopkins	13. Illinois	13. Pennsylvania
14. Iowa (Iowa City)	14. Minnesota	14. Northwestern
15.* Bryn Mawr	15. Stanford	15. Illinois
15.* Indiana		16. Minnesota
15.* Ohio State		17.* Duke
15.* Stanford		17.* Indiana
15.* Texas		19. North Carolina
		20. Washington (Seattle)

* Rank shared with another department.
† These 20 departments represent 27 percent of the 75 departments for which ratings were calculated.

POLITICAL SCIENCE

Leading Departments, by Rated Quality of Graduate Faculty

Institution†	All Respondents		Chairmen		Senior Scholars		Junior Scholars	
	Rank	Score	Rank	Score	Rank	Score	Rank	Score
"Distinguished"								
Yale..................	1	4.67	1	4.79	3	4.52	1	4.75
Harvard...............	2	4.60	2	4.70	1	4.60	2	4.53
California, Berkeley.....	3	4.51	3	4.51	2	4.56	3	4.44
Chicago...............	4	4.34	4	4.33	4	4.32	4	4.36
Columbia..............	5	4.08	5	4.17	5*	4.00	5	4.09
Princeton.............	6	4.04	6	4.14	5*	4.00	6	4.01
"Strong"								
M.I.T.................	7*	3.77	7	3.96	10	3.53	7	3.92
Wisconsin.............	7*	3.77	8*	3.66	7	3.76	9	3.84
Stanford..............	9	3.76	10	3.64	8	3.71	8	3.87
Michigan.............	10	3.63	11	3.56	9	3.57	10	3.73
Cornell...............	11	3.57	12	3.51	11	3.50	11	3.68
Northwestern..........	12	3.50	8*	3.66	12	3.35	12	3.55
U.C.L.A..............	13	3.39	13*	3.48	13	3.34	13	3.38
Indiana...............	14	3.34	13*	3.48	14	3.26	14	3.34
North Carolina........	15	3.23	15	3.29	15*	3.18	15	3.24
Minnesota............	16	3.16	16	3.12	15*	3.18	17	3.16
Illinois................	17	3.11	17*	3.09	17	3.16	18	3.07
Johns Hopkins..........	18	3.10	20	2.94	18	3.10	16	3.17

"Good" (10 departments arranged alphabetically):

Duke	Pennsylvania	Vanderbilt
Michigan State	Syracuse	Washington (St. Louis)
N.Y.U.	Texas	Washington (Seattle)
Ohio State		

"Adequate plus" (9 departments arranged alphabetically):

Brown	New School	Pittsburgh
Claremont	Oregon	Rutgers
Iowa (Iowa City)	Penn State	Virginia

† These tabulations and those for the effectiveness of the graduate program are based on ratings of the 64 institutions in the survey universe that reported the award of one or more doctorates in political science from July 1952 through June 1962.
* Rank and score shared with another department.

Profile of Respondents

Respondents	Number	Average Age	Average Number of Publications Since Highest Degree		Professional Meetings Attended in Last Four Years	
			Books	Articles	Regional	National
All respondents................	165	43.3	2.4	14	3.1	3.7
Chairmen....................	35	49.3	3.5	18	3.4	4.8
Senior scholars................	66	48.0	3.2	19	3.7	4.0
Junior scholars...............	64	35.1	1.1	5	2.4	2.8

Respondents' Division of Time for Professional Activities
(in percents)

Respondents	Instruction			Research and Writing	Administration	Other Professional	Other
	Undergraduate	Graduate	Total				
All respondents................	28	22	50	20	21	8	1
Chairmen....................	15	19	34	15	42	9	1
Senior scholars................	27	25	52	19	19	10	—
Junior scholars...............	35	22	57	23	12	6	2

POLITICAL SCIENCE

Leading Departments, by Rated Effectiveness of Graduate Program

Institution	All Respondents		Chairmen		Senior Scholars		Junior Scholars	
	Rank	Score	Rank	Score	Rank	Score	Rank	Score
"Extremely attractive"								
Yale...................	1	2.63	1	2.68	2	2.47	1	2.76
Harvard...............	2	2.57	2	2.66	1	2.59	2	2.52
California, Berkeley.....	3	2.33	3	2.38	3	2.40	4	2.24
Chicago...............	4	2.27	4	2.25	4	2.25	3	2.29
Princeton.............	5	2.20	5	2.19	5	2.18	5	2.22
Stanford..............	6	2.11	6	2.16	6	2.06	6	2.14
M.I.T.................	7	2.07	7	2.13	8	1.98	7	2.13
Wisconsin.............	8	2.05	8	2.03	7	2.02	8	2.09
"Attractive"								
Columbia.............	9	1.89	9	2.00	9	1.95	12	1.78
Michigan.............	10	1.84	10	1.83	10	1.80	9	1.88
Northwestern..........	11	1.81	11	1.81	11	1.79	11	1.82
Cornell...............	12	1.80	12	1.74	12	1.76	10	1.87
Indiana...............	13	1.61	14	1.57	13	1.65	13	1.60
North Carolina........	14	1.59	15	1.56	14	1.63	14*	1.57
Johns Hopkins.........	15*	1.53	17	1.44	15	1.61	17	1.50
U.C.L.A..............	15*	1.53	13	1.68	18	1.43	16	1.55

"Acceptable plus" (16 departments arranged alphabetically):

Claremont	N.Y.U.	Texas
Duke	Ohio State	Vanderbilt
Illinois	Oregon	Virginia
Iowa (Iowa City)	Pennsylvania	Washington (St. Louis)
Michigan State	Syracuse	Washington (Seattle)
Minnesota		

* Rank and score shared with another department.

High-Ranking Graduate Departments: Hughes, Keniston, and A.C.E. Studies

Top 11 Departments, Hughes Study, 1925	Top 15 Departments,[a] Keniston Study, 1957	Top 20[†] Departments, Rated Quality of Faculty, A.C.E. Study, 1964
1. Harvard	1. Harvard	1. Yale
2. Chicago	2. Chicago	2. Harvard
3. Columbia	3. California	3. California, Berkeley
4. Wisconsin	4. Columbia	4. Chicago
5. Illinois	5. Princeton	5. Columbia
6. Michigan	6. Michigan	6. Princeton
7. Princeton	7. Yale	7.* M.I.T.
8. Johns Hopkins	8. Wisconsin	7.* Wisconsin
9.* Iowa	9. Minnesota	9. Stanford
9.* Pennsylvania	10. Cornell	10. Michigan
11. California	11. Illinois	11. Cornell
	12. U.C.L.A.	12. Northwestern
	13. Stanford	13. U.C.L.A.
	14. Johns Hopkins	14. Indiana
	15. Duke	15. North Carolina
		16. Minnesota
		17. Illinois
		18. Johns Hopkins
		19. Duke
		20. Syracuse

* Rank shared with another department.
† These 20 departments represent 31 percent of the 64 departments for which ratings were calculated.
[a] Technical and specialized institutions were omitted from the Keniston study.

SOCIOLOGY

Leading Departments, by Rated Quality of Graduate Faculty

Institution†	All Respondents		Chairmen		Senior Scholars		Junior Scholars	
	Rank	Score	Rank	Score	Rank	Score	Rank	Score
"Distinguished"								
California, Berkeley[a]....	1	4.82	1	4.85	1	4.78	1	4.83
Harvard[b].............	2	4.65	2	4.62	2	4.64	2	4.67
Columbia.............	3	4.62	3	4.60	3	4.63	3	4.60
Chicago..............	4	4.41	4	4.37	4	4.45	4	4.39
Michigan.............	5	4.15	5	4.08	5	4.24	5	4.09
"Strong"								
Wisconsin.............	6	3.82	6	3.82	6	3.85	6	3.75
Cornell...............	7	3.63	7	3.62	7	3.73	8	3.51
Princeton.............	8	3.56	8	3.57	8	3.53	7	3.57
Minnesota............	9	3.44	9*	3.45	9	3.50	11	3.32
North Carolina........	10	3.35	9*	3.45	10	3.33	12	3.30
U.C.L.A..............	11	3.32	11	3.37	11	3.25	9	3.38
Stanford.............	12	3.28	14	3.26	12	3.21	10	3.35
Washington (Seattle)....	13	3.20	12	3.36	14	3.12	13	3.19
Northwestern..........	14	3.15	13	3.28	13	3.14	16	3.07
Yale.................	15	3.10	15*	3.14	16	3.04	15	3.12
Washington (St. Louis)[c]..	16	3.06	17	3.06	17	3.00	14	3.13
Michigan State........	17	3.05	15*	3.14	15	3.08	18	2.94

"Good" (7 departments arranged alphabetically):

Illinois	N.Y.U.	Pennsylvania
Indiana	Oregon	Texas
Johns Hopkins[b]		

"Adequate plus" (10 departments arranged alphabetically):

Brown	Ohio State	Purdue
Duke[c]	Penn State[c]	Southern California[c]
Iowa (Iowa City)	Pittsburgh	Washington State
New School		

† These tabulations and those for the effectiveness of the graduate program are based on ratings of 64 institutions in the survey universe that reported the award of one or more doctorates in sociology from July 1952 through June 1962. Three other institutions were reported as having awarded doctorates in the field during the period. However, their graduate deans indicate that doctoral study is not offered, and data pertaining to them have been eliminated from all calculations.
* Rank and score shared with another department.
[a] Doctoral study in sociology is offered in the Department of Sociology and Social Institutions.
[b] Doctoral study in sociology is offered in the Department of Social Relations.
[c] Doctoral study in sociology is offered in the Department of Sociology and Anthropology.

Profile of Respondents

Respondents	Number	Average Age	Average Number of Publications Since Highest Degree		Professional Meetings Attended in Last Four Years	
			Books	Articles	Regional	National
All respondents...............	157	44.4	2.6	22	3.5	4.2
Chairmen....................	36	48.9	3.5	40	4.5	5.2
Senior scholars...............	65	49.1	3.7	25	3.3	4.4
Junior scholars..............	56	35.7	.7	8	3.2	3.3

Respondents' Division of Time for Professional Activities
(in percents)

Respondents	Instruction			Research and Writing	Administration	Other Professional	Other
	Under-graduate	Graduate	Total				
All respondents...............	23	23	46	26	19	7	2
Chairmen....................	9	22	31	19	40	8	1
Senior scholars...............	23	24	47	27	15	8	3
Junior scholars..............	31	24	55	28	10	5	1

SOCIOLOGY

Leading Departments, by Rated Effectiveness of Graduate Program

Institution	All Respondents		Chairmen		Senior Scholars		Junior Scholars	
	Rank	Score	Rank	Score	Rank	Score	Rank	Score
"Extremely attractive"								
Harvard...............	1	2.50	1	2.53	2	2.52	1	2.45
California, Berkeley.....	2	2.41	4	2.19	1	2.55	2	2.38
Michigan..............	3	2.24	2	2.25	3	2.38	4	2.07
Chicago...............	4	2.22	3	2.23	4	2.30	3	2.14
Columbia..............	5	2.11	5	2.14	5	2.23	5	1.96
"Attractive"								
Wisconsin.............	6	1.99	6	2.12	6	2.00	6	1.90
Princeton.............	7	1.77	7	1.81	8	1.79	7	1.73
Cornell...............	8	1.75	9	1.78	9	1.77	8	1.71
Minnesota.............	9	1.72	8	1.80	7	1.90	12	1.47
North Carolina........	10	1.61	11*	1.69	10	1.61	11	1.55
Northwestern..........	11	1.58	10	1.77	11	1.59	14*	1.44
Stanford..............	12	1.57	15*	1.60	13	1.45	10	1.68
Johns Hopkins.........	13	1.53	13	1.66	19	1.32	9	1.70
U.C.L.A..............	14	1.51	15*	1.60	12	1.50	13	1.46

"Acceptable plus" (15 departments arranged alphabetically):

Brown	Michigan State	Pittsburgh
Duke	N.Y.U.	Texas
Illinois	Ohio State	Washington (St. Louis)
Indiana	Oregon	Washington (Seattle)
Iowa (Iowa City)	Pennsylvania	Yale

* Rank and score shared with another department.

High-Ranking Graduate Departments:
Hughes, Keniston, and A.C.E. Studies

Top 14 Departments, Hughes Study, 1925	Top 15 Departments, Keniston Study, 1957	Top 20† Departments, Rated Quality of Faculty, A.C.E. Study, 1964
1. Chicago	1. Harvard	1. California, Berkeley
2. Columbia	2. Columbia	2. Harvard
3. Wisconsin	3. Chicago	3. Columbia
4. Minnesota	4. Michigan	4. Chicago
5. Michigan	5. Cornell	5. Michigan
6. Harvard	6. California	6. Wisconsin
7. Missouri	7. Minnesota	7. Cornell
8. Pennsylvania	8. North Carolina	8. Princeton
9. North Carolina	9. Washington (Seattle)	9. Minnesota
10. Yale	10. Yale	10. North Carolina
11. Illinois	11. U.C.L.A.	11. U.C.L.A.
12. Cornell	12. Wisconsin	12. Stanford
13. Ohio State	13. Northwestern	13. Washington (Seattle)
14. Bryn Mawr	14. Ohio State	14. Northwestern
	15. Pennsylvania	15. Yale
		16. Washington (St. Louis)
		17. Michigan State
		18.* Indiana
		18.* Texas
		20. Johns Hopkins

* Rank shared with another department.
† These 20 departments represent 31 percent of the 64 departments for which ratings were calculated.

BACTERIOLOGY/MICROBIOLOGY

Leading Departments, by Rated Quality of Graduate Faculty

Institution[†]	All Respondents		Chairmen		Senior Scholars		Junior Scholars	
	Rank	Score	Rank	Score	Rank	Score	Rank	Score
"Distinguished"								
California, Berkeley.....	1	4.51	1	4.62	1	4.36	1	4.58
Rockefeller Inst.**......	2	4.31	2	4.48	2	4.29	2*	4.20
Illinois.................	3	4.21	3	4.45	4*	4.10	4	4.14
Wisconsin**............	4	4.14	4	4.25	3	4.25	6	3.92
Cal. Tech.**...........	5	4.11	5	4.08	4*	4.10	5	4.11
Harvard**.............	6	4.04	7	3.94	6*	3.96	2*	4.20
"Strong"								
Stanford**............	7	3.92	6	3.96	6*	3.96	7	3.82
Western Reserve........	8	3.65	8*	3.81	11	3.60	10	3.58
Johns Hopkins**........	9*	3.63	16*	3.46	10	3.61	8	3.76
Minnesota**............	9*	3.63	8*	3.81	8	3.68	14	3.40
Purdue**...............	11	3.57	19	3.44	14*	3.50	9	3.74
Washington (Seattle)....	12	3.55	10	3.76	17	3.46	12	3.45
Yale...................	13	3.52	11	3.61	13	3.51	13	3.44
Texas**................	14	3.51	12	3.56	9	3.67	17*	3.27
California, Davis**......	15	3.47	16*	3.46	19	3.41	11	3.52
Pennsylvania...........	16*	3.41	14*	3.50	14*	3.50	20	3.22
Rutgers**..............	16*	3.41	14*	3.50	18	3.43	16	3.31
Indiana**..............	18	3.39	18	3.45	21	3.36	15	3.38
Brandeis**.............	19	3.33	27	3.09	12	3.55	19	3.26
Chicago................	20*	3.32	13	3.52	22*	3.21	17*	3.27
Michigan..............	20*	3.32	21	3.40	20	3.39	21	3.17
N.Y.U.**..............	22	3.26	23	3.29	16	3.47	24	3.02
Columbia..............	23	3.19	22	3.32	22*	3.21	23	3.07
Pittsburgh**...........	24	3.07	20	3.41	26	3.04	28	2.87
Cornell................	25	3.06	29	3.00	24*	3.20	25	2.93
U.C.L.A.**............	26*	3.04	24	3.21	30	2.88	22	3.10
Yeshiva**[a]............	26*	3.04	26	3.10	24*	3.20	26*	2.90

"Good" (17 departments arranged alphabetically):

Cincinnati**	Maryland**	Oregon State**	Tufts[a]
Duke**	Michigan State**	Penn State	Tulane
Emory	North Carolina**	Rochester**	Washington (St. Louis)
Iowa (Iowa City)	Oregon**[a]	Southern California**	Washington State**
Iowa State (Ames)			

"Adequate plus" (18 departments arranged alphabetically):

Buffalo**	Kansas**	Nebraska**	St. Louis	Utah
Colorado**	Kansas State	Northwestern	Syracuse**	Vanderbilt
Florida**	Kentucky	Ohio State	Temple**	
George Washington	Massachusetts	Oklahoma**	Tennessee**	

[†] These tabulations and those for the effectiveness of the graduate program are based on ratings of 75 institutions. See page 18 for further explanation.
* Rank and score shared with another department.
** Study offered in a department other than department of bacteriology or microbiology *or* offered in more than one department.
[a] Doctorates reported in "biology" or "biological sciences, other." No more than half the respondents rated the department.

Profile of Respondents

Respondents	Number	Average Age	Average Number of Publications Since Highest Degree		Professional Meetings Attended in Last Four Years	
			Books	Articles	Regional	National
All respondents...............	156	44.7	.6	35	6.4	6.4
Chairmen....................	37	50.6	.8	49	6.6	7.4
Senior scholars...............	62	48.0	.9	46	7.5	6.3
Junior scholars...............	57	36.9	.2	13	5.1	6.0

Respondents' Division of Time for Professional Activities
(in percents)

Respondents	Instruction			Research and Writing	Administration	Other Professional	Other
	Undergraduate	Graduate	Total				
All respondents...............	22	26	48	27	17	6	2
Chairmen....................	16	20	36	18	35	8	3
Senior scholars...............	25	27	52	27	13	6	1
Junior scholars...............	23	28	51	33	9	4	3

BACTERIOLOGY/MICROBIOLOGY

Leading Departments, by Rated Effectiveness of Graduate Program

Institution	All Respondents		Chairmen		Senior Scholars		Junior Scholars	
	Rank	Score	Rank	Score	Rank	Score	Rank	Score
"Extremely attractive"								
California, Berkeley.....	1	2.46	2	2.44	2	2.33	1	2.62
Rockefeller Inst.........	2	2.32	3	2.40	5	2.26	4	2.34
Cal. Tech.............	3	2.31	7	2.17	4	2.27	2	2.41
Harvard..............	4	2.27	8	2.06	3	2.31	3	2.35
Illinois................	5	2.26	1	2.47	7	2.18	5	2.22
Wisconsin.............	6	2.23	4	2.30	1	2.35	7	2.04
Stanford..............	7	2.19	5	2.23	6	2.21	6	2.14
"Attractive"								
Washington (Seattle)....	8	1.95	6	2.19	13	1.86	10	1.88
Johns Hopkins..........	9	1.91	18	1.71	9*	1.98	9	1.98
Minnesota.............	10	1.90	10	1.97	11	1.92	12	1.83
California, Davis........	11	1.88	12	1.83	12	1.91	11	1.87
Western Reserve........	12	1.87	9	2.00	14*	1.83	13	1.82
Purdue...............	13	1.86	17	1.74	16	1.82	8	2.00
Yale.................	14	1.85	19	1.68	9*	1.98	14*	1.81
Texas................	15	1.79	13*	1.81	8	2.00	18	1.51
Indiana...............	16	1.71	13*	1.81	17	1.78	16	1.54
Brandeis..............	17*	1.68	32	1.33	18	1.76	14*	1.81
Michigan.............	17*	1.68	20	1.66	14*	1.83	19*	1.50
Pennsylvania..........	19	1.66	15	1.79	20*	1.71	19*	1.50
Chicago..............	20	1.65	11	1.84	22	1.65	17	1.52
Rutgers...............	21	1.61	21	1.63	20*	1.71	21	1.46
N.Y.U...............	22	1.53	23*	1.57	19	1.73	25	1.31

"Acceptable plus" (35 departments arranged alphabetically):

Buffalo	Maryland	Southern California
Cincinnati	Massachusetts	Syracuse
Colorado	Michigan State	Temple
Columbia	Nebraska	Tufts
Cornell	North Carolina	Tulane
Duke	Northwestern	U.C.L.A.
Emory	Ohio State	Utah
Florida	Oregon	Vanderbilt
Iowa (Iowa City)	Oregon State	Washington (St. Louis)
Iowa State (Ames)	Penn State	Washington State
Kansas	Pittsburgh	Yeshiva
Kansas State	Rochester	

* Rank and score shared with another department.

BIOCHEMISTRY

Leading Departments, by Rated Quality of Graduate Faculty

Institution†	All Respondents		Chairmen		Senior Scholars		Junior Scholars	
	Rank	Score	Rank	Score	Rank	Score	Rank	Score
"Distinguished"								
Harvard**.............	1	4.63	2	4.71	1	4.54	1	4.68
California, Berkeley.....	2	4.54	1	4.86	2	4.51	3	4.37
Stanford**.............	3	4.47	6	4.32	3	4.45	2	4.59
Rockefeller Inst.**......	4	4.34	4	4.35	4	4.36	4*	4.30
Wisconsin**...........	5	4.30	3	4.58	5	4.22	6	4.23
M.I.T.**ᵃ.............	6	4.25	5	4.34	6	4.17	4*	4.30
Cal. Tech.**...........	7	4.15	7	4.10	7	4.13	7	4.19
"Strong"								
Johns Hopkins**........	8	3.93	8	4.03	8	3.83	9	4.00
Brandeis..............	9	3.85	12	3.71	9	3.73	8	4.08
Illinois**..............	10	3.75	9	3.93	10*	3.71	10	3.68
Columbia**............	11	3.70	10	3.83	10*	3.71	13	3.56
Western Reserve**......	12	3.63	17	3.51	12	3.66	12	3.64
N.Y.U.**..............	13	3.60	11	3.72	15	3.49	11	3.67
Washington (Seattle)....	14	3.58	16	3.61	14	3.57	14	3.54
Duke**...............	15	3.54	14*	3.63	13	3.62	22	3.34
Michigan**............	16	3.47	18	3.44	16*	3.45	15	3.51
Pennsylvania**........	17*	3.42	20*	3.42	19	3.37	16	3.48
Yeshiva..............	17*	3.42	14*	3.63	16*	3.45	26*	3.11
Chicago..............	19	3.40	13	3.66	22	3.24	20	3.44
U.C.L.A.**............	20*	3.37	19	3.43	21	3.26	17	3.47
Yale.................	20*	3.37	24	3.31	20	3.32	18	3.46
Washington (St. Louis)**.	22	3.35	23	3.33	18	3.42	23	3.22
Tufts................	23	3.33	20*	3.42	23	3.23	21	3.39
Pittsburgh**...........	24*	3.21	25	3.23	24	3.21	25	3.18
Princeton**ᵃ...........	24*	3.21	27*	3.00	26*	3.15	19	3.45
Cornell..............	26	3.19	22	3.39	26*	3.15	28	3.10
California, Davis**......	27	3.16	26	3.03	25	3.17	24	3.21

"Good" (13 departments arranged alphabetically):

Indiana**	Minnesota**	Oregon State**	St. Louis	Vanderbilt**
Iowa (Iowa City)	Northwestern**	Purdue	Texas**	
Iowa State (Ames)	Oregon**	Rochester**	Utah**	

"Adequate plus" (13 departments arranged alphabetically):

Brown**	Florida	Ohio State**	Southern California**	Wayne State**
Colorado**	Florida State**	Penn State	Syracuse**	
Emory	North Carolina	Rutgers**	Tulane	

† These tabulations and those for the effectiveness of the graduate program are based on ratings of 75 institutions. See page 18 for further explanation.
* Rank and score shared with another department.
** Study offered in a department other than department of biochemistry *or* offered in more than one department.
ᵃ Doctorates reported in "biology" rather than "biochemistry."

Profile of Respondents

Respondents	Number	Average Age	Average Number of Publications Since Highest Degree		Professional Meetings Attended in Last Four Years	
			Books	Articles	Regional	National
All respondents................	152	43.5	.4	51	3.0	7.0
Chairmen....................	31	49.7	.8	91	3.9	8.5
Senior scholars................	69	47.0	.5	58	3.4	7.6
Junior scholars...............	52	35.4	.1	17	1.8	5.4

Respondents' Division of Time for Professional Activities
(in percents)

Respondents	Instruction			Research and Writing	Adminis-tration	Other Profes-sional	Other
	Under-graduate	Graduate	Total				
All respondents................	13	31	44	33	15	6	2
Chairmen....................	13	23	36	25	28	9	2
Senior scholars................	14	34	48	30	15	5	2
Junior scholars...............	13	33	46	41	7	4	2

BIOCHEMISTRY

Leading Departments, by Rated Effectiveness of Graduate Program

Institution	All Respondents		Chairmen		Senior Scholars		Junior Scholars	
	Rank	Score	Rank	Score	Rank	Score	Rank	Score
"Extremely attractive"								
California, Berkeley.....	1	2.63	1	2.83	1	2.58	2	2.57
Harvard..............	2	2.56	2	2.67	2	2.50	3	2.56
Stanford..............	3	2.52	4	2.53	3	2.44	1	2.62
M.I.T................	4*	2.42	5	2.50	5	2.30	4	2.55
Rockefeller Inst........	4*	2.42	3	2.58	4	2.32	6	2.45
Cal. Tech.............	6	2.33	7	2.29	6	2.26	5	2.46
Wisconsin.............	7	2.31	6	2.46	7	2.25	7	2.29
Johns Hopkins..........	8	2.17	9	2.13	8	2.15	8*	2.21
Brandeis..............	9	2.11	8	2.19	10	2.00	8*	2.21
"Attractive"								
Illinois................	10	1.99	10	2.07	9	2.03	11*	1.87
Washington (Seattle)....	11	1.93	11	2.04	11	1.96	15	1.82
Duke.................	12	1.90	13	1.93	12	1.91	13*	1.85
Western Reserve........	13	1.87	15	1.85	13	1.88	11*	1.87
U.C.L.A..............	14	1.78	19	1.73	16*	1.71	10	1.89
Yeshiva..............	15	1.74	18	1.74	14	1.81	21*	1.60
Princeton.............	16	1.72	25	1.56	16*	1.71	13*	1.85
Chicago..............	17	1.70	14	1.87	24	1.58	18	1.74
Columbia.............	18	1.69	12	2.00	20*	1.63	24	1.56
California, Davis........	19*	1.68	24	1.57	19	1.67	16	1.78
Michigan.............	19*	1.68	21	1.66	15	1.75	21*	1.60
Yale.................	21	1.67	20	1.71	23	1.59	17	1.76
Tufts.................	22	1.63	23	1.59	20*	1.63	19	1.65
Washington (St. Louis)..	23	1.62	22	1.65	18	1.68	26*	1.50
Cornell...............	24*	1.60	17	1.82	25*	1.50	23	1.58
Pennsylvania..........	24*	1.60	26	1.54	22	1.61	20	1.63
N.Y.U...............	26	1.55	16	1.83	27	1.41	25	1.55

"Acceptable plus" (28 departments arranged alphabetically):

Brown	Minnesota	Rutgers
Buffalo	North Carolina	St. Louis
Colorado	Northwestern	Southern California
Emory	Oregon	Syracuse
Florida	Oregon State	Texas
Florida State	Penn State	Tulane
Indiana	Pittsburgh	Utah
Iowa (Iowa City)	Purdue	Vanderbilt
Iowa State (Ames)	Rochester	Wayne State
Maryland		

* Rank and score shared with another department.

BOTANY

Leading Departments, by Rated Quality of Graduate Faculty

Institution†	All Respondents Rank	All Respondents Score	Chairmen Rank	Chairmen Score	Senior Scholars Rank	Senior Scholars Score	Junior Scholars Rank	Junior Scholars Score
"Distinguished"								
California, Berkeley.....	1	4.63	1	4.72	1	4.50	1	4.71
Harvard**a.............	2	4.25	2	4.31	2	4.25	3	4.20
Michigan..............	3	4.17	4	4.27	4	3.96	2	4.36
Wisconsin.............	4	4.02	3	4.28	5	3.92	4	4.00
"Strong"								
California, Davis........	5	3.92	10	3.60	3	3.98	5	3.97
Indiana...............	6	3.81	5*	3.95	7	3.79	6	3.76
Duke.................	7	3.80	8	3.80	6	3.90	9	3.68
Texas................	8	3.75	5*	3.95	9	3.68	8	3.74
Cal. Tech.**..........	9	3.73	9	3.61	8	3.75	7	3.75
Stanford**a...........	10	3.70	7	3.90	10	3.64	10	3.67
U.C.L.A..............	11	3.58	11	3.60	12	3.54	11	3.61
Cornell...............	12	3.46	14*	3.36	11	3.63	17	3.28
Michigan State........	13*	3.41	13	3.40	16	3.32	12	3.52
Purdue...............	13*	3.41	12	3.54	14	3.38	15*	3.38
Illinois...............	15	3.39	14*	3.36	13	3.41	15*	3.38
Yale**...............	16	3.30	17	3.27	15	3.36	18	3.22
North Carolina........	17	3.26	16	3.28	19*	3.13	14	3.42
Minnesota............	18	3.16	18	3.09	17	3.23	19	3.10
Claremont............	19	3.08	24	2.83	25	2.82	13	3.50
Chicago..............	20	3.02	23	2.90	19*	3.13	24	2.92
Pennsylvania..........	21	3.01	21*	3.00	18	3.20	31	2.72

"Good" (12 departments arranged alphabetically):

Columbia	Ohio State	Rutgers
Iowa (Iowa City)	Oregon State	Washington (St. Louis)
Iowa State (Ames)	Penn State	Washington (Seattle)
No. Carolina State	Rockefeller Inst.**	Washington State

"Adequate plus" (13 departments arranged alphabetically):

Florida	Nebraska	Syracuse**
Florida State**	Oklahoma	Tennessee
Kansas	Oregon**a	Texas A&M**
Maryland	Pittsburgh**	Utah
Missouri		

† These tabulations and those for the effectiveness of the graduate program are based on ratings of 61 institutions. See page 18 for further explanation.
* Rank and score shared with another department.
** Study offered in a department other than department of botany *or* offered in more than one department.
a Doctorates reported in "biology" rather than "botany."

Profile of Respondents

Respondents	Number	Average Age	Average Number of Publications Since Highest Degree Books	Average Number of Publications Since Highest Degree Articles	Professional Meetings Attended in Last Four Years Regional	Professional Meetings Attended in Last Four Years National
All respondents................	130	44.7	.6	27	3.8	3.9
Chairmen....................	22	49.4	1.2	38	4.3	4.4
Senior scholars................	58	50.3	.7	33	4.2	4.1
Junior scholars................	50	34.1	.3	16	3.0	3.3

Respondents' Division of Time for Professional Activities
(in percents)

Respondents	Instruction Under-graduate	Instruction Graduate	Instruction Total	Research and Writing	Administration	Other Professional	Other
All respondents................	26	26	52	24	18	5	1
Chairmen....................	13	23	36	16	42	5	1
Senior scholars................	24	29	53	25	14	6	1
Junior scholars...............	33	25	58	27	12	3	1

BOTANY

Leading Departments, by Rated Effectiveness of Graduate Program

Institution	All Respondents		Chairmen		Senior Scholars		Junior Scholars	
	Rank	Score	Rank	Score	Rank	Score	Rank	Score
"Extremely attractive"								
California, Berkeley.....	1	2.65	1	2.76	1	2.63	1	2.63
Michigan..............	2	2.33	3	2.50	3	2.23	2	2.37
Harvard..............	3	2.26	2	2.55	2	2.30	5*	2.07
Wisconsin............	4	2.13	4	2.35	5	2.14	8	2.00
California, Davis.......	5	2.10	11*	1.95	4	2.15	3	2.11
Duke................	6	2.05	6	2.26	6	2.04	10	1.95
Indiana..............	7*	2.04	8	2.18	8	1.94	4	2.10
Stanford.............	7*	2.04	5	2.27	9	1.92	5*	2.07
Texas...............	9	2.01	7	2.25	11	1.89	7	2.03
"Attractive"								
Cal. Tech.............	10*	1.91	9*	2.00	7	1.98	13	1.78
U.C.L.A.............	10*	1.91	9*	2.00	12	1.81	9	1.97
Michigan State........	12	1.81	15	1.91	13	1.77	12	1.81
Illinois...............	13	1.77	11*	1.95	14	1.76	15	1.70
Cornell..............	14*	1.75	17	1.81	10	1.91	17	1.52
Purdue..............	14*	1.75	11*	1.95	15	1.74	16	1.66
North Carolina........	16	1.73	11*	1.95	19	1.55	11	1.84
Yale.................	17	1.64	16	1.90	16	1.67	20	1.49
Claremont............	18	1.61	22*	1.47	17*	1.60	14	1.71
Minnesota............	19	1.59	18	1.71	17*	1.60	18*	1.50

"Acceptable plus" (26 departments arranged alphabetically):

Chicago	Missouri	Rockefeller Inst.
Colorado	Nebraska	Rutgers
Columbia	No. Carolina State	Syracuse
Florida	Ohio State	Tennessee
Florida State	Oklahoma	Washington (St. Louis)
Iowa (Iowa City)	Oregon	Washington (Seattle)
Iowa State (Ames)	Oregon State	Washington State
Kansas	Pennsylvania	West Virginia
Maryland	Penn State	

* Rank and score shared with another department.

High-Ranking Graduate Departments: Hughes, Keniston, and A.C.E. Studies

Top 15 Departments, Hughes Study, 1925	Top 15 Departments,[a] Keniston Study, 1957	Top 20[†] Departments, Rated Quality of Faculty, A.C.E. Study, 1964
1. Chicago	1. Harvard	1. California, Berkeley
2.* Columbia	2. California	2. Harvard
2.* Cornell	3. Wisconsin	3. Michigan
2.* Harvard	4. Michigan	4. Wisconsin
5. Wisconsin	5. Cornell	5. California, Davis
6. Michigan	6. Illinois	6. Indiana
7. Johns Hopkins	7. Yale	7. Duke
8. Illinois	8.* Indiana	8. Texas
9. Minnesota	8.* Minnesota	9. Cal. Tech.
10. California	8.* Pennsylvania	10. Stanford
11. Ohio State	11. Duke	11. U.C.L.A.
12. Stanford	12. U.C.L.A.	12. Cornell
13. Yale	13. Ohio State	13.* Michigan State
14. Pennsylvania	14. Stanford	13.* Purdue
15. Missouri	15. Columbia	15. Illinois
		16. Yale
		17. North Carolina
		18. Minnesota
		19. Claremont
		20. Chicago

* Rank shared with another department.
† These 20 departments represent 33 percent of the 61 departments for which ratings were calculated.
[a] Technical and specialized institutions were omitted from the Keniston study.

ENTOMOLOGY

Leading Departments, by Rated Quality of Graduate Faculty

Institution†	All Respondents		Chairmen		Senior Scholars		Junior Scholars	
	Rank	Score	Rank	Score	Rank	Score	Rank	Score
"Distinguished"								
California, Berkeley.....	1	4.56	1	4.52	1	4.56	1	4.58
"Strong"								
Illinois................	2	3.93	3*	3.94	2	3.97	3	3.85
Cornell...............	3	3.87	3*	3.94	3*	3.83	2	3.86
Wisconsin.............	4	3.76	2	4.05	6	3.58	4	3.83
Kansas...............	5	3.71	7	3.41	3*	3.83	5	3.73
Minnesota............	6	3.61	5	3.50	5	3.62	6	3.65
Ohio State**..........	7	3.38	6	3.44	7	3.42	8	3.26
California, Davis.......	8	3.32	8	3.27	8	3.23	7	3.48
Iowa State (Ames)**....	9	3.06	12	3.10	9	3.07	12*	3.00
Kansas State..........	10	3.04	9	3.21	10	2.94	11	3.03

"Good" (6 departments arranged alphabetically):

Johns Hopkins**	No. Carolina State**	Purdue
Michigan State	Oregon State	Rutgers

"Adequate plus" (8 departments arranged alphabetically):

Connecticut**	Massachusetts	Virginia Polytech.
Louisiana State	Penn State	Washington State**
Maryland	Texas A&M	

† These tabulations and those for the effectiveness of the graduate program are based on ratings of the 31 institutions in the survey universe that reported the award of at least one doctorate in entomology from July 1952 through June 1962.
* Rank and score shared with another department.
** Study offered in a department other than department of entomology *or* offered in more than one department.

Profile of Respondents

Respondents	Number	Average Age	Average Number of Publications Since Highest Degree		Professional Meetings Attended in Last Four Years	
			Books	Articles	Regional	National
All respondents...............	90	44.6	.4	39	3.5	3.9
Chairmen....................	19	50.1	.4	61	4.4	5.7
Senior scholars................	42	49.1	.5	47	3.2	3.7
Junior scholars...............	29	34.2	.2	15	3.2	3.2

Respondents' Division of Time for Professional Activities
(in percents)

Respondents	Instruction			Research and Writing	Adminis-tration	Other Profes-sional	Other
	Under-graduate	Graduate	Total				
All respondents...............	15	23	38	35	19	5	4
Chairmen....................	8	20	28	21	44	7	—
Senior scholars................	15	23	38	35	18	5	5
Junior scholars...............	19	25	44	43	5	4	5

ENTOMOLOGY

Leading Departments, by Rated Effectiveness of Graduate Program

Institution	All Respondents		Chairmen		Senior Scholars		Junior Scholars	
	Rank	Score	Rank	Score	Rank	Score	Rank	Score
"Extremely attractive"								
California, Berkeley.....	1	2.57	1	2.67	1	2.65	1	2.41
Cornell...............	2	2.09	3	2.00	2	2.15	2	2.07
Illinois................	3	2.05	4*	1.94	3	2.11	3	2.04
"Attractive"								
Kansas...............	4*	1.92	8	1.69	4	2.00	4	1.95
Wisconsin.............	4*	1.92	2	2.38	7	1.76	5	1.88
Minnesota............	6	1.86	4*	1.94	5	1.84	6	1.84
California, Davis........	7	1.73	4*	1.94	6	1.78	7*	1.52
Ohio State............	8	1.62	7	1.76	8	1.70	11	1.40

"Acceptable plus" (14 departments arranged alphabetically):

Connecticut	Massachusetts	Purdue
Iowa State (Ames)	Michigan State	Rutgers
Johns Hopkins	No. Carolina State	Virginia Polytech.
Kansas State	Oregon State	Washington State
Maryland	Penn State	

* Rank and score shared with another department.

PHARMACOLOGY

Leading Departments, by Rated Quality of Graduate Faculty

Institution†	All Respondents		Chairmen		Senior Scholars		Junior Scholars	
	Rank	Score	Rank	Score	Rank	Score	Rank	Score
"Distinguished"								
Harvard**	1	4.35	2	4.55	1	4.47	1	4.21
Michigan	2	4.11	1	4.70	3	4.13	3	3.90
Pennsylvania	3	4.07	4*	4.22	2	4.23	4	3.88
Yale	4	4.02	4*	4.22	5	4.08	5	3.87
"Strong"								
Utah	5	3.98	13	3.80	4	4.12	2	3.93
Iowa (Iowa City)	6	3.75	6*	4.00	11	3.65	6	3.75
Yeshiva	7	3.72	6*	4.00	6*	4.00	8	3.42
Emory**	8	3.68	6*	4.00	10	3.70	7	3.57
Washington (St. Louis)	9	3.61	14	3.62	6*	4.00	13	3.22
Cornell[a]	10	3.60	6*	4.00	8	3.90	14	3.17
Minnesota**	11	3.55	10*	3.90	12	3.63	12	3.34
California[b]	12	3.52	3	4.25	13	3.35	10	3.36
Stanford	13	3.49	20	3.11	9	3.81	11	3.35
Illinois	14	3.44	10*	3.90	14	3.27	9	3.41
Rochester	15	3.26	12	3.88	17	3.21	17	3.04
Johns Hopkins	16	3.12	16	3.33	18	3.18	19	2.94
Chicago	17	3.10	15	3.44	23	2.94	16	3.08
Kansas	18	3.05	18*	3.20	26	2.90	15	3.11
Vanderbilt	19*	3.02	22*	3.00	15*	3.22	21	2.83
Washington (Seattle)	19*	3.02	18*	3.20	20*	3.00	18	2.96

"Good" (8 departments arranged alphabetically):

Buffalo	Northwestern	Western Reserve
Columbia**	Tulane	Wisconsin**
George Washington	U.C.L.A.	

"Adequate plus" (12 departments arranged alphabetically):

Boston U.**	Maryland	Texas**
Cincinnati	Pittsburgh	Tufts
Florida	Purdue[e]	Virginia
Georgetown	Southern California	West Virginia

† These tabulations and those for the effectiveness of the graduate program are based on ratings of 52 institutions. See page 18 for further explanation.

* Rank and score shared with another department.

** Study offered in a department other than department of pharmacology, *or* offered in more than one department.

[a] No doctorates reported in pharmacology. Doctoral study in the field is offered at the Cornell Medical School in New York City, not on the Ithaca campus.

[b] The institutional identification shown on the questionnaire was "U. of California, Berkeley." Approximately one-quarter of the department's raters changed the line to read "U. of California, San Francisco." Doctoral study in pharmacology is offered by the San Francisco Medical Center; study in comparative pharmacology and toxicology is offered in an intercampus program involving Berkeley, Davis, and the San Francisco Medical Center.

[e] Doctorates reported in "pharmacy," not "pharmacology."

Profile of Respondents

Respondents	Number	Average Age	Average Number of Publications Since Highest Degree		Professional Meetings Attended in Last Four Years	
			Books	Articles	Regional	National
All respondents	74	43.3	.8	53	3.8	7.7
Chairmen	11	53.9	1.8	114	9.0	13.2
Senior scholars	26	46.2	1.1	73	2.6	7.6
Junior scholars	37	36.9	.2	21	3.0	6.1

Respondents' Division of Time for Professional Activities
(in percents)

Respondents	Instruction			Research and Writing	Administration	Other Professional	Other
	Under-graduate	Graduate	Total				
All respondents	22	20	42	32	16	7	2
Chairmen	14	17	31	18	35	14	—
Senior scholars	25	20	45	29	18	7	1
Junior scholars	22	21	43	39	9	5	4

PHARMACOLOGY

Leading Departments, by Rated Effectiveness of Graduate Program

Institution	All Respondents		Chairmen		Senior Scholars		Junior Scholars	
	Rank	Score	Rank	Score	Rank	Score	Rank	Score
"Extremely attractive"								
Harvard	1	2.32	2	2.56	1	2.43	1	2.17
Michigan	2	2.25	1	2.73	2	2.19	2	2.13
Yale	3	2.17	3	2.50	3	2.13	4	2.08
Pennsylvania	4	2.16	4	2.40	5	2.10	3	2.12
"Attractive"								
Yeshiva	5	2.00	9*	2.00	6*	2.00	5*	2.00
Utah	6	1.95	11	1.91	6*	2.00	7	1.93
Iowa (Iowa City)	7	1.93	9*	2.00	11	1.81	5*	2.00
California[a]	8	1.91	6	2.25	9	1.86	10	1.81
Stanford	9	1.90	19*	1.50	4	2.14	9	1.85
Washington (St. Louis)	10	1.84	7	2.11	8	1.95	14	1.62
Emory	11*	1.82	15	1.88	13	1.68	8	1.89
Minnesota	11*	1.82	8	2.09	10	1.85	11*	1.69
Cornell	13	1.79	5	2.30	12	1.79	15	1.58
Rochester	14	1.65	12*	1.90	14	1.67	16	1.54
Illinois	15	1.63	16	1.82	19	1.45	11*	1.69
Washington (Seattle)	16	1.62	17	1.80	17*	1.47	13	1.67
Chicago	17	1.56	12*	1.90	20*	1.44	17	1.50
Johns Hopkins	18	1.52	14	1.89	16	1.50	20	1.38

"Acceptable plus" (26 departments arranged alphabetically):

Boston U.	Kansas	Tennessee
Buffalo	Maryland	Texas
California, Davis	Northwestern	Tufts
Cincinnati	Ohio State	Tulane
Columbia	Oklahoma	U.C.L.A.
Florida	Pittsburgh	Vanderbilt
George Washington	Purdue	Virginia
Georgetown	Southern California	West Virginia
		Western Reserve
		Wisconsin

*Rank and score shared with another department.
[a]See note b, opposite page.

PHYSIOLOGY

Leading Departments, by Rated Quality of Graduate Faculty

Institution†	All Respondents		Chairmen		Senior Scholars		Junior Scholars	
	Rank	Score	Rank	Score	Rank	Score	Rank	Score
"Distinguished"								
Harvard**	1	4.52	1	4.53	1	4.58	1	4.42
Rockefeller Inst.**	2	4.18	2	4.13	3	4.08	2	4.32
"Strong"								
Johns Hopkins**	3	3.97	3*	4.08	6	3.91	3	3.93
Washington (Seattle)** ..	4	3.96	3*	4.08	5	3.93	4	3.87
California, Berkeley** ...	5	3.90	11*	3.54	2	4.20	5*	3.80
Cal. Tech.**	6	3.85	7*	3.72	4	3.96	5*	3.80
Minnesota**	7	3.73	5	3.90	11*	3.69	10	3.63
Pennsylvania**	8	3.70	6	3.78	10	3.73	11	3.60
Michigan**	9	3.69	11*	3.54	8*	3.74	7	3.74
Columbia**	10	3.62	16*	3.33	7	3.75	9	3.64
Chicago**	11	3.57	15	3.43	8*	3.74	14*	3.46
Rochester**	12	3.55	7*	3.72	18*	3.50	14*	3.46
U.C.L.A.**	13	3.54	14	3.45	18*	3.50	8	3.65
Cornell**	14	3.52	13	3.47	14	3.66	18	3.37
Princeton**ᵃ	15	3.50	19*	3.27	13	3.67	17	3.38
Illinois	16	3.49	16*	3.33	17	3.51	12	3.55
Wisconsin**	17	3.42	29	2.86	11*	3.69	13	3.51
Duke**	18	3.41	18	3.28	15*	3.52	19	3.36
Western Reserve**	19	3.39	10	3.60	22	3.40	22	3.19
Buffalo	20	3.37	9	3.66	25*	3.10	16	3.42
Yale**	21	3.29	26	2.95	18*	3.50	21	3.23
Yeshivaᵇ	22	3.25	23	3.11	21	3.46	23	3.16
Indiana**	23	3.24	21	3.26	23	3.37	29	3.04
Stanford	24	3.21	31*	2.81	15*	3.52	27	3.10
Washington (St. Louis)..	25	3.11	24*	3.00	27	3.07	20	3.25
Northwestern	26	3.05	19*	3.27	25*	3.10	36	2.80
Oregon**ᵇ	27	3.02	28	2.87	28	3.04	26	3.11

"Good" (15 departments arranged alphabetically):

Brown**ᵇ	Iowa (Iowa City)**	Rice**ᵇ	Tulane**
California, Davis**	Michigan State	Rutgers**	Utah**
Emory**	N.Y.U.**	Syracuse**	Vanderbilt**
Florida**ᵇ	Pittsburgh**ᵃ	Tufts	

"Adequate plus" (14 departments arranged alphabetically):

Cincinnati	Iowa State (Ames)**	Ohio State	Texas**
Colorado**	Kansas**	Oklahoma**	Wayne State**
Connecticut**	Maryland**	St. Louis**	
Florida State**	North Carolina**	Tennessee**	

† These tabulations and those for the effectiveness of the graduate program are based on ratings of 71 institutions. See page 18 for further explanation.
* Rank and score shared with another department.
** Study offered in a department other than department of physiology *or* offered in more than one department.
ᵃ Doctorate reported in "biology" rather than in "physiology."
ᵇ Doctorates reported in "biology" or "biological sciences, other" rather than in "physiology"; no more than half the respondents rated the department.

Profile of Respondents

Respondents	Number	Average Age	Average Number of Publications Since Highest Degree		Professional Meetings Attended in Last Four Years	
			Books	Articles	Regional	National
All respondents...............	117	43.4	.6	40	3.4	7.0
Chairmen..................	27	49.4	.6	66	4.6	7.1
Senior scholars..............	47	47.3	.8	48	4.2	7.7
Junior scholars..............	43	35.5	.3	15	1.9	6.3

Respondents' Division of Time for Professional Activities
(in percents)

Respondents	Instruction			Research and Writing	Adminis-tration	Other Professional	Other
	Under-graduate	Graduate	Total				
All respondents...............	19	26	45	32	17	6	1
Chairmen..................	14	20	34	28	27	8	3
Senior scholars..............	20	25	45	28	19	7	—
Junior scholars..............	21	30	51	39	7	4	—

PHYSIOLOGY

Leading Departments, by Rated Effectiveness of Graduate Program

Institution	All Respondents		Chairmen		Senior Scholars		Junior Scholars	
	Rank	Score	Rank	Score	Rank	Score	Rank	Score
"Extremely attractive"								
Harvard	1	2.40	1	2.36	2	2.49	1	2.32
Rockefeller Inst	2	2.25	2	2.29	4	2.27	3	2.21
California, Berkeley	3	2.24	7	2.00	1	2.56	5*	2.03
Washington (Seattle)	4	2.18	3	2.18	6	2.12	2	2.26
Cal. Tech	5	2.17	5	2.06	3	2.36	4	2.05
Johns Hopkins	6	2.15	4	2.16	5	2.26	5*	2.03
"Attractive"								
Minnesota	7	1.97	8	1.89	8*	2.03	7	1.96
Pennsylvania	8	1.95	6	2.05	10	2.00	8	1.83
U.C.L.A.	9	1.86	11*	1.81	16*	1.91	9*	1.82
Michigan	10	1.84	16	1.74	11	1.97	15	1.73
Illinois	11	1.83	9	1.87	20	1.88	11*	1.77
Rochester	12	1.82	17	1.72	13*	1.94	13*	1.74
Columbia	13	1.81	21	1.65	13*	1.94	13*	1.74
Cornell	14*	1.80	11*	1.81	18*	1.89	17*	1.67
Princeton	14*	1.80	18*	1.67	12	1.96	17*	1.67
Yale	16	1.79	26*	1.50	7	2.05	22	1.58
Chicago	17*	1.78	23*	1.58	16*	1.91	11*	1.77
Wisconsin	17*	1.78	34	1.32	8*	2.03	9*	1.82
Duke	19	1.74	23*	1.58	13*	1.94	19	1.63
Western Reserve	20	1.71	13*	1.80	23	1.73	20	1.62
Stanford	21*	1.69	26*	1.50	18*	1.89	23	1.57
Yeshiva	21*	1.69	22	1.63	21	1.75	16	1.69
Oregon	23	1.67	18*	1.67	22	1.74	21	1.59
Buffalo	24*	1.65	10	1.83	27	1.62	24	1.56
Indiana	24*	1.65	13*	1.80	25	1.68	26	1.52
Pittsburgh	26	1.52	35*	1.29	24	1.72	28	1.42

"Acceptable plus" (29 departments arranged alphabetically):

Brown	Michigan State	Syracuse
California, Davis	N.Y.U.	Tennessee
Colorado	North Carolina	Texas
Emory	Northwestern	Tufts
Florida	Ohio State	Tulane
Florida State	Oklahoma	Utah
Iowa (Iowa City)	Oklahoma State	Vanderbilt
Iowa State (Ames)	Rice	Washington (St. Louis)
Kansas	Rutgers	Wayne State
Maryland	Southern California	

* Rank and score shared with another department.

PSYCHOLOGY

Leading Departments, by Rated Quality of Graduate Faculty

Institution†	All Respondents		Chairmen		Senior Scholars		Junior Scholars	
	Rank	Score	Rank	Score	Rank	Score	Rank	Score
"Distinguished"								
Harvard.............	1	4.58	3	4.58	1*	4.53	1	4.62
Stanford.............	2	4.56	1	4.76	1*	4.53	2	4.46
Michigan.............	3	4.40	4	4.54	3	4.36	3	4.33
California, Berkeley.....	4*	4.35	2	4.61	4*	4.32	5	4.21
Yale.................	4*	4.35	5	4.45	4*	4.32	4	4.31
Illinois..............	6	4.08	6	4.33	6	4.09	7	3.87
"Strong"								
Minnesota............	7	3.98	7	4.21	8	3.94	8	3.86
Wisconsin............	8	3.97	8	4.00	7	3.97	6	3.95
Brown...............	9	3.73	13	3.71	9	3.88	11	3.59
Iowa (Iowa City).......	10	3.66	11*	3.73	12	3.64	9*	3.62
Pennsylvania..........	11	3.63	11*	3.73	13	3.58	9*	3.62
Indiana..............	12	3.62	9	3.83	14	3.52	12	3.56
U.C.L.A.............	13	3.58	14	3.68	10	3.67	14	3.40
Columbia............	14	3.54	10	3.79	11	3.66	18	3.24
Johns Hopkins.........	15	3.44	15	3.54	15	3.51	17	3.28
Northwestern..........	16	3.43	16	3.44	17	3.40	13	3.45
Chicago..............	17	3.37	18	3.38	18	3.38	16	3.33
Duke................	18	3.34	19*	3.35	19	3.30	15	3.36
Cornell..............	19	3.33	17	3.41	16	3.45	19	3.13
Ohio State...........	20	3.24	19*	3.35	20	3.26	20	3.12
Princeton............	21	3.14	22	3.22	21*	3.13	21	3.08
Michigan State........	22	3.02	23	3.09	24	3.00	23	3.00
North Carolina........	23	3.01	21	3.26	25	2.96	25	2.84

"Good" (14 departments arranged alphabetically):

Carnegie Tech.	Oregon	Southern California
Clark	Penn State	Texas
Colorado	Pittsburgh	Washington (St. Louis)
Kansas	Purdue	Washington (Seattle)
N.Y.U.	Rochester	

"Adequate plus" (23 departments arranged alphabetically):

Arizona	Florida	Rutgers
Boston U.	Florida State	Syracuse
Brandeis	George Peabody	Tufts
Bryn Mawr	Kansas State	Vanderbilt
Buffalo	Maryland	Virginia
Cincinnati	Massachusetts	Washington State
Connecticut	Missouri	Wayne State
	Nebraska	Western Reserve

†These tabulations and those for the effectiveness of the graduate program are based on ratings of the 88 institutions in the survey universe that reported the award of one or more doctorates in psychology from July 1952 through June 1962.
* Rank and score shared with another department.

Profile of Respondents

Respondents	Number	Average Age	Average Number of Publications Since Highest Degree		Professional Meetings Attended in Last Four Years	
			Books	Articles	Regional	National
All respondents...............	198	43.2	1.1	27	3.9	3.7
Chairmen...................	47	49.2	1.7	36	4.1	4.3
Senior scholars...............	76	48.7	1.5	39	3.8	4.5
Junior scholars..............	75	34.1	.3	10	3.9	2.6

Respondents' Division of Time for Professional Activities
(in percents)

Respondents	Instruction			Research and Writing	Administration	Other Professional	Other
	Under-graduate	Graduate	Total				
All respondents...............	17	28	45	24	21	8	1
Chairmen...................	7	21	28	15	48	8	—
Senior scholars...............	16	31	47	27	17	9	1
Junior scholars..............	25	31	56	28	9	6	1

PSYCHOLOGY

Leading Departments, by Rated Effectiveness of Graduate Program

Institution	All Respondents		Chairmen		Senior Scholars		Junior Scholars	
	Rank	Score	Rank	Score	Rank	Score	Rank	Score
"Extremely attractive"								
Stanford	1	2.58	1	2.72	1	2.54	1	2.51
Michigan	2	2.36	2	2.49	4*	2.25	3	2.39
Harvard	3	2.35	5*	2.21	2	2.38	2	2.41
Yale	4	2.34	3	2.40	3	2.27	4	2.38
California, Berkeley	5	2.23	5*	2.21	4*	2.25	5	2.22
Illinois	6	2.14	4	2.25	7	2.16	8	2.03
Wisconsin	7	2.08	8*	2.05	8	2.09	6	2.10
Minnesota	8	2.06	7	2.11	9	2.01	7	2.06
"Attractive"								
Brown	9	1.97	11	1.86	6	2.19	10	1.82
Indiana	10	1.87	8*	2.05	11	1.85	12	1.77
Pennsylvania	11	1.86	12*	1.83	12	1.83	9	1.91
Johns Hopkins	12	1.79	12*	1.83	10	1.95	16	1.59
Northwestern	13*	1.78	14	1.82	13*	1.72	11	1.81
U.C.L.A.	13*	1.78	10	1.89	13*	1.72	13	1.76
Iowa (Iowa City)	15	1.67	17	1.67	16	1.66	14*	1.67
Columbia	16	1.63	18	1.66	15	1.69	18	1.54
Duke	17	1.61	15	1.69	19	1.50	14*	1.67
Chicago	18	1.60	19	1.64	18	1.59	17	1.57
Cornell	19	1.57	16	1.68	17	1.60	21	1.44

"Acceptable plus" (32 departments arranged alphabetically):

Brandeis	Michigan State	Rutgers
Carnegie Tech.	Missouri	Southern California
Clark	N.Y.U.	Syracuse
Colorado	North Carolina	Texas
Connecticut	Ohio State	Tufts
Florida	Oregon	Vanderbilt
George Peabody	Penn State	Virginia
Kansas	Pittsburgh	Wayne State
Kansas State	Princeton	Washington (St. Louis)
Maryland	Purdue	Washington (Seattle)
Massachusetts	Rochester	

* Rank and score shared with another department.

High-Ranking Graduate Departments: Hughes, Keniston, and A.C.E. Studies

Top 15 Departments, Hughes Study, 1925	Top 15 Departments, Keniston Study, 1957	Top 20† Departments, Rated Quality of Faculty, A.C.E. Study, 1964
1. Columbia	1. Harvard	1. Harvard
2. Harvard	2. Michigan	2. Stanford
3. Chicago	3. Yale	3. Michigan
4. Cornell	4. California	4.* California, Berkeley
5. Johns Hopkins	5. Stanford	4.* Yale
6. Iowa	6. Minnesota	6. Illinois
7. Stanford	7. Illinois	7. Minnesota
8. Michigan	8. Iowa	8. Wisconsin
9. Princeton	9. Wisconsin	9. Brown
10. Yale	10. Chicago	10. Iowa (Iowa City)
11. Ohio State	11. Columbia	11. Pennsylvania
12.* Illinois	12. Indiana	12. Indiana
12.* Minnesota	13. Ohio State	13. U.C.L.A.
14. Wisconsin	14. Cornell	14. Columbia
15. Clark	15. Johns Hopkins	15. Johns Hopkins
		16. Northwestern
		17. Chicago
		18. Duke
		19. Cornell
		20. Ohio State

* Rank shared with another department.
† These 20 departments represent 23 percent of the 88 departments for which ratings were calculated.

ZOOLOGY

Leading Departments, by Rated Quality of Graduate Faculty

Institution†	All Respondents		Chairmen		Senior Scholars		Junior Scholars	
	Rank	Score	Rank	Score	Rank	Score	Rank	Score
"Distinguished"								
California, Berkeley.....	1	4.67	1	4.73	1	4.64	1	4.63
Harvard**a............	2	4.56	2	4.67	2	4.51	2	4.52
Rockefeller Inst.**......	3	4.31	3	4.34	3	4.32	3	4.25
Stanford**a...........	4	4.09	4	4.14	6	4.10	4	4.02
Johns Hopkins**a.......	5	4.02	8	3.81	4	4.19	5	4.00
"Strong"								
Yale**................	6	3.96	5	4.06	8	3.89	6	3.94
Indiana..............	7	3.95	6	4.00	5	4.15	13	3.63
U.C.L.A.............	8	3.85	9	3.79	7	3.97	9	3.74
Wisconsin............	9	3.81	7	3.90	12	3.65	7	3.91
Michigan.............	10	3.80	10	3.75	9	3.77	8	3.88
Chicago..............	11	3.70	11	3.72	11	3.69	11*	3.68
Princeton**a.........	12	3.62	12	3.58	15	3.58	11*	3.68
Illinois..............	13	3.60	13	3.54	13	3.64	14	3.58
Columbia.............	14	3.50	21	3.24	10	3.72	15	3.47
Cornell..............	15	3.48	19	3.29	14	3.61	16	3.45
Duke................	16	3.44	18	3.37	18	3.29	10	3.72
Western Reserve**a.....	17	3.36	17	3.38	17	3.34	17*	3.36
Texas...............	18	3.31	14	3.48	19	3.25	20	3.21
Pennsylvania..........	19	3.29	16	3.39	23	3.15	17*	3.36
Minnesota............	20	3.21	22	3.15	21	3.21	19	3.24
Washington (Seattle)....	21	3.20	20	3.25	20	3.24	21	3.08
Northwestern**a........	22	3.18	24*	3.06	16	3.39	24	3.02
Purdue**a............	23	3.15	15	3.40	25	3.02	22	3.06
Brown**a.............	24	3.09	24*	3.06	22	3.20	25*	3.00

"Good" (11 departments arranged alphabetically):

California, Davis	Michigan State	Rutgers
Iowa (Iowa City)	North Carolina	Washington (St. Louis)
Iowa State (Ames)	Rice**a	Washington State
Kansas	Rochester**	

"Adequate plus" (14 departments arranged alphabetically):

Colorado**	Massachusetts	Pittsburgh**
Connecticut	Missouri	Southern California**
Floridaa	Ohio State	Syracuse
Florida State**	Oregon State	Tulane**
Maryland	Penn State	

† These tabulations and those for the effectiveness of the graduate program are based on ratings of 64 institutions. See page 18 for further explanation.
* Rank and score shared with another department.
** Study offered in a department other than department of zoology *or* offered in more than one department.
a Doctorates reported in "biology" rather than "zoology."

Profile of Respondents

Respondents	Number	Average Age	Average Number of Publications Since Highest Degree		Professional Meetings Attended in Last Four Years	
			Books	Articles	Regional	National
All respondents................	126	45.8	.9	31	3.3	5.8
Chairmen..................	35	50.0	1.1	39	3.1	5.6
Senior scholars..............	51	51.2	1.2	44	3.9	6.4
Junior scholars..............	40	34.2	.4	10	2.8	5.3

Respondents' Division of Time for Professional Activities
(in percents)

Respondents	Instruction			Research and Writing	Administration	Other Professional	Other
	Under-graduate	Graduate	Total				
All respondents................	26	21	47	26	21	5	2
Chairmen..................	17	17	34	16	44	6	1
Senior scholars..............	26	26	52	26	14	6	2
Junior scholars..............	33	20	53	34	9	4	2

ZOOLOGY

Leading Departments, by Rated Effectiveness of Graduate Program

Institution	All Respondents		Chairmen		Senior Scholars		Junior Scholars	
	Rank	Score	Rank	Score	Rank	Score	Rank	Score
"Extremely attractive"								
California, Berkeley.....	1	2.58	1	2.75	2	2.38	1	2.71
Harvard..............	2	2.50	2	2.47	1	2.50	2	2.53
Stanford..............	3	2.27	3	2.28	3	2.28	4*	2.24
Johns Hopkins..........	4*	2.17	8*	2.03	5	2.20	3	2.27
Yale.................	4*	2.17	6	2.16	6	2.14	6	2.19
Rockefeller Inst........	6	2.16	5	2.22	8	2.10	7	2.17
Indiana..............	7	2.14	4	2.23	4	2.21	10	1.93
Wisconsin.............	8	2.12	7	2.07	9*	2.05	4*	2.24
Michigan.............	9	2.09	8*	2.03	7	2.11	8	2.12
"Attractive"								
U.C.L.A...............	10	1.95	12*	1.87	9*	2.05	11	1.89
Princeton.............	11	1.88	10	2.00	14	1.83	12*	1.82
Illinois...............	12	1.87	11	1.94	12	1.87	12*	1.82
Chicago..............	13	1.84	12*	1.87	11	1.90	14*	1.74
Cornell..............	14	1.76	21	1.66	13	1.84	14*	1.74
Duke................	15*	1.75	12*	1.87	21	1.52	9	1.94
Western Reserve.......	15*	1.75	12*	1.87	17	1.67	16	1.71
Pennsylvania..........	17	1.67	17	1.84	18	1.61	19	1.57
Columbia.............	18	1.66	22	1.60	15*	1.68	17	1.70
Washington (Seattle)....	19	1.61	19	1.69	15*	1.68	23	1.44
Texas................	20	1.58	16	1.86	24	1.39	20	1.54
Purdue..............	21	1.52	18	1.73	30	1.24	18	1.64

"Acceptable plus" (26 departments arranged alphabetically):

Brown	Massachusetts	Rutgers
California, Davis	Michigan State	Penn State
Colorado	Minnesota	Pittsburgh
Connecticut	North Carolina	Southern California
Florida	Northwestern	Syracuse
Florida State	Ohio State	Tulane
Iowa (Iowa City)	Oregon State	Washington (St. Louis)
Iowa State (Ames)	Rice	Washington State
Kansas	Rochester	

* Rank and score shared with another department.

High-Ranking Graduate Departments: Hughes, Keniston, and A.C.E. Studies

Top 15 Departments, Hughes Study, 1925	Top 15 Departments,[a] Keniston Study, 1957	Top 20[†] Departments, Rated Quality of Faculty, A.C.E. Study, 1964
1. Columbia	1. Harvard	1. California, Berkeley
2. Chicago	2. California	2. Harvard
3. Harvard	3. Columbia	3. Rockefeller Inst.
4. Yale	4. Indiana	4. Stanford
5. Johns Hopkins	5. Yale	5. Johns Hopkins
6. Princeton	6. Johns Hopkins	6. Yale
7. Illinois	7. Wisconsin	7. Indiana
8.* Michigan	8. U.C.L.A.	8. U.C.L.A.
8.* Wisconsin	9. Princeton	9. Wisconsin
10. California	10. Chicago	10. Michigan
11. Cornell	11. Michigan	11. Chicago
12. Stanford	12. Pennsylvania	12. Princeton
13.* Bryn Mawr	13. Cornell	13. Illinois
13.* Minnesota	14. Stanford	14. Columbia
13.* Ohio State	15. Illinois	15. Cornell
		16. Duke
		17. Western Reserve
		18. Texas
		19. Pennsylvania
		20. Minnesota

* Rank shared with another department.
† These 20 departments represent 31 percent of the 64 departments for which ratings were calculated.
a Technical and specialized institutions were omitted from the Keniston study.

ASTRONOMY

Leading Departments, by Rated Quality of Graduate Faculty

Institution†	All Respondents		Chairmen		Senior Scholars		Junior Scholars	
	Rank	Score	Rank	Score	Rank	Score	Rank	Score
"Distinguished"								
Cal. Tech.............	1	4.81	2	4.46	1	4.91	1	4.91
Princeton.............	2	4.62	1	4.66	2	4.53	2	4.69
Chicago..............	3	4.12	3	4.38	5	3.87	3	4.22
California, Berkeley.....	4	4.10	4	4.23	4	4.03	4*	4.08
Harvard..............	5	4.08	5	4.00	3	4.11	4*	4.08
"Strong"								
Yale.................	6	3.39	6	3.61	6	3.29	6	3.35
Wisconsin............	7	3.25	7	3.38	7	3.24	8	3.18
Michigan.............	8	3.20	8	3.23	8	3.16	7	3.22

"Good" (2 departments arranged alphabetically):
Colorado   Indiana

"Adequate plus" (2 departments arranged alphabetically):
Case   Columbia

† These tabulations and those for the effectiveness of the graduate program are based on ratings of the 16 institutions in the survey universe that reported the award of one or more doctorates in astronomy from July 1952 through June 1962.
* Rank and score shared with another department.

Profile of Respondents

Respondents	Number	Average Age	Average Number of Publications Since Highest Degree		Professional Meetings Attended in Last Four Years	
			Books	Articles	Regional	National
All respondents...............	62	43.2	.9	41	4.6	6.7
Chairmen...................	13	49.2	1.4	57	11.1	7.2
Senior scholars...............	26	48.0	1.2	58	3.5	7.3
Junior scholars...............	23	33.5	.2	12	2.0	5.9

Respondents' Division of Time for Professional Activities
(in percents)

Respondents	Instruction			Research and Writing	Administration	Other Professional	Other
	Undergraduate	Graduate	Total				
All respondents...............	17	22	39	32	18	8	4
Chairmen...................	8	20	28	19	31	12	10
Senior scholars...............	13	22	35	35	18	9	3
Junior scholars...............	26	24	50	35	10	5	1

ASTRONOMY

Leading Departments, by Rated Effectiveness of Graduate Program

Institution	All Respondents		Chairmen		Senior Scholars		Junior Scholars	
	Rank	Score	Rank	Score	Rank	Score	Rank	Score
"Extremely attractive"								
Cal. Tech...............	1	2.80	1	2.54	1	2.86	1	2.89
Princeton..............	2	2.49	2	2.17	2	2.52	2	2.65
California, Berkeley.....	3	2.13	3	2.15	3	2.12	4	2.11
"Attractive"								
Harvard..............	4	1.98	6	1.69	4	1.92	3	2.26
Wisconsin.............	5	1.77	5	1.77	5	1.71	6	1.84
Chicago..............	6	1.70	4	2.08	7	1.46	7	1.75
Michigan.............	7	1.68	7	1.54	6	1.56	5	1.94

"Acceptable plus" (5 departments arranged alphabetically):

Case	Columbia	Yale
Colorado	Indiana	

High-Ranking Graduate Departments: Hughes, Keniston, and A.C.E. Studies

Top 8 Departments, Hughes Study, 1925	Top 13 Departments,[a] Keniston Study, 1957	Top 16† Departments, Rated Quality of Faculty, A.C.E. Study, 1964
1. California	1. California	1. Cal. Tech.
2. Chicago	2. Chicago	2. Princeton
3. Michigan	3. Michigan	3. Chicago
4. Princeton	4. Harvard	4. California, Berkeley
5. Yale	5. Princeton	5. Harvard
6. Harvard	6. Indiana	6. Yale
7.* Northwestern	7. Ohio State	7. Wisconsin
7.* Wisconsin	8. Yale	8. Michigan
	9. Wisconsin	9. Indiana
	10. Pennsylvania	10. Colorado
	11. Columbia	11. Case
	12. Illinois	12. Columbia
	13. Northwestern	13. Pennsylvania
		14. Northwestern
		15. Georgetown
		16. Virginia

* Rank shared with another department.
† These 16 departments are all those surveyed in this field.
[a] Technical and specialized institutions were omitted from the Keniston study.

CHEMISTRY

Leading Departments, by Rated Quality of Graduate Faculty

Institution†	All Respondents		Chairmen		Senior Scholars		Junior Scholars	
	Rank	Score	Rank	Score	Rank	Score	Rank	Score
"Distinguished"								
Harvard...............	1	4.95	1	4.96	1	4.97	1	4.92
Cal. Tech.............	2	4.72	2	4.81	2	4.75	2	4.61
California, Berkeley.....	3	4.68	3	4.75	3	4.71	3	4.59
M.I.T.................	4	4.55	4	4.57	4	4.57	4	4.50
Stanford..............	5	4.32	5	4.36	5	4.38	5	4.22
Illinois................	6	4.13	6	4.26	6	4.10	6	4.07
"Strong"								
Columbia.............	7*	4.00	7*	4.06	9	3.97	7*	3.98
Wisconsin.............	7*	4.00	7*	4.06	8	3.98	7*	3.98
U.C.L.A..............	9	3.92	10	3.91	7	4.05	10	3.77
Chicago...............	10	3.91	9	4.02	10	3.93	9	3.82
Cornell...............	11	3.77	12	3.80	11	3.84	11	3.67
Yale..................	12	3.76	11	3.88	12	3.79	12	3.65
Princeton.............	13	3.67	13	3.78	13	3.71	13	3.55
Northwestern..........	14	3.52	14	3.71	15	3.53	14	3.38
Minnesota............	15	3.51	15	3.58	14	3.65	16	3.31
Iowa State (Ames)......	16	3.40	16	3.51	16	3.43	18	3.28
Ohio State............	17*	3.37	18	3.42	17*	3.40	17	3.30
Purdue................	17*	3.37	20	3.34	17*	3.40	15	3.33
Michigan..............	19	3.25	17	3.48	19	3.25	22	3.07
Indiana...............	20	3.24	19	3.37	21*	3.20	19	3.17
Washington (Seattle)....	21	3.18	21	3.31	26	3.13	20*	3.13
Johns Hopkins..........	22	3.17	27	3.15	21*	3.20	20*	3.13
Texas.................	23	3.14	25	3.17	23	3.19	23	3.03
Penn State............	24	3.13	22*	3.21	25	3.16	24	3.01
Brooklyn Polytech.......	25	3.08	24	3.19	27	3.12	26*	2.93
Florida State..........	26*	3.06	26	3.16	20	3.21	29*	2.84
Rice..................	26*	3.06	29*	3.11	24	3.17	28	2.90
Brown................	28	3.02	28	3.13	28	3.02	26*	2.93

"Good" (19 departments arranged alphabetically):

Brandeis	Florida	Notre Dame	Southern California
California, Davis	Iowa (Iowa City)	Oregon	Utah
Carnegie Tech.	Kansas	Pennsylvania	Washington (St. Louis)
Colorado	Michigan State	Pittsburgh	Wayne State
Duke	North Carolina	Rochester	

"Adequate plus" (18 departments arranged alphabetically):

Arizona	Ill. Inst. of Tech.	Nebraska	Virginia
Case	Kansas State	Oregon State	Washington State
Cincinnati	Louisiana State	Rensselaer	Western Reserve
Delaware	Maryland	Rutgers	
Georgia Tech.	N.Y.U.	Vanderbilt	

† These tabulations and those for the effectiveness of the graduate program are based on ratings of the 96 institutions in the survey universe that reported the award of one or more doctorates in chemistry from July 1952 through June 1962.
* Rank and score shared with another department.

Profile of Respondents

Respondents	Number	Average Age	Average Number of Publications Since Highest Degree		Professional Meetings Attended in Last Four Years	
			Books	Articles	Regional	National
All respondents................	218	42.4	.7	44	3.3	6.2
Chairmen...................	50	49.7	1.4	74	3.3	7.6
Senior scholars................	86	47.6	.7	58	4.6	6.6
Junior scholars...............	82	32.8	.2	12	1.9	5.0

Respondents' Division of Time for Professional Activities
(in percents)

Respondents	Instruction			Research and Writing	Administration	Other Professional	Other
	Undergraduate	Graduate	Total				
All respondents................	22	29	51	18	23	7	1
Chairmen...................	10	19	29	12	49	9	1
Senior scholars................	23	29	52	19	19	9	1
Junior scholars...............	28	34	62	21	11	5	—

CHEMISTRY

Leading Departments, by Rated Effectiveness of Graduate Program

Institution	All Respondents		Chairmen		Senior Scholars		Junior Scholars	
	Rank	Score	Rank	Score	Rank	Score	Rank	Score
"Extremely attractive"								
Harvard...............	1	2.75	2	2.71	1	2.84	1	2.69
Cal. Tech.............	2	2.73	1	2.83	2	2.78	2	2.62
California, Berkeley.....	3	2.63	3	2.65	3	2.65	3	2.60
M.I.T................	4	2.50	4	2.52	4*	2.51	4	2.47
Stanford..............	5	2.39	5	2.39	4*	2.51	5	2.28
Illinois................	6*	2.18	6	2.33	6	2.22	8	2.05
Wisconsin.............	6*	2.18	7	2.24	8	2.18	6	2.14
U.C.L.A.............	8	2.02	9*	2.04	7	2.21	13	1.81
Columbia.............	9	2.01	11*	2.00	14	1.92	7	2.11
"Attractive"								
Cornell...............	10	1.99	8	2.07	9	2.00	9	1.94
Chicago..............	11	1.95	13	1.98	10	1.97	10	1.91
Princeton.............	12	1.94	9*	2.04	12	1.94	11	1.87
Yale.................	13	1.92	11*	2.00	11	1.96	12	1.83
Northwestern..........	14	1.84	14*	1.84	13	1.93	14	1.74
Minnesota............	15	1.72	14*	1.84	15	1.77	16	1.59
Iowa State (Ames)......	16*	1.58	24	1.59	17*	1.62	17	1.52
Michigan.............	16*	1.58	16	1.74	16	1.66	24	1.38
Indiana...............	18	1.56	18	1.71	20	1.58	20	1.43
Johns Hopkins.........	19	1.55	20*	1.64	27*	1.45	15	1.60
Ohio State............	20*	1.53	26	1.55	17*	1.62	21	1.42
Washington (Seattle)....	20*	1.53	20*	1.64	24*	1.49	18	1.51
Purdue...............	22	1.52	28	1.53	17*	1.62	22*	1.40
Rice.................	23	1.51	22	1.63	21	1.57	26	1.35

"Acceptable plus" (37 departments arranged alphabetically):

Arizona	Ill. Inst. of Tech.	Oregon State
Brandeis	Iowa (Iowa City)	Pennsylvania
Brooklyn Polytech.	Kansas	Penn State
Brown	Kansas State	Pittsburgh
California, Davis	Lousiana State	Rochester
Carnegie Tech.	Maryland	Rutgers
Case	Michigan State	Southern California
Colorado	N.Y.U.	Texas
Delaware	Nebraska	Utah
Duke	North Carolina	Washington (St. Louis)
Florida	Notre Dame	Washington State
Florida State	Oregon	Wayne State
Georgia Tech.		

* Rank and score shared with another department.

High-Ranking Graduate Departments: Hughes, Keniston, and A.C.E. Studies

Top 15 Departments, Hughes Study, 1925	Top 16 Departments,[a] Keniston Study, 1957	Top 20† Departments, Rated Quality of Faculty, A.C.E. Study, 1964
1. Harvard	1. Harvard	1. Harvard
2. M.I.T.	2. California	2. Cal. Tech.
3. California	3. Illinois	3. California, Berkeley
4. Chicago	4. Chicago	4. M.I.T.
5. Yale	5. Wisconsin	5. Stanford
6. Cal. Tech.	6. Yale	6. Illinois
7. Cornell	7. Cornell	7.* Columbia
8. Illinois	8. Columbia	7.* Wisconsin
9. Princeton	9. Minnesota	9. U.C.L.A.
10. Columbia	10. U.C.L.A.	10. Chicago
11. Johns Hopkins	11. Princeton	11. Cornell
12. Michigan	12.* Northwestern	12. Yale
13. Wisconsin	12.* Washington (Seattle)	13. Princeton
14.* Ohio State	14. Michigan	14. Northwestern
14.* Stanford	15. Stanford	15. Minnesota
	16. Ohio State	16. Iowa State (Ames)
		17.* Ohio State
		17.* Purdue
		19. Michigan
		20. Indiana

* Rank shared with another department.
† These 20 departments represent 21 percent of the 96 departments for which ratings were calculated.
[a] Technical and specialized institutions were omitted from the Keniston study.

GEOLOGY

Leading Departments, by Rated Quality of Graduate Faculty

Institution†	All Respondents		Chairmen		Senior Scholars		Junior Scholars	
	Rank	Score	Rank	Score	Rank	Score	Rank	Score
"Distinguished"								
Harvard................	1	4.45	2	4.51	1	4.40	1	4.45
California, Berkeley.....	2*	4.38	3	4.37	2	4.39	2	4.38
Cal. Tech.............	2*	4.38	1	4.58	3*	4.27	3	4.35
Columbia.............	4	4.28	4	4.25	3*	4.27	4	4.29
"Strong"								
Princeton..............	5	3.98	5	4.19	7	3.93	8	3.87
M.I.T.................	6	3.96	7	3.88	6	4.04	7	3.90
Stanford..............	7	3.94	6	4.00	5	4.13	9	3.64
Penn State............	8	3.82	8	3.83	8	3.72	6	3.92
Yale..................	9	3.76	10	3.58	9	3.69	5	3.96
U.C.L.A..............	10	3.67	9	3.72	10	3.67	10	3.60
Johns Hopkins.........	11*	3.50	12	3.50	14	3.44	11	3.56
Texas.................	11*	3.50	11	3.54	12	3.52	12	3.43
Wisconsin.............	13	3.45	14	3.40	11	3.58	15	3.30
Minnesota.............	14	3.37	13	3.48	15	3.39	16	3.25
Illinois................	15*	3.32	17	3.27	13	3.49	18	3.12
Michigan..............	15*	3.32	18	3.22	16	3.33	14	3.36
Chicago...............	17	3.30	15	3.36	17	3.19	13	3.40
Northwestern..........	18	3.19	16	3.30	18	3.18	19	3.10
Rice..................	19	3.12	19	3.00	19	3.11	17	3.21

"Good" (3 departments arranged alphabetically):

Indiana	Ohio State	Washington (Seattle)

"Adequate plus" (15 departments arranged alphabetically):

Arizona	Kansas	Oregon
Cincinnati	Louisiana State	Southern California
Colorado	Michigan State	Utah
Cornell	Missouri	Virginia Polytech.
Iowa (Iowa City)	Oklahoma	Wyoming

† These tabulations and those for the effectiveness of the graduate program are based on ratings of 55 institutions in the survey universe that reported the award of one or more doctorates in geology from July 1952 through June 1962. One other institution was reported as having awarded doctorates in the field during that period. However, its graduate dean indicates that doctoral study is not offered, and data pertaining to it have been eliminated from all calculations.
* Rank and score shared with another department.

Profile of Respondents

Respondents	Number	Average Age	Average Number of Publications Since Highest Degree		Professional Meetings Attended in Last Four Years	
			Books	Articles	Regional	National
All respondents................	158	45.0	.8	27	4.1	6.1
Chairmen....................	37	50.3	1.2	36	4.3	7.0
Senior scholars...............	68	51.1	1.1	37	5.0	6.6
Junior scholars...............	53	34.1	.2	9	2.8	4.7

Respondents' Division of Time for Professional Activities
(in percents)

Respondents	Instruction			Research and Writing	Adminis-tration	Other Profes-sional	Other
	Under-graduate	Graduate	Total				
All respondents................	21	28	49	22	19	7	3
Chairmen....................	14	19	33	15	43	7	1
Senior scholars...............	20	30	50	22	15	8	4
Junior scholars...............	28	32	60	25	8	4	2

GEOLOGY

Leading Departments, by Rated Effectiveness of Graduate Program

Institution	All Respondents		Chairmen		Senior Scholars		Junior Scholars	
	Rank	Score	Rank	Score	Rank	Score	Rank	Score
"Extremely attractive"								
Harvard.............	1	2.38	1	2.43	1	2.34	2	2.40
California, Berkeley.....	2	2.33	4	2.19	2	2.32	1	2.44
Cal. Tech............	3	2.20	2*	2.31	6	2.10	3	2.25
Stanford.............	4	2.19	2*	2.31	3	2.25	7*	2.00
Princeton............	5	2.14	5	2.17	4*	2.13	5	2.15
Columbia............	6	2.12	6	2.03	4*	2.13	4	2.18
M.I.T...............	7	2.01	7*	1.94	7	1.98	6	2.08
"Attractive"								
Yale................	8	1.93	9	1.86	8	1.90	7*	2.00
Penn State...........	9	1.86	11	1.80	9	1.82	9	1.94
U.C.L.A.............	10	1.80	7*	1.94	10*	1.81	13	1.71
Texas...............	11	1.79	14	1.69	10*	1.81	10	1.83
Johns Hopkins........	12	1.77	13	1.76	13	1.75	11	1.82
Wisconsin............	13	1.76	12	1.77	12	1.77	12	1.73
Minnesota...........	14	1.71	10	1.83	15	1.64	14	1.69
Rice................	15	1.62	17*	1.47	14	1.65	15	1.68
Michigan............	16	1.53	17*	1.47	17	1.58	16	1.50

"Acceptable plus" (18 departments arranged alphabetically):

Arizona	Indiana	Ohio State
Chicago	Kansas	Southern California
Cincinnati	Louisiana State	Utah
Colorado	Michigan State	Virginia Polytech.
Cornell	Missouri	Washington (Seattle)
Illinois	Northwestern	Wyoming

* Rank and score shared with another department.

High-Ranking Graduate Departments:
Hughes, Keniston, and A.C.E. Studies

Top 15 Departments, Hughes Study, 1925	Top 15 Departments,[a] Keniston Study, 1957	Top 20[†] Departments, Rated Quality of Faculty, A.C.E. Study, 1964
1. Chicago	1. Columbia	1. Harvard
2.* Columbia	2. Harvard	2.* California, Berkeley
2.* Yale	3. California	2.* Cal. Tech.
4. Harvard	4. Yale	4. Columbia
5. Wisconsin	5. Princeton	5. Princeton
6. Johns Hopkins	6. Stanford	6. M.I.T.
7. California	7. Johns Hopkins	7. Stanford
8. Stanford	8. Wisconsin	8. Penn State
9. Cornell	9. Michigan	9. Yale
10. Princeton	10. Chicago	10. U.C.L.A.
11. Minnesota	11. Illinois	11.* Johns Hopkins
12. Michigan	12. Northwestern	11.* Texas
13. Illinois	13. Minnesota	13. Wisconsin
14. Iowa	14. U.C.L.A.	14. Minnesota
15. Ohio State	15. Cornell	15.* Illinois
		15.* Michigan
		17. Chicago
		18. Northwestern
		19. Rice
		20. Ohio State

* Rank shared with another department.
† These 20 departments represent 36 percent of the 55 departments for which ratings were calculated.
ᵃ Technical and specialized institutions were omitted from the Keniston study.

MATHEMATICS

Leading Departments, by Rated Quality of Graduate Faculty

Institution†	All Respondents		Chairmen		Senior Scholars		Junior Scholars	
	Rank	Score	Rank	Score	Rank	Score	Rank	Score
"Distinguished"								
Harvard..............	1	4.85	1	4.91	1	4.87	3	4.78
California, Berkeley.....	2	4.81	2	4.85	3	4.80	1*	4.80
Princeton.............	3	4.79	3	4.69	2	4.81	1*	4.80
Chicago..............	4	4.60	4	4.62	4	4.65	4	4.51
M.I.T................	5	4.39	5	4.41	5	4.43	5	4.31
Stanford.............	6	4.19	8	4.06	6	4.21	7	4.23
Yale.................	7	4.13	6*	4.11	9	4.03	6	4.26
N.Y.U...............	8	4.10	6*	4.11	7	4.15	8*	4.01
Columbia............	9	4.02	9	3.97	8	4.04	8*	4.01
"Strong"								
Wisconsin............	10	3.88	10	3.91	11	3.93	10	3.78
Michigan............	11	3.86	11	3.82	10	4.00	11	3.67
Illinois..............	12	3.74	12	3.79	12	3.84	13	3.57
Cornell..............	13	3.70	13	3.72	13	3.80	14	3.54
Cal. Tech............	14	3.66	14	3.54	14	3.73	12	3.60
Minnesota...........	15	3.48	17	3.42	16	3.52	15	3.44
U.C.L.A.............	16	3.47	15	3.50	15	3.53	16	3.34
Washington (Seattle)....	17	3.39	16	3.46	18	3.39	17	3.31
Brown...............	18	3.36	18	3.38	17	3.41	19*	3.26
Brandeis.............	19	3.24	21	3.20	21	3.22	18	3.29
Johns Hopkins........	20	3.23	23	3.12	19	3.34	23	3.11
Northwestern.........	21	3.21	20	3.23	20	3.24	22	3.13
Pennsylvania.........	22	3.15	22	3.18	25	3.10	21	3.18
Purdue..............	23	3.14	25	3.00	24	3.12	19*	3.26
Virginia.............	24	3.13	19	3.32	22	3.17	24	2.90
Indiana.............	25	3.02	24	3.05	23	3.13	25	2.82

"Good" (7 departments arranged alphabetically):

Duke	Ohio State	Rochester
Maryland	Rice	Tulane
North Carolina		

"Adequate plus" (14 departments arranged alphabetically):

Carnegie Tech.	Notre Dame	Texas
Colorado	Oregon	Washington (St. Louis)
Iowa (Iowa City)	Penn State	Wayne State
Kansas	Southern California	Yeshiva
Michigan State	Syracuse	

† These tabulations and those for the effectiveness of the graduate program are based on ratings of the 8 institutions in the survey universe that reported the award of one or more doctorates in mathematics from July 1952 through June 1962.
* Rank and score shared with another department.

Profile of Respondents

Respondents	Number	Average Age	Average Number of Publications Since Highest Degree		Professional Meetings Attended in Last Four Years	
			Books	Articles	Regional	National
All respondents...............	178	43.5	.9	21	4.4	4.5
Chairmen...................	35	49.4	1.6	27	5.9	5.1
Senior scholars...............	81	48.5	1.2	30	4.5	5.7
Junior scholars...............	62	33.4	.2	7	3.5	2.7

Respondents' Division of Time for Professional Activities

(in percents)

Respondents	Instruction			Research and Writing	Adminis-tration	Other Profes-sional	Other
	Under-graduate	Graduate	Total				
All respondents...............	19	28	47	25	21	6	1
Chairmen...................	10	19	29	16	50	5	—
Senior scholars...............	17	30	47	28	18	7	—
Junior scholars...............	26	32	58	27	9	4	2

MATHEMATICS

Leading Departments, by Rated Effectiveness of Graduate Program

Institution	All Respondents		Chairmen		Senior Scholars		Junior Scholars	
	Rank	Score	Rank	Score	Rank	Score	Rank	Score
"Extremely attractive"								
Princeton..............	1	2.66	1	2.57	1	2.84	2	2.50
Harvard...............	2	2.53	2	2.51	2	2.52	1	2.55
California, Berkeley.....	3	2.44	4	2.29	4	2.47	3	2.48
Stanford..............	4	2.43	5	2.24	3	2.51	4	2.45
M.I.T................	5	2.38	3	2.47	6	2.35	5	2.38
Chicago..............	6	2.35	6	2.17	5	2.42	6	2.37
Yale.................	7	2.26	7	2.15	7	2.34	7	2.22
Wisconsin............	8	2.08	8	2.06	9	2.13	8	2.04
Cornell..............	9	2.01	10	1.97	8	2.14	10	1.87
"Attractive"								
Cal. Tech............	10*	1.99	11	1.81	11	2.07	9	2.00
Michigan.............	10*	1.99	9	2.03	10	2.12	14	1.77
N.Y.U...............	12	1.87	12*	1.77	12	1.96	11*	1.81
Illinois...............	13*	1.79	15	1.59	13	1.88	13	1.80
Washington (Seattle)....	13*	1.79	12*	1.77	15	1.79	11*	1.81
Columbia.............	15	1.73	14*	1.65	14	1.80	16	1.69
Minnesota............	16	1.65	14*	1.65	17	1.72	18	1.54
Brandeis..............	17*	1.63	20	1.43	19	1.67	15	1.74
Brown................	17*	1.63	19	1.45	18	1.70	17	1.65
U.C.L.A..............	17*	1.63	16	1.56	16	1.75	19	1.51
Northwestern..........	20	1.52	17*	1.47	21	1.60	20	1.46

"Acceptable plus" (24 departments arranged alphabetically):

Carnegie Tech.	North Carolina	Rochester
Colorado	Notre Dame	Southern California
Duke	Ohio State	Syracuse
Indiana	Oregon	Texas
Johns Hopkins	Pennsylvania	Tulane
Kansas	Penn State	Virginia
Maryland	Purdue	Washington (St. Louis)
Michigan State	Rice	Yeshiva

* Rank and score shared with another department.

High-Ranking Graduate Departments: Hughes, Keniston, and A.C.E. Studies

Top 13 Departments, Hughes Study, 1925	Top 16 Departments,[a] Keniston Study, 1957	Top 20† Departments, Rated Quality of Faculty, A.C.E. Study, 1964
1. Chicago	1. Harvard	1. Harvard
2. Harvard	2. Chicago	2. California, Berkeley
3. Princeton	3. Princeton	3. Princeton
4. Illinois	4. California	4. Chicago
5. Columbia	5. Michigan	5. M.I.T.
6. Yale	6. Yale	6. Stanford
7. Cornell	7. Columbia	7. Yale
8. Wisconsin	8. N.Y.U.	8. N.Y.U.
9. Johns Hopkins	9. Stanford	9. Columbia
10. Michigan	10. Cornell	10. Wisconsin
11. California	11. Wisconsin	11. Michigan
12. Pennsylvania	12. Illinois	12. Illinois
13. Minnesota	13. Ohio State	13. Cornell
	14. Minnesota	14. Cal. Tech.
	15.* Pennsylvania	15. Minnesota
	15.* Texas	16. U.C.L.A.
		17. Washington (Seattle)
		18. Brown
		19. Brandeis
		20. Johns Hopkins

* Rank shared with another department.
† These 20 departments represent 25 percent of the 81 departments for which ratings were calculated.
[a] Technical and specialized institutions are omitted from the Keniston study.

PHYSICS

Leading Departments, by Rated Quality of Graduate Faculty

Institution†	All Respondents		Chairmen		Senior Scholars		Junior Scholars	
	Rank	Score	Rank	Score	Rank	Score	Rank	Score
"Distinguished"								
California, Berkeley.....	1	4.78	1	4.86	1*	4.78	1*	4.73
Cal. Tech...............	2	4.77	2	4.79	1*	4.78	1*	4.73
Harvard................	3	4.71	3	4.74	3	4.75	4	4.61
Princeton..............	4	4.60	4	4.62	4	4.56	3	4.63
Stanford...............	5	4.47	5	4.51	6	4.50	5	4.38
M.I.T.................	6	4.45	6	4.48	5	4.55	7	4.28
Columbia..............	7	4.32	7	4.45	7	4.26	6	4.29
Illinois................	8	4.10	8	4.18	9	4.14	8	4.00
Cornell................	9	4.07	9	4.14	10	4.10	9	3.96
"Strong"								
Chicago................	10	4.00	10	3.95	8	4.16	10	3.81
Yale..................	11	3.77	11	3.87	11	3.73	11	3.74
Wisconsin..............	12	3.69	12	3.77	12	3.70	12	3.59
Michigan..............	13*	3.46	14	3.48	13	3.52	14	3.32
Rochester..............	13*	3.46	16	3.42	14	3.48	13	3.45
Pennsylvania...........	15	3.37	15	3.45	15*	3.39	16	3.26
Maryland..............	16	3.35	17	3.35	15*	3.39	15	3.29
Minnesota.............	17	3.31	13	3.50	17	3.30	18	3.13
Washington (Seattle)....	18	3.16	18	3.20	19	3.18	20	3.06
Johns Hopkins..........	19*	3.12	20*	3.02	18	3.19	19	3.08
U.C.L.A...............	19*	3.12	20*	3.02	21	3.14	17	3.15
Carnegie Tech.........	21	3.09	19	3.05	20	3.16	21*	3.02

"Good" (17 departments arranged alphabetically):

Brandeis	Iowa State (Ames)	Purdue
Brown	Michigan State	Rice
Case	N.Y.U.	Rutgers
Colorado	Northwestern	Syracuse
Duke	Ohio State	Washington (St. Louis)
Indiana	Pittsburgh	

"Adequate plus" (11 departments arranged alphabetically):

Brooklyn Polytech.	Notre Dame	Southern California
Florida State	Oregon	Texas
Iowa (Iowa City)	Penn State	Virginia
North Carolina	Rensselaer	

† These tabulations and those for the effectiveness of the graduate program are based on ratings of the 86 institutions in the survey universe that reported the award of one or more doctorates in physics from July 1952 through June 1962.

* Rank and score shared with another department.

Profile of Respondents

Respondents	Number	Average Age	Average Number of Publications Since Highest Degree		Professional Meetings Attended in Last Four Years	
			Books	Articles	Regional	National
All respondents...............	190	42.0	.5	28	3.3	8.3
Chairmen....................	43	47.5	.4	37	2.5	8.5
Senior scholars...............	82	46.6	.8	37	3.9	9.4
Junior scholars...............	65	33.1	.1	10	2.9	6.9

Respondents' Division of Time for Professional Activities
(in percents)

Respondents	Instruction			Research and Writing	Administration	Other Professional	Other
	Under-graduate	Graduate	Total				
All respondents...............	19	28	47	23	22	7	1
Chairmen....................	13	19	32	14	47	7	1
Senior scholars...............	19	29	48	23	20	8	2
Junior scholars...............	22	35	57	29	8	5	—

PHYSICS

Leading Departments, by Rated Effectiveness of Graduate Program

Institution	All Respondents		Chairmen		Senior Scholars		Junior Scholars	
	Rank	Score	Rank	Score	Rank	Score	Rank	Score
"Extremely attractive"								
Princeton..............	1	2.61	2*	2.63	4	2.58	1	2.65
Cal. Tech.............	2	2.60	1	2.71	1	2.64	3*	2.50
Stanford..............	3	2.57	2*	2.63	3	2.59	2	2.52
Harvard...............	4	2.56	4	2.53	2	2.62	3*	2.50
California, Berkeley.....	5	2.42	5	2.49	5	2.39	5	2.42
M.I.T.................	6	2.26	8	2.08	6	2.32	6	2.30
Cornell...............	7	2.22	6	2.35	7	2.23	7	2.12
Illinois...............	8	2.15	7	2.18	8	2.19	8	2.09
"Attractive"								
Wisconsin.............	9	1.97	9	2.06	9	2.00	11	1.86
Chicago...............	10*	1.92	11	2.00	10	1.90	10	1.89
Yale..................	10*	1.92	12	1.94	12	1.86	9	1.97
Columbia.............	12	1.89	10	2.03	11	1.88	12	1.82
Rochester.............	13	1.75	16	1.74	13	1.81	13	1.66
Michigan..............	14	1.71	14*	1.76	14	1.75	14	1.61
Washington (Seattle)....	15	1.65	14*	1.76	16	1.67	18	1.53
Pennsylvania...........	16	1.64	13	1.77	18	1.65	16*	1.54
Maryland.............	17	1.61	22	1.47	15	1.68	15	1.60
Minnesota.............	18	1.59	17	1.61	17	1.66	21*	1.48
Johns Hopkins..........	19	1.52	18*	1.56	19	1.62	25	1.35

"Acceptable plus" (29 departments arranged alphabetically):

Brandeis	Iowa State (Ames)	Rensselaer
Brooklyn Polytech.	Michigan State	Rice
Brown	N.Y.U.	Rutgers
Carnegie Tech.	North Carolina	Southern California
Case	Northwestern	Syracuse
Colorado	Notre Dame	Texas
Duke	Ohio State	U.C.L.A.
Florida State	Penn State	Virginia
Indiana	Pittsburgh	Washington (St. Louis)
Iowa (Iowa City)	Purdue	

* Rank and score shared with another department.

High-Ranking Graduate Departments: Hughes, Keniston, and A.C.E. Studies

Top 14 Departments, Hughes Study, 1925	Top 15 Departments,[a] Keniston Study, 1957	Top 20[†] Departments, Rated Quality of Faculty, A.C.E. Study, 1964
1. Chicago	1. California	1. California, Berkeley
2. Harvard	2. Harvard	2. Cal. Tech.
3. Cal. Tech.	3. Columbia	3. Harvard
4.* Princeton	4. Princeton	4. Princeton
4.* Yale	5. Chicago	5. Stanford
6. Wisconsin	6. Stanford	6. M.I.T.
7. Columbia	7. Cornell	7. Columbia
8. Johns Hopkins	8. Illinois	8. Illinois
9. Michigan	9. Michigan	9. Cornell
10. Cornell	10. Wisconsin	10. Chicago
11. Minnesota	11. Yale	11. Yale
12. California	12. Minnesota	12. Wisconsin
13. Stanford	13. Pennsylvania	13.* Michigan
14. Iowa (Iowa City)	14. Ohio State	13.* Rochester
	15. Johns Hopkins	15. Pennsylvania
		16. Maryland
		17. Minnesota
		18. Washington (Seattle)
		19.* Johns Hopkins
		19.* U.C.L.A.

* Rank shared with another department.
† These 20 departments represent 23 percent of the 86 departments for which ratings were calculated.
[a] Technical and specialized institutions were omitted from the Keniston study.

CHEMICAL ENGINEERING

Leading Departments, by Rated Quality of Graduate Faculty

Institution†	All Respondents		Chairmen		Senior Scholars		Junior Scholars	
	Rank	Score	Rank	Score	Rank	Score	Rank	Score
"Distinguished"								
Wisconsin............	1	4.43	3	4.31	1	4.52	1	4.38
M.I.T...............	2	4.36	1	4.54	2	4.49	7	4.02
Minnesota...........	3*	4.25	5*	4.18	5	4.20	2	4.37
Princeton...........	3*	4.25	2	4.32	4	4.22	4	4.21
California, Berkeley.....	5	4.24	7	4.05	3	4.29	3	4.31
Delaware............	6*	4.13	5*	4.18	6	4.11	5	4.11
Michigan............	6*	4.13	4	4.29	7	4.05	6	4.09
"Strong"								
Illinois..............	8	3.80	8	3.75	8	3.80	8	3.84
Cal. Tech...........	9	3.53	9	3.62	9	3.56	11	3.38
Northwestern........	10*	3.42	11	3.44	10	3.37	10	3.45
Stanford............	10*	3.42	13	3.28	11	3.32	9	3.72
Texas...............	12	3.35	10	3.45	12	3.29	12*	3.33
Carnegie Tech........	13	3.33	12	3.42	13	3.26	12*	3.33
Rice................	14	3.18	14	3.08	14	3.20	14	3.21
Washington (Seattle)....	15	3.05	16	2.96	15*	3.06	15	3.12

"Good" (11 departments arranged alphabetically):

Brooklyn Polytech.	Iowa State (Ames)	Purdue
Columbia	Johns Hopkins	Rensselaer
Cornell	N.Y.U.	Yale
Ill. Inst. of Tech.	Ohio State	

"Adequate plus" (15 departments arranged alphabetically):

Case	No. Carolina State	Penn State
Cincinnati	Oklahoma	Rochester
Kansas	Oklahoma State	Syracuse
Lehigh	Oregon State	Tennessee
Maryland	Pennsylvania	Washington (St. Louis)

† These tabulations and those for the effectiveness of the graduate program are based on ratings of the 56 institutions in the survey universe that reported the award of one or more doctorates in chemical engineering from July 1952 through June 1962.

* Rank and score shared with another department.

Profile of Respondents

Respondents	Number	Average Age	Average Number of Publications Since Highest Degree		Professional Meetings Attended in Last Four Years	
			Books	Articles	Regional	National
All respondents...............	144	43.4	.6	25	3.7	5.7
Chairmen....................	37	48.6	.7	28	3.7	6.6
Senior scholars...............	63	46.5	.8	34	4.3	5.9
Junior scholars...............	44	34.2	.2	10	2.8	4.8

Respondents' Division of Time for Professional Activities
(in percents)

Respondents	Instruction			Research and Writing	Administration	Other Professional	Other
	Under-graduate	Graduate	Total				
All respondents...............	23	29	52	15	23	10	1
Chairmen....................	16	20	36	10	42	11	1
Senior scholars...............	23	29	52	16	21	10	1
Junior scholars...............	27	35	62	16	11	9	2

CHEMICAL ENGINEERING

Leading Departments, by Rated Effectiveness of Graduate Program

Institution	All Respondents		Chairmen		Senior Scholars		Junior Scholars	
	Rank	Score	Rank	Score	Rank	Score	Rank	Score
"Extremely attractive"								
Wisconsin.............	1	2.49	1	2.45	1	2.53	1	2.46
Princeton.............	2	2.37	2	2.44	4	2.30	3	2.41
Minnesota............	3	2.36	5*	2.29	2	2.35	2	2.45
California, Berkeley.....	4	2.32	3	2.41	3	2.32	4	2.21
Delaware.............	5	2.16	5*	2.29	6	2.07	6	2.17
M.I.T................	6	2.14	4	2.38	5	2.21	9	1.80
Michigan.............	7	2.06	7	2.24	7*	2.04	8	1.95
Illinois................	8	2.05	8	2.06	7*	2.04	7	2.06
"Attractive"								
Stanford..............	9	1.88	10	1.74	9	1.81	5	2.18
Northwestern..........	10	1.68	11*	1.73	10	1.68	10	1.61
Cal. Tech.............	11	1.65	9	1.83	12	1.66	13*	1.45
Texas.................	12	1.63	11*	1.73	11	1.67	13*	1.45
Carnegie Tech.........	13	1.58	13	1.68	13*	1.58	12	1.47
Rice..................	14	1.55	14	1.61	13*	1.58	15	1.42
Washington (Seattle)....	15	1.53	16	1.45	15	1.56	11	1.58

"Acceptable plus" (22 departments arranged alphabetically):

Brooklyn Polytech.	Maryland	Purdue
Case	N.Y.U.	Rensselaer
Columbia	No. Carolina State	Rochester
Cornell	Ohio State	Tennessee
Ill. Inst. of Tech.	Oklahoma	Washington (St. Louis)
Iowa State (Ames)	Oregon State	Yale
Johns Hopkins	Pennsylvania	
Lehigh	Penn State	

* Rank and score shared with another department.

CIVIL ENGINEERING

Leading Departments, by Rated Quality of Graduate Faculty

Institution†	All Respondents		Chairmen		Senior Scholars		Junior Scholars	
	Rank	Score	Rank	Score	Rank	Score	Rank	Score
"Distinguished"								
California, Berkeley.....	1	4.52	1	4.61	1	4.42	1	4.57
Illinois................	2	4.40	2	4.54	2	4.37	2	4.36
M.I.T................	3	4.17	3	4.22	3	4.22	4	4.07
Cal. Tech.............	4	4.09	4	3.95	4	4.06	3	4.19
"Strong"								
Stanford..............	5	3.86	5	3.84	5	3.93	5	3.78
Purdue................	6	3.70	6	3.80	6	3.75	6	3.58
Michigan.............	7	3.62	7	3.72	7	3.65	8	3.51
Cornell...............	8	3.42	8	3.45	9	3.45	11	3.34
Northwestern..........	9	3.41	10	3.27	10	3.40	9	3.48
Columbia.............	10	3.37	9	3.29	8	3.58	16	3.13
Wisconsin.............	11	3.22	14	3.00	13	3.08	7	3.53
Texas................	12	3.14	11	3.16	16	3.05	12*	3.24
Lehigh...............	13*	3.12	15	2.95	11	3.23	17	3.06
Washington (Seattle)....	13*	3.12	12	3.05	14*	3.07	12*	3.24
Minnesota............	15	3.08	17*	2.85	12	3.13	15	3.14

"Good" (14 departments arranged alphabetically):

Carnegie Tech.	Iowa State (Ames)	Penn State
Florida	Johns Hopkins	Princeton
Georgia Tech.	Michigan State	Rensselaer
Harvard	No. Carolina State	U.C.L.A.
Ill. Inst. of Tech.	Ohio State	

"Adequate plus" (8 departments arranged alphabetically):

Colorado	N.Y.U.	Texas A&M
Iowa (Iowa City)	Oregon State	Yale
Missouri	Pennsylvania	

† These tabulations and those for the effectiveness of the graduate program are based on ratings of the 40 institutions in the survey universe that reported the award of one or more doctorates in civil engineering from July 1952 through June 1962.
* Rank and score shared with another department.

Profile of Respondents

Respondents	Number	Average Age	Average Number of Publications Since Highest Degree		Professional Meetings Attended in Last Four Years	
			Books	Articles	Regional	National
All respondents................	118	43.9	.5	19	9.1	7.3
Chairmen....................	22	50.0	.5	27	8.6	9.9
Senior scholars................	52	49.0	.8	25	11.4	7.5
Junior scholars...............	44	34.0	.1	8	6.6	5.8

Respondents' Division of Time for Professional Activities
(in percents)

Respondents	Instruction			Research and Writing	Adminis- tration	Other Profes- sional	Other
	Under- graduate	Graduate	Total				
All respondents................	17	28	45	19	22	12	1
Chairmen....................	10	23	33	9	46	11	—
Senior scholars................	16	26	42	20	23	14	1
Junior scholars...............	23	33	56	22	10	11	1

CIVIL ENGINEERING

Leading Departments, by Rated Effectiveness of Graduate Program

Institution	All Respondents		Chairmen		Senior Scholars		Junior Scholars	
	Rank	Score	Rank	Score	Rank	Score	Rank	Score
"Extremely attractive"								
California, Berkeley.....	1	2.61	1	2.75	1	2.53	1	2.62
Illinois.................	2	2.32	2	2.59	4	2.19	2	2.31
Stanford...............	3	2.17	4	2.11	3	2.22	3	2.16
M.I.T.................	4	2.15	3	2.23	2	2.24	5	2.02
Cal. Tech.............	5	2.12	5*	2.05	5	2.17	4	2.11
"Attractive"								
Purdue................	6	1.86	5*	2.05	6*	1.80	7	1.81
Cornell................	7	1.79	7	2.00	6*	1.80	9*	1.67
Michigan..............	8*	1.76	8	1.86	8	1.78	9*	1.67
Northwestern..........	8*	1.76	9	1.81	9	1.71	8	1.80
Wisconsin..............	10	1.62	10*	1.56	13*	1.45	6	1.87
Washington (Seattle)....	11	1.51	10*	1.56	16	1.42	11	1.61

"Acceptable plus" (24 departments arranged alphabetically):

Carnegie Tech.	Iowa State (Ames)	Oregon State
Colorado	Johns Hopkins	Pennsylvania
Columbia	Lehigh	Penn State
Florida	Michigan State	Princeton
Georgia Tech.	Minnesota	Rensselaer
Harvard	N.Y.U.	Texas
Ill. Inst. of Tech.	No. Carolina State	Texas A&M
Iowa (Iowa City)	Ohio State	U.C.L.A.

* Rank and score shared with another department.

ELECTRICAL ENGINEERING

Leading Departments, by Rated Quality of Graduate Faculty

Institution†	All Respondents		Chairmen		Senior Scholars		Junior Scholars	
	Rank	Score	Rank	Score	Rank	Score	Rank	Score
"Distinguished"								
M.I.T.	1	4.78	1	4.96	1	4.85	1	4.60
Stanford	2	4.68	2	4.76	2	4.75	2	4.55
California, Berkeley	3	4.38	3	4.62	3	4.34	3	4.25
Illinois	4	4.13	4	4.17	4	4.14	4	4.07
"Strong"								
Cal. Tech.	5	3.98	5	4.04	6	3.90	5	4.02
Brooklyn Polytech	6	3.94	7	3.76	5	4.11	6	3.87
Michigan	7	3.68	8	3.70	7	3.76	9	3.57
Harvard	8	3.60	6	3.81	8	3.44	7	3.60
Purdue	9	3.51	9	3.52	9	3.43	8	3.58
Columbia	10*	3.34	18	3.20	12	3.28	10	3.56
Wisconsin	10*	3.34	14	3.30	10	3.39	15	3.28
Carnegie Tech.	12	3.33	11	3.47	14*	3.21	12	3.37
Pennsylvania	13	3.29	19	3.19	14*	3.21	11	3.48
Johns Hopkins	14	3.28	13	3.41	13	3.25	16	3.20
Cornell	15	3.25	16	3.26	11	3.34	21	3.10
Minnesota	16*	3.24	10	3.50	17	3.16	17	3.17
Princeton	16*	3.24	12	3.45	14*	3.21	20	3.13
Syracuse	18	3.16	21	3.15	19	3.02	13	3.34
N.Y.U.	19	3.13	17	3.21	18	3.07	18	3.15
U.C.L.A.	20	3.08	22	3.13	22	2.89	14	3.29
Ohio State	21	3.04	15	3.27	21	2.91	23*	3.00
Case	22	3.02	20	3.18	20	2.95	23*	3.00

"Good" (9 departments arranged alphabetically):

Brown	Northwestern	Texas
Iowa State (Ames)	Penn State	Washington (Seattle)
Michigan State	Rensselaer	Yale

'Adequate plus" (13 departments arranged alphabetically):

Arizona	Lehigh	Pittsburgh
Colorado	Maryland	Southern California
Florida	New Mexico	Utah
Georgia Tech.	Oklahoma State	Washington (St. Louis)
Ill. Inst. of Tech.		

† These tabulations and those for the effectiveness of the graduate program are based on ratings of the 54 institutions in the survey universe that reported the award of one or more doctorates in electrical engineering from July 1952 through June 1962.
* Rank and score shared with another department.

Profile of Respondents

Respondents	Number	Average Age	Average Number of Publications Since Highest Degree		Professional Meetings Attended in Last Four Years	
			Books	Articles	Regional	National
All respondents	128	43.1	1.3	13	5.1	6.7
Chairmen	25	49.9	1.4	16	5.2	8.5
Senior scholars	53	46.9	2.2	19	6.0	7.8
Junior scholars	50	35.7	.2	6	4.1	4.7

Respondents' Division of Time for Professional Activities
(in percents)

Respondents	Instruction			Research and Writing	Administration	Other Professional	Other
	Under-graduate	Graduate	Total				
All respondents	21	27	48	16	26	9	2
Chairmen	9	12	21	10	57	10	2
Senior scholars	20	29	49	18	22	8	3
Junior scholars	28	32	60	17	14	9	—

ELECTRICAL ENGINEERING

Leading Departments, by Rated Effectiveness of Graduate Program

Institution	All Respondents		Chairmen		Senior Scholars		Junior Scholars	
	Rank	Score	Rank	Score	Rank	Score	Rank	Score
"Extremely attractive"								
Stanford..............	1	2.59	2	2.64	1	2.71	1	2.44
M.I.T.................	2	2.45	1	2.76	2	2.54	3	2.20
California, Berkeley.....	3	2.44	3	2.52	3	2.49	2	2.35
Illinois...............	4	2.23	4	2.33	4	2.28	4	2.13
Cal. Tech.............	5	2.06	6	2.00	5	2.11	5	2.05
Harvard..............	6	2.04	5	2.17	6	2.00	6	1.97
"Attractive"								
Michigan..............	7	1.85	7	1.87	7	1.92	7	1.77
Brooklyn Polytech.......	8*	1.78	8	1.80	9	1.88	8*	1.68
Princeton..............	8*	1.78	10	1.71	8	1.90	8*	1.68
Johns Hopkins..........	10	1.68	11	1.63	10	1.76	11	1.65
Purdue................	11	1.61	12	1.56	11	1.71	14	1.55
Wisconsin..............	12	1.59	13	1.55	13	1.60	12	1.61
Cornell...............	13	1.54	15	1.48	12	1.68	17	1.44
Carnegie Tech.........	14	1.52	14	1.50	15	1.48	13	1.58

"Acceptable plus" (23 departments arranged alphabetically):

Arizona	Maryland	Pittsburgh
Brown	Michigan State	Rensselaer
Case	Minnesota	Syracuse
Columbia	N.Y.U.	Texas
Florida	Northwestern	U.C.L.A.
Georgia Tech.	Ohio State	Washington (Seattle)
Ill. Inst. of Tech.	Pennsylvania	Yale
Iowa State (Ames)	Penn State	

* Rank and score shared with another department.

MECHANICAL ENGINEERING

Leading Departments, by Rated Quality of Graduate Faculty

Institution†	All Respondents		Chairmen		Senior Scholars		Junior Scholars	
	Rank	Score	Rank	Score	Rank	Score	Rank	Score
"Distinguished"								
M.I.T.	1	4.61	1	4.76	1	4.56	1	4.57
Cal. Tech.	2	4.20	2	4.28	2*	4.00	2	4.44
Stanford	3	4.14	3	4.19	2*	4.00	3	4.31
"Strong"								
California, Berkeley	4	3.83	5	3.94	4	3.83	4	3.75
Minnesota	5	3.72	4	4.05	6	3.61	7	3.68
Purdue	6	3.65	6*	3.61	5	3.63	6	3.70
Brown	7	3.58	6*	3.61	7	3.56	9	3.60
Harvard	8	3.54	13	3.22	8	3.53	5	3.73
Michigan	9	3.50	9	3.55	9*	3.40	8	3.65
Illinois	10	3.33	10	3.30	12	3.28	11	3.44
Cornell	11	3.32	16	3.15	11	3.38	12	3.32
Northwestern	12	3.27	8	3.57	14*	3.18	16	3.20
Columbia	13	3.26	14*	3.21	13	3.27	13*	3.26
Johns Hopkins	14	3.23	12	3.23	9*	3.40	22	2.96
Case	15	3.20	14*	3.21	14*	3.18	15	3.21
Princeton	16	3.19	11	3.26	16	3.10	13*	3.26
U.C.L.A.	17	3.12	19*	2.94	17	3.02	10	3.47

"Good" (10 departments arranged alphabetically):

Brooklyn Polytech.	Ohio State	Rensselaer
Carnegie Tech.	Pennsylvania	Rice
Ill. Inst. of Tech.	Penn State	Wisconsin
N.Y.U.		

"Adequate plus" (11 departments arranged alphabetically):

Georgia Tech.	Michigan State	Syracuse
Iowa State (Ames)	Oklahoma State	Texas
Lehigh	Pittsburgh	Yale
Maryland	Southern California	

† These tabulations and those for the effectiveness of the graduate program are based on ratings of the 47 institutions in the survey universe that reported the award of one or more doctorates in mechanical engineering from July 1952 through June 1962.

* Rank and score shared with another department.

Profile of Respondents

Respondents	Number	Average Age	Average Number of Publications Since Highest Degree		Professional Meetings Attended in Last Four Years	
			Books	Articles	Regional	National
All respondents	119	43.8	.7	16	4.4	6.9
Chairmen	21	48.3	1.2	28	4.2	11.4
Senior scholars	58	46.6	.8	19	5.2	7.0
Junior scholars	40	37.1	.2	7	3.3	4.4

Respondents' Division of Time for Professional Activities
(in percents)

Respondents	Instruction			Research and Writing	Administration	Other Professional	Other
	Undergraduate	Graduate	Total				
All respondents	20	26	46	17	27	9	1
Chairmen	8	15	23	9	55	11	2
Senior scholars	17	28	45	19	26	9	1
Junior scholars	31	29	60	20	12	8	—

MECHANICAL ENGINEERING

Leading Departments, by Rated Effectiveness of Graduate Program

Institution	All Respondents		Chairmen		Senior Scholars		Junior Scholars	
	Rank	Score	Rank	Score	Rank	Score	Rank	Score
"Extremely attractive"								
M.I.T.	1	2.41	2	2.50	1	2.31	1	2.53
Cal. Tech.	2	2.38	1	2.61	3	2.26	3	2.42
Stanford	3	2.36	3	2.33	2	2.30	2	2.47
California, Berkeley	4	2.09	4	2.19	4	2.10	4	2.00
"Attractive"								
Minnesota	5	1.94	6	2.06	5	1.88	5	1.96
Harvard	6	1.86	11	1.87	6	1.87	8	1.86
Michigan	7	1.82	9*	1.88	9	1.74	6	1.90
Purdue	8	1.81	7	2.00	10	1.72	9	1.84
Brown	9	1.79	5	2.18	7	1.78	12	1.64
Cornell	10	1.75	9*	1.88	8	1.75	11	1.67
Princeton	11	1.68	12	1.86	14	1.45	7	1.88
Illinois	12	1.62	16	1.53	13	1.61	10	1.71
Case	13	1.59	15	1.56	11	1.71	17*	1.40
Johns Hopkins	14	1.54	14	1.73	12	1.64	21	1.32
Northwestern	15	1.51	8	1.89	16	1.41	17*	1.40

"Acceptable plus" (21 departments arranged alphabetically):

Brooklyn Polytech.	Maryland	Pittsburgh
Carnegie Tech.	Michigan State	Rensselaer
Columbia	N.Y.U.	Rice
Georgia Tech.	Ohio State	Texas
Ill. Inst. of Tech.	Oklahoma State	U.C.L.A.
Iowa State (Ames)	Pennsylvania	Wisconsin
Lehigh	Penn State	Yale

* Rank and score shared with another department.

IV · *A Review of Selected Disciplines*

UPON REVIEW OF THE DATA in the preceding chapter, the reader may well ask how reliable the various ratings are. The study staff, anticipating this question and anxious to find the answer, selected four fields for somewhat more detailed analysis. A small panel of experts in each of the four fields was chosen with the advice of the appropriate professional association to provide a group of judges selected on a different basis from that used for the larger sample. In addition it was thought useful to analyze the judgments of the main body of respondents in relation to such factors as the institutions from which they had received their highest degrees, the departments at which they were employed at the time of the survey, the scholarly publications records of departments, the level of faculty salaries, and so on. Furthermore, it was felt that variations in regional assessments and in the percentage of informed response might reveal factors about departments and survey procedures that are not apparent when only an average of judgments is reported.

The four fields selected for detailed analysis were economics, English, physics, and political science. The first three were chosen as representative fields in, respectively, the social sciences, the humanities, and the natural sciences; political science was added so that comparisons could be made between the A.C.E. study and the study by Somit and Tanenhaus published in 1964.[1]

In this chapter, the focus is on several selected disciplines, in an effort to relate subjective ratings to background factors and certain "objective" factors involving departments. In chapter 5, several different types of indices are correlated with over-all institutional ratings. Both types of comparisons are useful in attempting to measure the reliability of subjective opinion surveys.

ECONOMICS

Select panel

In his 1924 and 1934 studies Hughes used panels of selected experts to judge the quality of graduate programs. In one sense all the participants in the 1964 survey were experts; that is, they were selected for their scholarly competence and positions of leadership. In economics, an additional small, select panel was chosen, with advice from the American Economic Association. Picked to represent expertise in this field were four recent presidents of the association, the editors of four major economics journals, and seven additional distinguished scholars to give balance to the panel with respect to regional representation and institutional type. About a third of the recommended panel members were already participants in the study; the others were queried separately in the summer and fall of 1964. They received the identical questionnaire, and had no information available to them other than that which the original 173 respondents had received. Twelve of the 15 invited panelists completed the questionnaires.

Table 8 shows the rank order of the leading departments as rated on Question A (faculty quality) by the original sample (as a unit and by subgroups) and by the small panel of experts. The small panel shows greater variance with the over-all rankings than does any of the three age and rank subgroups. The rank correlation with the over-all ranking was .911 for the experts panel, .949 for the chairmen, .990 for the junior scholars, and .991 for the senior scholars. Clearly, of the subgroups, the small panel is the poorest predictor of the over-all rank of departments (although this does not necessarily mean that the over-all rank is "right" and the experts' view "wrong").

Of particular interest are the small panel's placing Yale and M.I.T. in a tie position for the leader above Harvard, its boost to departments at Stanford, Minnesota, and Carnegie Tech., and its relative downgrading of Chicago and Wisconsin.

[1] Albert Somit and Joseph Tanenhaus, *American Political Science: A Profile of a Discipline* (New York: Atherton Press, 1964).

TABLE 8: *Comparison of Faculty Quality Ratings of High-ranking Economics Departments, by Rating Group*

INSTITUTION	RANK				
	All Respondents	Chairmen	Senior Scholars	Junior Scholars	Select Panel
Harvard	1	1*	1	1*	3
M.I.T.	2	1*	2	1*	1*
Chicago	3	5	3	3*	5
Yale	4	3	5	3*	1*
California, Berkeley	5	7	4	5	6
Stanford	6	4	6	6	4
Princeton	7	6	7	7	7
Michigan	8	9*	9	8	8
Columbia	9	9*	8	9*	11*
Wisconsin	10	8	10	9*	13*
Minnesota	11	13	11	11	9*
Northwestern	12	11	12	13	11*
Carnegie Tech.	13	12	14	12	9*
Pennsylvania	14	14	13	15	13*
Johns Hopkins	15	15	15	14	15*
U.C.L.A.	16	19	16	16	15*

* Rank shared with another department.

Rank ordering sometimes magnifies small differences in raw scores. Figure 2 therefore shows diagrammatically the quality scores assigned to the 71 doctorate-granting economics departments by the large survey sample and by the experts panel. Although there are a few departments where the disagreement between the panel and the larger sample is quite noticeable, in general there is a close fit. The small panel tended to give slightly higher scores to most of the departments in the 3.0 to 5.0 range and somewhat lower scores to the weaker departments, as indicated by the divergence of the plotted points from the 45° line of equal rating.

Table 9 and Figure 3 show the relationship of the experts panel's assessment of the effectiveness of doctoral programs (Question B) to the assessment by the 173 respondents. Among the leading

departments, the panel was more favorably disposed to Northwestern and Johns Hopkins than was the over-all group, and rated these two institutions considerably higher on this question than on Question A. By contrast, Columbia and Michigan fared less well in the experts' judgment. As the scatter diagram indicates, the panelists rated most departments higher on Question B than the 173 respondents did.

A comparison of the views of all respondents on the two questions reveals a tendency for the smaller departments—primarily in the private universities—to improve their rank on Question B over Question A, and for the larger departments —particularly those in urban locations—to slip. M.I.T. bumps Harvard for the first position, and Stanford, Wisconsin, Northwestern, Carnegie Tech., and Johns Hopkins move up by two

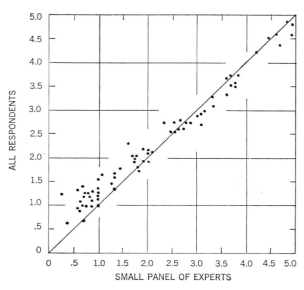

FIG. 2—Faculty quality ratings of 71 economics departments, as judged by all respondents and by a panel of experts.

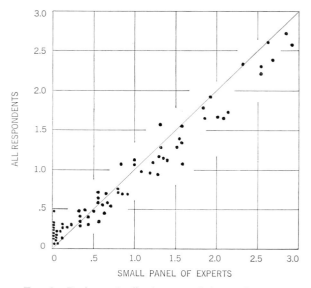

FIG. 3—Ratings of effectiveness of doctoral programs of 71 economics departments, as judged by all respondents and by a panel of experts.

TABLE 9: *Comparison of Ratings of Effectiveness of the Doctoral Program of High-ranking Economics Departments, by Rating Group*

INSTITUTION	RANK				
	All Respondents	Chairmen	Senior Scholars	Junior Scholars	Select Panel
M.I.T.	1	2	1	1	2
Harvard	2	4	2	3	4
Yale	3	1	3	2	1
Stanford	4	3	4	5	3
California, Berkeley	5	6	6	4	7
Princeton	6	5	5	7	5*
Chicago	7	7	7	6	5*
Wisconsin	8	9*	8	8	11
Michigan	9	9*	9	9	13
Northwestern	10	8	11	12	8
Carnegie Tech	11	12	12	10	10
Johns Hopkins	12*	15	10	11	9
Minnesota	12*	9*	14	13	12
Columbia	14	14	13	14	21*
Pennsylvania	15	13	15	15	14*

* Rank shared with another department.

or more rank positions. Columbia and Chicago decline most markedly on Question B.

From a careful review of the data, it appears that many of the differences between the ratings provided by the experts panel and the general survey participants result from the small size of the panel. Ratings derived from randomly picked groups of a dozen returns will frequently differ from the average ratings provided by a much larger sample; therefore, the apparent difference in the experts' views may be more a statistical phenomenon than a true one. Many of the Hughes 1924 panels numbered only 25–30 persons, and the Keniston panels of chairmen averaged fewer than 20 members; thus some similar distortions may have been reflected in these earlier ratings. Future evaluation panels, in our view, should number a minimum of 50 in order to reduce this possible distortion.

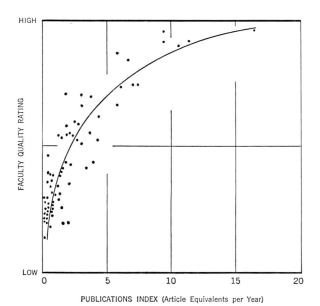

FIG. 4—Relationship of rated quality of graduate faculty to index of publications, 71 economics departments.

Publications index

A few respondents returned critical notes suggesting that the most prestigious departments do not always include the most creative or productive scholars. Although a number of individual examples can be cited in support of this view, it seemed useful to attempt to document this point. No easy way to measure "creativity" could be devised, and, therefore, a measure of productivity was elected. Six major journals in the field of economics—journals which publish most of the general theoretical and expository articles, not the highly specialized contributions in public finance, labor economic history, or land economics—were selected, and all articles, shorter communications, and book reviews were tallied for a four-year period (June 1960–June 1964).[2] To provide some weighting, it was assumed that four short communications or eight book reviews were the equivalent of one substantive article.

Similarly, all books reviewed in the *American Economic Review*, the official journal of the American Economic Association, during the same four-year period were tallied. A theoretical or research book was counted as the equivalent of six articles, a textbook as three articles, and an edited collection as two articles. Thus weighted, publications originating in each department were aggregated and converted to an article equivalents index, the distribution ranging from a high of approximately twenty a year at Harvard to none for a few departments.

No two people will agree on the precise weight-

[2] These journals were: *American Economic Review, Quarterly Journal of Economics, Journal of Political Economy, Review of Economics and Statistics, Econometrica,* and *Southern Economic Journal.* Before inclusion of the last named, a careful survey was made to ensure that this was not primarily a regional journal unduly favoring a few institutions. Only two of the leading four departments represented by articles were Southern, and they had only four articles each out of nearly one hundred in the four-year period.

ing that should be given various types of publications, but the above system seemed a reasonable approach. Various other weights were tried, and they produced little change in the relative standing of departments on such a scholarly productivity index. Ideally "bonuses" should be assigned to the most imaginative contributions, but no reasonable system could be devised without initiating another subjective opinion study.

Figure 4 arrays the departments by the index of faculty quality from chapter 3 and the publications index. An approximate line of best fit has been drawn in, showing the relationship between these two factors.

It is immediately apparent from Figure 4 that there is a high degree of concentration of publications in a few departments. The ten most productive departments (nine of which are also among the first ten in the subjective measure of faculty quality) accounted for 56 percent of all publications reviewed for this four-year period; the 25 most productive departments accounted for nearly 90 percent. At the other extreme, more than two dozen departments averaged no more than one article a year, and ten of the Ph.D.-granting departments averaged no more than one book review a year. Amidst all the current controversy over the "publish or perish" dictum, there appears little evidence that this has applicability below the most distinguished departments in economics (or alternatively, that at some institutions no distinction is made whether or not a scholar publishes in the mainstream of reputable journals or his book warrants even a short book review). Certainly, although the fit is not perfect, there is a clear correlation between reputation of a department and the scholarly productivity of its members.[3]

Institutional background

The institutional background of a respondent is bound to have some influence on his judgment of some departments. One can argue the case two ways: (*a*) an individual is likely to have considerably more objective knowledge about his own current department and his Ph.D. alma mater, or

[3] It should be noted in passing, however, that this conclusion works both ways, for *ceteris paribus* Professor X probably has a somewhat easier task getting his work published in major journals if his address is Cambridge or Berkeley.

TABLE 10: *Difference between Mean Scores of All Respondents and Ratings by Alumni, Quality of Graduate Faculty, Economics Departments*

DEPARTMENTS WITH FOUR OR MORE ALUMNUS RATERS	NUMBER OF ALUMNUS RATERS	AVERAGE DIFFERENCE FROM MEAN SCORES OF 173 RESPONDENTS	
		Amount	Percent
Harvard	27	+.15	3.1
Illinois	14	+.50	18.4
Chicago	13	+.36	7.9
California, Berkeley	10	+.31	6.9
Wisconsin	10	+.13	3.5
Princeton	9	+.24	5.7
Michigan	7	+.72	19.4
Columbia	6	+.46	12.4
Cornell	6	+.88	29.7
Johns Hopkins	4	−.28	8.5
North Carolina	4	+.53	19.5
Pennsylvania	4	+.68	20.5
Yale	4	+.44	9.6
Average for 37 departments with alumni raters	156	.50	22.3

(*b*) an individual is more likely to be biased in favor of the institutions where he is currently employed and from which he received his highest degree. Whichever may be the more appropriate conclusion, we attempted to measure the impact of such institutional attachments on the judgments of our participating scholars.

In Table 10 are listed all the universities which granted the doctorate to four or more of the respondents in economics. The difference between the mean score on quality of graduate faculty given to a department by its alumni and by the whole sample is shown in column 2. The average difference was .50 on a scale ranging from zero to a maximum of five. Since the mean raw score for the 71 departments was approximately 2.2, this represents a judgment about one-fifth higher than that provided by all raters of a particular department. A summary of the alumnus ratings in the four disciplines treated in this chapter is given in Table 11.

A similar check was made to distinguish the ratings scholars gave to their own current departments from those provided by outsiders. In this case individual institutions cannot be identified, for the samples were so small that identification would violate the confidentiality of the information provided. However, the average difference from

TABLE 11: *Difference between Mean Scores of Alumnus Raters and of All Respondents, by Score Ranges, Quality of Graduate Faculty, Four Disciplines*

FIELD OF STUDY	AVERAGE DIFFERENCE IN SCORES				
	Over-all Departmental Scores				All Departments
	>4.00	3.01–4.00	2.00–3.00	<2.00	
Economics	.25	.44	.79	1.09	.50
English	.19	.46	.77	.57	.39
Physics	.24	.37	.66	.91	.42
Political science	.29	.51	.85	1.41	.50

TABLE 12: *Difference between Mean Scores of Employee Raters and of All Respondents, by Score Ranges, Quality of Graduate Faculty, Four Disciplines*

FIELD OF STUDY	AVERAGE DIFFERENCE IN SCORES				All Departments
	Over-all Departmental Scores				
	>4.00	3.01–4.00	2.00–3.00	<2.00	
Economics...............	.40	.55	.96	1.05	.89
English.................	.39	.60	.90	1.06	.86
Physics.................	.43	.48	.55	1.25	.81
Political science..........	.50	.64	.80	1.01	.82

the mean raw score of economics departments was .89, representing a judgment about one-third higher than that given by all raters. Table 12 compares the economics figures with those of the three other fields discussed in this chapter.

It is obvious that most scholars exhibit considerable institutional loyalty in favoring their alma mater and present departments, and it might be expected that if one corrected for these biases the list of leading departments would be sharply altered. This assumption was tested by creating a "clean" rating for each department in which the respondents' ratings of their own Ph.D. and employing institutions were removed. Somewhat surprisingly, there was almost no difference between the rank order produced by the clean version and the total response, as is shown in Table 13. When the responses were limited to those not connected with a department, the average score fell for each department, but the ranking was almost unaltered. M.I.T. bumped Harvard in the number one spot, but no other change occurred among the first 20. For the 71 departments, 47 retained precisely the same rank, 19 changed rank by only one position, three changed by two positions, and two by three positions.

TABLE 13: *Ratings of Quality of Graduate Faculty, High-ranking Economics Departments, by All Respondents and by Those without Close Institutional Affiliation*

INSTITUTION	RATINGS BY:			
	All Respondents		Non-employee— Non-alumnus Respondents	
	Rank	Score	Rank	Score
Harvard...........	1	4.82	2	4.79
M.I.T.............	2	4.80	1	4.80
Chicago...........	3	4.57	3*	4.54
Yale..............	4	4.56	3*	4.54
California, Berkeley..	5	4.50	5	4.48
Stanford...........	6	4.36	6	4.35
Princeton..........	7	4.22	7	4.20
Michigan..........	8	3.72	8	3.68
Columbia..........	9	3.71	9	3.67
Wisconsin..........	10	3.68	10	3.65
Minnesota.........	11	3.56	11	3.55
Northwestern.......	12	3.51	12	3.49
Carnegie Tech......	13	3.48	13	3.48
Pennsylvania.......	14	3.33	14	3.32
Johns Hopkins......	15	3.29	15	3.29
U.C.L.A...........	16	3.08	16	3.06

* Rank and score shared with another department.

On reflection it is apparent why institutional loyalty makes little difference to the over-all rank of a department. The large biases were in favor of current employing institution, but the design of our sample gave fairly equal weight to each department being rated (at least two respondents, and not more than four, for each Ph.D.-granting department). The smaller biases favored the Ph.D. alma mater, but as Table 10 indicated, there were only 13 departments with as many as four alumni in the sample, and only five departments with as many as ten. In addition, the few departments with the most alumni among the respondents were very strong by anyone's estimate, and their alumnus ratings were not very different from those by outsiders. By contrast, the weaker departments, where the alumnus biases were significantly large, were seldom represented by more than one or two alumni—hardly sufficient to influence the average judgment of 173 respondents.

It is difficult to design a sample that would eliminate (or cancel out) all possible biases, although some future survey might find this an interesting task to attempt. It might be accomplished by assembling a roster of respondents, as this study did, and also asking each department to provide a list of ten or so of its most knowledgeable Ph.D. graduates over the last quarter century. Using these two sources, one could then construct a list which would give equal (or some predetermined weighted) alumnus representation for each department. The design of the present study minimized the influence of biases in favor of the institution where the respondent was currently employed, but had no control factor for institution of highest degree. However, in view of the insignificant difference in rank order resulting from the outsiders' view (after removing alumnus and employee ratings), there seems to be little value to be gained by such a complicated procedure.

Regional variations

As indicated in an earlier chapter, the regional location of respondents has some effect on the ratings they give to departments in various parts of the country. The regional differences result primarily from two factors: (a) persons who have spent most of their adult years in a particular region develop a sense of regional loyalty to their

TABLE 14: *Regional Ratings of Quality of Graduate Faculty of*
Leading Economics Departments

INSTITUTION	ALL RESPONDENTS		RESPONDENTS, BY REGION							
			East		Midwest		South		West	
	Rank	Score	Rank	Score	Rank	Score	Rank	Score	Rank	Score
Harvard.....................	1	4.82	1	4.81	1	4.89	2	4.64	1	4.91
M.I.T........................	2	4.80	3	4.71	2	4.85	1	4.79	2	4.87
Chicago.....................	3	4.57	4	4.63	5	4.50	3	4.62	4	4.43
Yale........................	4	4.56	2	4.74	4	4.55	5	4.35	5	4.41
California, Berkeley..........	5	4.50	5	4.41	3	4.60	4	4.39	3	4.62
Stanford....................	6	4.36	6	4.37	6	4.36	7	4.28	6	4.37
Princeton...................	7	4.22	7	4.30	7	4.12	6	4.32	7	4.04
Michigan....................	8	3.72	9	3.69	9	3.75	9	3.54	8	3.91
Columbia....................	9	3.71	8	3.76	12	3.58	8	3.79	11	3.66
Wisconsin...................	10	3.68	10	3.51	8	3.93	13	3.45	9	3.87
Minnesota..................	11	3.56	13	3.47	11	3.68	11	3.48	12	3.58
Northwestern...............	12	3.51	11*	3.48	13	3.46	12	3.47	10	3.69
Carnegie Tech...............	13	3.48	11*	3.48	10	3.69	10	3.50	19	3.00
Pennsylvania................	14	3.33	14	3.38	15	3.34	16	3.25	13	3.22
Johns Hopkins..............	15	3.29	15	3.22	14	3.35	14	3.33	14	3.20
U.C.L.A....................	16	3.08	18	2.82	16	3.12	15	3.30	15	3.17

* Rank and score shared with another department.

neighboring institutions, and (*b*) raters usually have more knowledge and information about nearby universities, and (as indicated in a succeeding section of this chapter) there is a direct correlation between knowledge about a department and the quality rating given to it.

Table 14 illustrates the average rating provided by respondents in the four regions of the country to the "Distinguished" and "Strong" departments of economics. While there is quite a high degree of consistency in most ratings, the regional variation is fairly marked for some departments. Among the "Distinguished" departments, for example, Yale scored 4.74 in the East, but only 4.35 in the South; Princeton, on the other hand, received its highest rating in the South and was rated considerably lower by the Westerners. Among the "Strong" departments, Wisconsin scored .48 higher in the Midwest than in the South, Carnegie Tech .69 higher in the Midwest than in the West, and U.C.L.A. .48 higher in the South than in the East.

A careful review of all the data for the 71 economics departments indicates certain consistent patterns, which are summarized in Table 15. The Easterners were generally the least lenient raters, as evidenced by the fact that the mean score given to departments was .10 below the over-all average for all respondents. Easterners were hard on everyone, even themselves, as shown by the fact that they were the only regional group that gave lower ratings to their own institutions than did economists living in other parts of the country. The Midwesterners were the most representative, living up to their central position in the country by showing the least regional bias of any group. The Southerners were relatively generous to everyone, but most particularly to themselves. (Or conversely, all other regions showed more bias against Southern departments than against any others.) The Westerners were most lenient with all institutions, but at least favored themselves less than they did the Midwestern departments.

The data summarized in Table 15 underline the necessity for achieving a relatively equitable balance of respondents from all sections of the country in such an opinion survey. However, if one

TABLE 15: *Ratings of Quality of Graduate Faculty, Economics Departments,*
by Raters' Current Region

RATERS' REGION OF EMPLOYMENT	DEPARTMENTS LOCATED IN:				ALL DEPARTMENTS
	East	Midwest	South	West	
	Average Rating				
East...................	2.36	2.13	1.46	2.47	2.14
Midwest...............	2.39	2.26	1.54	2.52	2.21
South.................	2.41	2.31	1.90	2.65	2.32
West..................	2.45	2.41	1.60	2.72	2.34
All raters..............	2.39	2.26	1.64	2.57	2.24
	Percentage Difference from Over-all Mean				
East...................	−1.3	−5.8	−11.0	−3.9	−4.5
Midwest...............	—	—	−6.1	−1.9	−1.3
South.................	+.8	+2.2	+15.9	+3.1	+3.6
West..................	+2.5	+6.6	−2.4	+5.8	+4.5

had to use a small sample of respondents, a good case might be made for choosing predominantly persons living near the geographical center of the country.

Faculty salaries

In the case of economics the study was fortunate in having one additional datum with which to compare our ratings. The chairmen of some thirty of the major departments regularly meet and exchange information of interest to the profession. As an outgrowth of these meetings, Francis Boddy, professor of economics and associate dean of the Graduate School at the University of Minnesota, has made a series of annual surveys of salaries in 45 of the leading departments of economics. The confidential information gathered by him was joined with the study's information on the departmental quality ratings and was used to test, by means of multiple regression techniques, the relationship between rated departmental quality and salary levels.

If the faculty quality index is used as the dependent variable and six salary levels as the independent variables, the multiple correlation coefficient (R) is .851. This finding indicates that nearly three-fourths of the variation in quality can be accounted for by variation in salary levels. The zero-order correlation (r) between quality and the mean salary level of "superior full professors" (the upper third within the rank) alone

was .794. It is important to note that the relationship between quality and mean salary level decreased systematically with decreasing professional status and rank. Thus, the quality index correlates .794, .754, .470, .357, and .181, respectively, with the average salary of "superior full professors," full professors, "superior associate professors," associate professors, and assistant professors. These findings support the impression that the scholarly reputation of a department rests heavily on its distinguished full professors. The less prestigious universities compete more evenly for young assistant professors; thus the low coefficient. This would seem to be true for two reasons: (*a*) the poorer institutions can better afford to compete for promising young scholars in the $6,000–$9,000 range than they can in the $15,000–$25,000 range, and (*b*) the universities near the top can rely to a considerable extent on their prestige rather than pecuniary rewards in attracting the aspiring young scholar. Thus scholarly talent is somewhat more evenly distributed among universities in the lower ranks, but tends to become more highly concentrated at the highest ranks in a few institutions which have preferred environments and resources.

Departmental prestige

Another consideration of interest is how the quality of a scholar's current department influences his views of other departments. After the returns were tallied, the respondents in economics

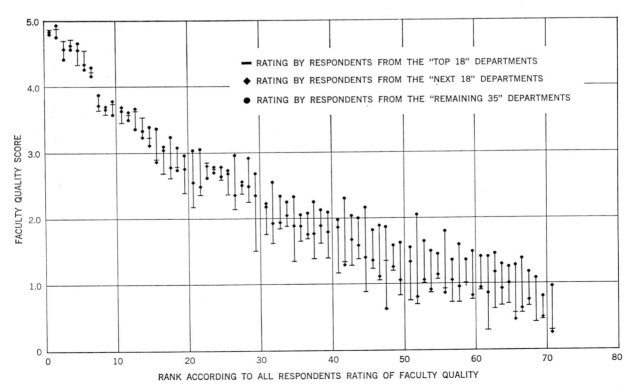

Fig. 5—Rated quality of faculty, as judged by respondents in economics departments in the first quarter, second quarter, and second half of rankings.

were categorized into three groups: those currently employed in departments rated as being in the upper quarter, the second quarter, and the lower half of the rated quality of graduate faculty list. Figure 5 plots the ratings by these three groups for the 71 departments. The scholars from the top departments apparently thought the best were better and the worst were poorer than did their colleagues in the less distinguished departments, although there are a few exceptions to this generalization. Nevertheless the rank ordering of departments would have been little altered had we used only one of the groups for our entire sample, and we were quite satisfied that in economics the view from the top is not markedly different than that from other vantage points.

Finally, an attempt was made to test our questionnaire design and to interpret the meaning of the response when our judges declined to provide a rating and checked "insufficient information." It had been anticipated that many respondents, when asked to judge departments about which they had little or no information, would be torn between giving a low rating (assuming that if they did not know something positive about a department, it must be quite poor) and giving no rating at all. Judging by the returns, and by conversations later with many who had participated in the study, it appears that most respondents bent over backward to be fair and gave no score to a department about which they felt uninformed. The percentage of returns giving some rating to a specified department ranged all the way from 98 percent for seven of the leading departments to 35 percent for one quite small department. The average response rate was about 70 percent.

Figure 6 plots the quality score given to departments against the percentage of respondents who provided some positive rating. There is a clear correlation between the two; the good departments are well known, and poorer departments are most frequently the ones about which little is known.[4] The few exceptions were institutions like Claremont Graduate School, which, though rated quite highly by persons who were familiar with its department, because of its relative newness in this field and small degree output, was not well known in the Eastern half of the country.

Before leaving the field of economics, a word should be added about departmental organization of graduate work. Most of the 71 economics departments included in our survey were organized, formal departments in the arts and sciences division of the university. In a number of cases, however, where there were variations in the organization of doctoral work in economics, the ratings

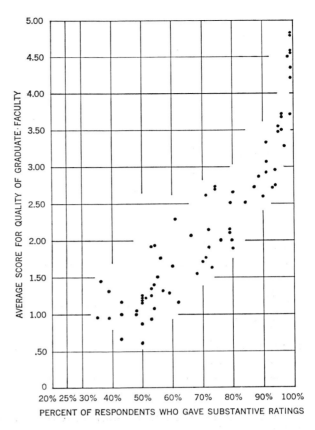

Fig. 6—Rated quality of economics faculty, by percent of respondents providing ratings.

may not accurately assess the quality of a university's economics faculty.

Three cases may be distinguished. (1) In several institutions graduate work in economics is not offered in the school of arts and sciences, but a doctoral program is offered within another organizational unit (for example, in the School of Business Administration at the University of Florida, in the Graduate School of Industrial Administration at Carnegie Tech.). (2) In many universities, graduate faculty in economics are found in both a department of economics in arts and sciences and a school of business administration. We have no way of knowing the extent to which raters lumped the two faculties together in making their judgments, or whether they omitted from their consideration economists in organizational units other than the arts and sciences division. (3) In some land-grant universities, economics and agricultural economics are separate departments and in others they are not. It is our impression that where a combined department had a dominant emphasis upon agricultural economics, it did not fare as well as it might have if a larger proportion of agricultural specialists had been included in the sample of respondents. Iowa State, for example, may have been penalized because its economics doctorate is awarded by a Department of Eco-

---

[4] See below, p. 117, for a summary discussion of this point and a hypothesis which might be drawn from the data.

nomics and Sociology which traditionally has had a strong agricultural emphasis.

In some subject areas, such as Romance languages and biology, variations in departmental structure or in the organization of degree programs are an even more common problem and are dealt with in footnotes in the appropriate tables in chapter 3.

ENGLISH

Select panel

For comparative purposes a panel of 15 experts was selected after consultation with the Modern Language Association, the National Council of Teachers of English, the College English Association, and the English specialist of the U.S. Office of Education. The panel members, consisting of those who were thought to be most knowledgeable about graduate education in English, were drawn as follows: five from the East, four from the Midwest, three from the Far West, and three from the South. They took their Ph.D. degrees at ten different universities; half have since taught at an average of three different institutions. Their combined firsthand teaching experience represented 23 private universities, 16 state universities, four private colleges, one foreign university, and one high school. Their average age was 51.7; they have written an average of 40.7 articles and 6.4 books. Fields of specialization covered the periods from medieval through modern British literature as well as criticism and language; four members of the panel were specialists in American literature.

Besides teaching experience, the panelists had an overview of the field through professional activity; past presidents of the major English organizations and past editors of major professional journals were represented on the panel, as were those with administrative experience as department chairmen, graduate deans, and provosts. One-fifth of the recommended panel members were already participants in the study; the others were queried separately in the fall of 1964. They received the identical questionnaire, and had no information available to them other than that which the original respondents had received.

Table 16 shows the rank order of the leading English departments according to Question A as determined by all respondents, by the three subgroups in the original sample, and by the small panel of experts. The small panel shows greater variance from the over-all ratings than does any of the three subgroups. For the 23 "Distinguished" and "Strong" departments the rank correlation with the over-all rating was .886 for the select panel, .967 for the chairmen, .974 and .982 for the senior and junior scholars respectively. The most marked disagreements between the small panel and the larger sample were in the panel's downgrading of Wisconsin, Michigan, Minnesota, North Carolina, Stanford, and Pennsylvania. Lest

TABLE 16: *Comparison of Faculty Quality Ratings of High-ranking English Departments, by Rating Group*

INSTITUTION	RANK				
	All Respondents	Chairmen	Senior Scholars	Junior Scholars	Select Panel
Yale.................	1	1	1	1	1
Harvard...............	2	2	2	2	3
California, Berkeley......	3	3	3	3	2
Princeton..............	4	5	4	4	5
Columbia..............	5	4	5	5	4
Chicago...............	6	9	6	7	6
Stanford...............	7	6	11*	6	10*
Cornell................	8	8	7	8	7
Wisconsin.............	9	7	10	9	13
Indiana...............	10	10*	9	11	8
Illinois...............	11*	10*	8	13	10*
Johns Hopkins..........	11*	12	11*	10	9
Michigan..............	13	13	13	12	18*
U.C.L.A..............	14	15*	14	14	12
Minnesota..............	15	17	17*	15	21*
Northwestern...........	16	14	19	16	14
North Carolina..........	17	18*	15	17*	21*
Pennsylvania...........	18	18*	16	21	21*
Washington (Seattle).....	19	21	17*	20	15
Duke..................	20	15*	20	19	16*
N.Y.U................	21	20	21	17*	16*
Brown.................	22	24	22	22	26
Texas.................	23	22	23	24*	18*

* Rank shared with another department.

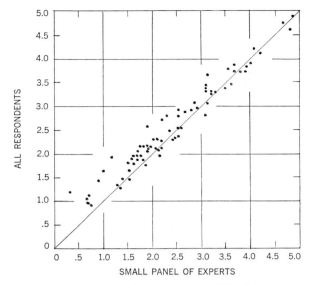

FIG. 7—Faculty quality ratings of 74 English departments, as judged by all respondents and by a panel of experts.

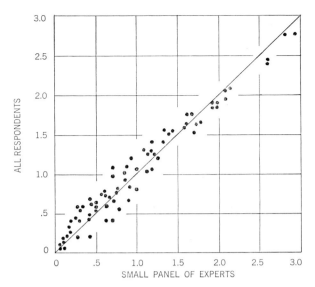

FIG. 8—Ratings of effectiveness of doctoral programs of 74 English departments, as judged by all respondents and by a panel of experts.

one suspect some bias against the large public university, it should be noted that the panel gave higher ratings than did any of the three subgroups of respondents to California (Berkeley), Indiana, U.C.L.A., Washington (Seattle), and Texas.

Figure 7 plots the select panel's ratings for quality of faculty against those of the over-all sample. As was the case in the other disciplines reviewed in this chapter, the panel members were somewhat harsher critics than the 185 participants in the spring 1964 questionnaire survey. The small size of the panel probably accounts for some of the irregularities between the ratings of the two groups, although in general there was a fairly close correlation in the ratings provided by the differently selected samples.

Table 17 and Figure 8 present a comparison of the select panel and over-all group ratings on the effectiveness of doctoral programs.

Publications index

To measure productivity, five major journals [5] in the field of English were selected in consultation with officers of the three major professional associations. All articles, shorter notes, and book reviews were tallied for a four-year period (June 1960–June 1964). To provide weighting, it was

[5] The journals were *American Literature, Modern Philology, PMLA, Studies in Philology,* and *Philological Quarterly.* The first four were also sampled by Bernard Berelson in his *Graduate Education in the United States* (New York: McGraw-Hill Book Co., 1960).

TABLE 17: *Comparison of Ratings of Effectiveness of the Doctoral Program of High-ranking English Departments, by Rating Group*

INSTITUTION	All Respondents	Chairmen	Senior Scholars	Junior Scholars	Select Panel
Harvard.................	1*	2	2	1	2
Yale....................	1*	1	1	2	1
California, Berkeley......	3	3	4	3	3*
Princeton...............	4	4	3	4	3*
Stanford................	5	5	5	5	5
Cornell.................	6	6	7	6	6*
Chicago................	7	10	6	8	6*
Indiana................	8*	8	8	10*	8*
Johns Hopkins..........	8*	11	9	7	10*
Columbia..............	10	7	10	10*	8*
Wisconsin..............	11	9	13*	9	10*
Michigan...............	12	13	11	12	15
Illinois.................	13	12	12	14	16*
North Carolina.........	14	14	13*	18	12
Northwestern..........	15*	15	17	15	13
U.C.L.A...............	15*	18	15	16	16*
Duke..................	17	16*	16	19	18*
Minnesota.............	18	16*	20	17	23*
Pennsylvania...........	19	20	18	20	20*
Washington (Seattle).....	20	19	19	21	14

* Rank shared with another department.

assumed that four short notes or eight book reviews were the equivalent of a substantive article. Similarly, all books reviewed in the selected journals were tallied for the same four-year period. A theoretical or research book was counted as the equivalent of six articles, a bibliographical study as three articles, and an edited work [6] or translation as two articles. Thus weighted, publications originating in each department were aggregated and converted to an article equivalents index, the distribution ranging from a high of nearly twenty per year to none for a few departments.

Figure 9 arrays the departments by the index of faculty quality and the publications index and displays a moderately high degree of concentration of publications in a few departments. The ten most productive departments (only six of which are also among the first ten in rated quality of faculty) accounted for 41 percent of all publications reviewed for this four-year period; the leading 25 departments produced approximately 75 percent. At the other extreme, 23 doctorate-granting departments averaged no more than one article a year, and seven departments averaged no more than one book review a year.

It is apparent from Figure 9 that the correlation between reputation of the faculty of English departments and their publications records, although strongly positive, is not nearly as close as it is in

[6] Textual editing of a major sort, such as that of preparing a manuscript or collating editions, was counted as a substantive book of research.

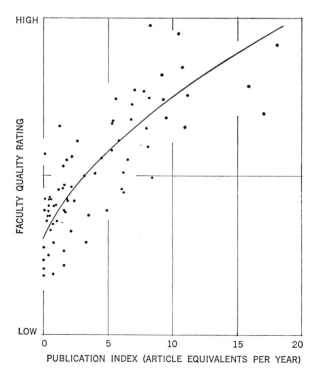

FIG. 9—Relationship of rated quality of graduate faculty to index of publications, 74 English departments.

economics and political science. A number of factors may account for this. First, there appears to be a somewhat broader distribution of talent in English than in the social or physical sciences; for example, it is not unusual to find highly productive scholars in English literature in the smaller colleges, whereas this is the exception rather than the rule in, say, economics or physics. Second, the scholar in non-humanities areas finds many alternative channels for his creative energies—in consulting, part-time employment, government service, and technical advisory roles to industry, public agencies, and foreign governments. By contrast, the literary humanist (as distinguished from the artist with his various mediums of expression) finds few creative outlets other than writing. Thus the publication of books and articles is the primary means of expression of the professor of English, and it is not surprising that a publications index in this field exhibits a lesser degree of concentration in a few major university departments. Third, English is a core subject at the undergraduate level in every college or university, and therefore even the university with no Ph.D. program will have a large faculty. In economics or physics, the size of faculty is more closely related to the number of graduate students taught. The publications index, as constructed, may tend to favor the large department and partially obscure qualitative differences. Fourth, if the respondents selected for the various fields are representative, the data included in the tables of profiles of respondents in chapter 3 suggest another possibility. It appears that the quantity of publications (as weighted in the index above) on an annual basis is higher for the junior scholars in English (and political science) than for the senior scholars, whereas the reverse is true for economics. That is, the typical distinguished economist, as he ages, has a constant productivity rate, measured purely by numbers of articles and books, while the professor of English (or political science) has a slightly decreasing rate.[7] It has already been indicated in a preceding section that the younger talent in any discipline is likely to be much more equally distributed among institutions than the distinguished senior scholars purely for economic reasons (even the less well-known and less well-endowed institutions can afford to compete vigorously for bright young assistant and associate professors, although they may be priced out of the market for the better senior professors).

[7] Judging the number of years in a scholarly career by the elapsed time between the average age at which the doctorate is received in the three fields and the average age of respondents, the annual productivity rates in article equivalents are as follows:

Field	Junior Scholars	Senior Scholars
Economics	1.9	1.9
English	2.7	2.0
Political science	2.5	2.1

This difference in productivity between English and economics might partially account for poorer correlation between a department's scholarly reputation and the volume of publications produced by its faculty.

Finally, the accessibility of publication facilities undoubtedly has some effect on the publications records of departments. The institutions publishing the periodicals used in computing our index ranked somewhat higher on the publications index than they did on the assessment of faculty quality. It may also be relevant that all but one of the "Distinguished" and "Strong" English departments were in universities with university presses, whereas only six of the 35 lowest rated departments had access to a home university press.

Institutional background

Respondents to the questionnaire were obviously better informed about departments of which they were currently members or from which they had obtained their doctorates, but it is problematic whether this made them more or less objective about the departments to which they had personal ties. To determine the extent of possible bias, we first separated out the ratings given by alumni to their Ph.D. alma mater. Table 18 lists all the universities which granted the doctorate to four or more of the respondents in English. The difference between the average rating given by alumni and the over-all average of the 185 respondents on quality of graduate faculty is shown in column 2, and the percentage difference is given in column 3.

While alumni of all of the leading departments except Cornell gave a higher rating to their alma mater than did non-alumni, the department at the University of Texas was the only one for which the difference was greater than 20 percent. Similar analyses were made for the other three fields surveyed in this chapter. Professors of English were less inclined to give preferential ratings to their Ph.D. alma mater than economists, political scientists, or physicists. Table 11, above, compares the alumnus ratings of quality of graduate faculty for the four fields. The greatest difference between professors of English and those in the other three fields was for departments which scored below 2.0; English alumni who received their doctorates from the poorer rated departments scored these departments only about one-third higher than non-alumni did, while alumni in the three other disciplines gave 60–100 percent higher scores to their doctoral institutions. Professors of English apparently had less institutional loyalty—or were more objective—than their confreres in the other academic fields.

The second check on the effect of institutional background was made by separating out the ratings professors gave to the departments where they were employed in 1964. Because the number of respondents in each department was so small (not

TABLE 18: *Difference between Mean Scores of All Respondents and Ratings by Alumni, Quality of Graduate Faculty, English Departments*

DEPARTMENTS WITH FOUR OR MORE ALUMNUS RATERS	NUMBER OF ALUMNUS RATERS	AVERAGE DIFFERENCE FROM MEAN SCORES OF 185 RESPONDENTS	
		Amount	Percent
Harvard.............	29	+.14	2.9
Yale................	23	+.04	.8
Chicago............	11	+.59	15.1
Columbia...........	9	+.64	15.6
North Carolina.......	8	+.39	11.6
Princeton...........	8	+.29	6.9
Wisconsin...........	8	+.34	9.0
Michigan............	7	+.66	18.2
Iowa (Iowa City).....	6	+.54	18.2
California, Berkeley...	5	+.16	3.5
Cornell.............	5	−.03	.8
Illinois..............	5	+.28	7.5
Johns Hopkins........	5	+.53	14.2
Pennsylvania.........	5	+.47	14.1
Northwestern.........	4	+.35	10.3
Stanford............	4	+.14	3.6
Texas...............	4	+.96	31.6
Average for 35 departments with alumni raters............	177	.39	14.9

more than four), the confidentiality of the responses would be violated by a report of these by department. However, the difference between the average rating by professors of their own current department and the rating provided by the over-all sample was .86. This is somewhat lower than the average difference in economics, but above that for physics and political science (see Table 12 above).

The third step in assessing the extent of possible distortion caused by the institutional background of the respondents was to recompute the ratings to omit entirely the ratings given to departments by both their alumni and teaching staff. This provided a ranking entirely by "outsiders"—what might be described as the most objective but least well-informed view. The rankings and scores by these outsiders and by the total sample are shown in Table 19. Omitting the views of those with close institutional affiliation had almost no effect on the rank order of departments; although the average score for each department fell slightly, its relative position remained almost precisely the same. Among the "Distinguished" and "Strong" departments, if one interprets the ties favorably, there was not a single change in rank position among the 23 departments. There was only one instance (Chicago) where the raw score differed by more than .04. For the entire list of 74 departments, the rank position of 66 departments did not change at all, while four departments changed by only one position, two changed by two positions, and two in the lower half of the list changed by four positions. Thus it can be seen that the inclusion of varying numbers of persons who received their degrees from, or were currently employed in, doctorate-granting departments had almost no effect on

TABLE 19: *Ratings of Quality of Graduate Faculty, High-ranking English Departments, by All Respondents and by Those without Close Institutional Affiliation*

INSTITUTION	RATINGS BY:			
	All Respondents		Non-employee— Non-alumnus Respondents	
	Rank	Score	Rank	Score
Yale..............	1	4.87	1	4.86
Harvard...........	2	4.75	2	4.72
California, Berkeley..	3	4.59	3	4.58
Princeton.........	4	4.21	4	4.19
Columbia.........	5	4.11	5	4.08
Chicago...........	6	3.91	6*	3.84
Stanford..........	7	3.86	6*	3.84
Cornell...........	8	3.83	8	3.83
Wisconsin.........	9	3.78	9	3.76
Indiana...........	10	3.73	10	3.72
Illinois...........	11*	3.72	12	3.70
Johns Hopkins......	11*	3.72	11	3.69
Michigan..........	13	3.63	13	3.59
U.C.L.A..........	14	3.48	14	3.49
Minnesota.........	15	3.42	15	3.41
Northwestern.......	16	3.40	16	3.39
North Carolina.....	17	3.36	17*	3.32
Pennsylvania.......	18	3.33	17*	3.32
Washington (Seattle)	19	3.30	19	3.28
Duke.............	20	3.28	20	3.26
N.Y.U............	21	3.26	21	3.23
Brown............	22	3.06	22	3.06
Texas.............	23	3.04	23	3.01

* Rank and score shared with another department.

the over-all ratings. Institutional loyalty, therefore, did not appear to introduce any marked bias into the assessment of faculty quality.

Regional variations

Table 20 indicates the ratings given by respondents living in four regions of the country to the "Distinguished" and "Strong" departments as measured by quality of the graduate faculty. The general pattern is similar to that in the other disciplines reviewed in this chapter, for respondents in the various regions tend to favor their own neighboring institutions. The rating of English departments by Easterners, however, is interesting in that they do not particularly favor themselves. Except for Columbia and Cornell, where the raters in the East were in almost exact agreement with scholars from other regions, all Eastern departments were rated lower by themselves than by outsiders. This is particularly noticeable in the cases of Princeton, Pennsylvania, and N.Y.U.

Significant differences in opinion can be seen in the difference of .47 between the Eastern and Southern ratings of Princeton, .46 between the Eastern and Western views of Stanford, .60 between the Eastern and Southern views of Pennsylvania, .69 between the Southern and Western opinions of Washington (Seattle), .47 between the Southern and Western reputations of Brown, and .58 in the Eastern and Southern ratings of Texas.

Table 21 summarizes the regional assessment of departmental strength in the four major sectors of the country.

American versus British literature specialists

To determine whether the respondents' area of specialization within the field of English had any marked effect on their rating of graduate departments, the respondents were identified as specialists in American or British literature, and separate tallies were made of the ratings of the two groups. About 75 percent of the respondents were specialists in British literature and about 20 percent, specialists in American literature, as shown in Table 22.

TABLE 20: *Regional Ratings of Quality of Graduate Faculty of Leading English Departments*

INSTITUTION	ALL RESPONDENTS		RESPONDENTS, BY REGION							
			East		Midwest		South		West	
	Rank	Score	Rank	Score	Rank	Score	Rank	Score	Rank	Score
Yale.....................	1	4.87	1	4.83	1	4.89	1	4.85	1	4.92
Harvard..................	2	4.75	2	4.66	2	4.82	2	4.76	2	4.75
California, Berkeley..........	3	4.59	3	4.52	3	4.57	3	4.57	3	4.73
Princeton.................	4	4.21	5	3.98	4	4.29	4	4.45	6	4.10
Columbia.................	5	4.11	4	4.12	5	4.12	5	4.00	4	4.24
Chicago..................	6	3.91	7	3.73	6	4.05	9	3.78	5	4.14
Stanford.................	7	3.86	11	3.57	8	3.96	7	3.95	7	4.03
Cornell..................	8	3.83	6	3.83	7	3.98	11	3.70	14	3.70
Wisconsin................	9	3.78	10	3.61	10	3.80	6	3.97	12*	3.73
Indiana..................	10	3.73	8	3.70	9	3.82	14	3.59	10*	3.75
Illinois..................	11*	3.72	12	3.55	11	3.77	8	3.82	12*	3.73
Johns Hopkins.............	11*	3.72	9	3.64	12	3.71	10	3.75	9	3.80
Michigan.................	13	3.63	13	3.46	13	3.67	12	3.65	8	3.82
U.C.L.A.................	14	3.48	15*	3.26	15	3.52	17	3.53	15	3.67
Minnesota................	15	3.42	15*	3.26	19	3.33	18	3.52	10*	3.75
Northwestern..............	16	3.40	17	3.20	14	3.56	20	3.28	17	3.57
North Carolina............	17	3.36	14	3.38	21	3.18	15	3.57	19	3.34
Pennsylvania..............	18	3.33	20	3.03	18	3.37	13	3.63	18	3.37
Washington (Seattle)........	19	3.30	21	2.97	16	3.49	25	2.94	16	3.63
Duke....................	20	3.28	18	3.12	20	3.23	16	3.54	22	3.21
N.Y.U...................	21	3.26	19	3.07	17	3.48	21	3.20	21	3.26
Brown...................	22	3.06	22	2.93	22	3.17	28	2.86	20	3.33
Texas...................	23	3.04	25*	2.75	23	3.05	19	3.33	24	3.07

* Rank and score shared with another department.

TABLE 21: *Ratings of Quality of Graduate Faculty, English Departments, by Raters' Current Region*

RATERS' REGION OF EMPLOYMENT	DEPARTMENTS LOCATED IN:				ALL DEPART-MENTS
	East	Midwest	South	West	
	Average Rating				
East	2.62	2.65	2.01	2.47	2.46
Midwest	2.77	2.79	2.06	2.59	2.58
South	2.60	2.68	2.16	2.62	2.52
West	2.82	2.87	2.13	2.77	2.67
All raters	2.70	2.74	2.08	2.60	2.55
	Percentage Difference from Over-all Mean				
East	−3.0	−3.3	−3.4	−5.0	−3.5
Midwest	+2.6	+1.8	−1.0	−.4	+1.2
South	−3.7	−2.2	+3.9	+.8	−1.2
West	+4.4	+4.7	+2.4	+6.5	+4.7

TABLE 22: *Breakdown of English Department Respondents, by Area of Specialization*

Specialty	Chairmen	Professors	Total	%
British [a]	40	98	138	75
American [b]	10	26	36	19
Unidentified	—	11	11	6
Total	50	135	185	100

[a] Includes 4, language; 2, comparative literature; 2, composition and writing; and 2, criticism specialists, for a total of 7.3 percent of total British.

[b] Includes 5 who are both British *and* American specialists.

Table 23 sets forth in rank order the scores of the top 23 English departments as determined by four categories of specialists—chairmen and non-chairmen specializing in American literature and chairmen and non-chairmen specializing in British literature—and compares these to the rating of the total identified group of 174. The relatively small

number represented in the American specialist chairmen's group probably accounts for the fact the ratings of this group show the greatest variation from the ratings of the total group.

Closest to the over-all ratings were those of the British specialist scholars, who were numerically the largest group. They differed enough, however, to interchange the ranks of Wisconsin and Johns Hopkins between ninth and twelfth positions. American literature specialists rated Berkeley above Harvard and generally boosted the departments noted as strong in their special area—Indiana, N.Y.U., Duke, and Texas.

As Table 23 indicates, the difference between the American and British literature specialists was minor for most departments. Only in the ratings given by American specialist chairmen to N.Y.U. and Texas was the deviation from the over-all

TABLE 23: *Quality of English Faculty in Leading Departments as Rated by American and British Literature Specialists*

INSTITUTION	TOTAL GROUP [a]	AMERICAN LITERATURE		BRITISH LITERATURE	
		Chairmen	Professors	Chairmen	Professors
Yale	4.86	4.90	4.80	4.95	4.84
Harvard	4.74	4.60	4.50	4.84	4.78
California, Berkeley	4.58	4.70	4.53	4.58	4.57
Princeton	4.19	4.20	4.23	4.17	4.19
Columbia	4.13	4.50	4.11	4.17	4.08
Chicago	3.94	3.80	3.92	3.87	3.98
Cornell	3.83	3.70	3.73	3.87	3.86
Stanford	3.82	3.60	3.76	4.00	3.79
Wisconsin	3.76	3.90	3.72	3.90	3.69
Illinois	3.73	3.87	3.65	3.72	3.74
Indiana	3.73	3.90	3.88	3.65	3.71
Johns Hopkins	3.70	3.40	3.50	3.76	3.76
Michigan	3.62	3.30	3.53	3.67	3.65
U.C.L.A.	3.46	3.20	3.65	3.43	3.45
Minnesota	3.41	3.20	3.38	3.48	3.41
Northwestern	3.40	3.50	3.30	3.45	3.40
North Carolina	3.35	3.42	3.37	3.28	3.36
Pennsylvania	3.31	3.30	3.60	3.29	3.23
N.Y.U.	3.29	3.66	3.47	3.21	3.23
Washington (Seattle)	3.28	3.22	3.45	3.32	3.32
Duke	3.26	3.55	3.47	3.31	3.16
Brown	3.01	3.10	3.29	2.88	2.96
Texas	3.01	3.55	3.04	3.07	2.93

[a] These ratings are the averages from 174 respondents who were identified as American or British specialists, and differ slightly from the scores given for all 185 respondents in chapter 3.

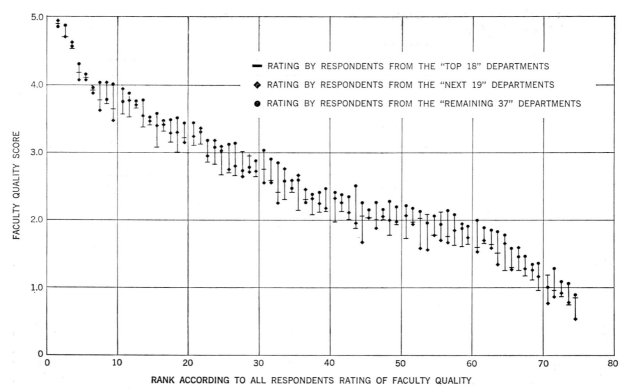

FIG. 10—Rated quality of faculty, as judged by respondents in English departments in the first quarter, second quarter, and second half of rankings.

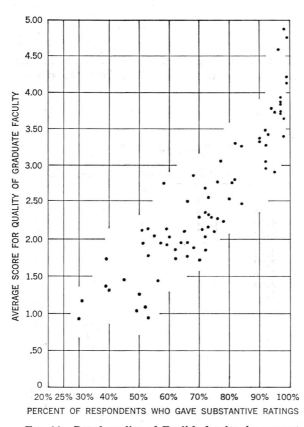

FIG. 11—Rated quality of English faculty, by percent of respondents providing ratings.

score as high as 10 percent. The average difference between the ratings given by the two sets of chairmen was ± .21, but only ± .14 for the non-chairmen. Even though these differences are not very great, they indicate the need to achieve an equitable balance of representatives from subfields within a discipline. Our sample, composed of 185 scholars, appears to reflect the distribution of faculty within English departments.

Departmental prestige

In order to assess the influence of the prestige of the respondents' current departments on the ratings given to other departments, after the initial quality rankings were determined, the scores were recomputed on another basis. Respondents were divided into three groups: those in departments which rated among the top quarter, the second quarter, and the lower half, on the basis of Question A (quality of faculty).

As in the case of other fields reviewed in this chapter, the average scores by respondents in these three groups were inversely related to the quality of current employing institution; that is, respondents from the poorer departments tended to rate all departments higher than did those from the better departments. In the case of English there are some interesting differences in the judgments of the three groups. Raters in the departments falling into the second half of the rank-ordered list placed Harvard above Yale (perhaps a "halo effect") and gave a substantially better rating to Stanford, Wisconsin, Illinois, Minnesota, and Pennsylvania than did the judges from departments in the upper half. Judges from departments in the top quarter were less kind to Minnesota and Pennsylvania than the other judges. Scholars from departments in the second quarter, despite the fact that they were the in-between group both in the quality of their own departments and in the intermediate median score they assigned to departments, were either the highest or the lowest raters for the first ten departments; below the first ten their scores generally fell between the upper quarter and lower half categories.

Figure 10 plots the scores by these three groups for all departments of English. As can be readily seen by the symbols, the raters from departments in the top quarter were most commonly the stern-est judges, and those from departments in the lower half in most cases gave the highest scores.

Finally, Figure 11 shows the relationship between the average rating of faculty quality given to departments and the percentage of respondents who had sufficient information to make a judgment. The leading 18 departments were rated by at least 90 percent of the participating scholars; the median departments were rated by 73 percent. Only seven departments were rated by less than 50 percent; the lowest response rate was 30 percent. As in the case of other fields reviewed in this chapter, there is a high positive correlation between quality rating and percentage response. Seldom is a department well known for being poor; or, obversely, when dubious about the quality of a department, respondents frequently checked "insufficient information."

PHYSICS

Select panel

A small panel of experts was selected with advice from the American Institute of Physics. Fifteen distinguished physicists, chosen with a regard for regional and institutional balance, were sent the same questionnaire in the summer of 1964 which the 190 respondents to the original survey had completed in the spring. Twelve of the 15 returned usable replies.

Table 24 shows the ranking of the "Distinguished" and "Strong" physics departments in the opinion of the large sample (as a unit and individually) and the small panel of experts. By and large,

the panel was in fairly close agreement with the view of all respondents, though there were a few exceptions. Princeton and Maryland were ranked five positions lower by the panel than by the total group of respondents, and Columbia, Minnesota, and Washington (Seattle) were each moved up three positions. In physics, unlike the other three disciplines reviewed in this chapter, the department chairmen were good predictors of the over-all ranking; members of the experts panel, perhaps because of the small size of the sample, were more frequently at odds with the over-all ranking. The chairmen, even though they com-

TABLE 24: *Comparison of Faculty Quality Ratings of High-ranking Physics Departments, by Rating Group*

INSTITUTION	All Respondents	Chairmen	Senior Scholars	Junior Scholars	Select Panel
California, Berkeley......	1	1	1*	1*	2
Cal. Tech..............	2	2	1*	1*	1
Harvard..............	3	3	3	4	3
Princeton..............	4	4	4	3	9*
Stanford..............	5	5	6	5	6
M.I.T.................	6	6	5	7	4*
Columbia..............	7	7	7	6	4*
Illinois..............	8	8	9	8	9*
Cornell..............	9	9	10	9	7
Chicago..............	10	10	8	10	8
Yale..................	11	11	11	11	11
Wisconsin..............	12	12	12	12	13
Michigan..............	13*	14	13	14	12
Rochester..............	13*	16	14	13	16*
Pennsylvania..........	15	15	15*	16	16*
Maryland..............	16	17	15*	15	21
Minnesota..............	17	13	17	18	14
Washington (Seattle).....	18	18	19	20	15
Johns Hopkins..........	19*	20*	18	19	20
U.C.L.A...............	19*	20*	21	17	18
Carnegie Tech..........	21	19	20	21*	22

* Rank shared with another department.

prised only 23 percent of all respondents, were in precise agreement with the over-all ranking through the first 12 departments. Minnesota and U.C.L.A. were the only institutions for which the rankings provided by the three subgroups differed by as much as four positions, and in these cases the rank ordering somewhat exaggerates the relatively small differences in the raw scores given to these departments by the respondent groups. The rank correlation with the over-all ratings was .930 for the select panel, .979 for the chairmen, .988 and .989 for the senior and junior scholars respectively.

Figure 12 plots the scores of the experts panelists and of all respondents for the 86 doctorate-

granting physics departments. As can be seen by the predominance of points above the 45° diagonal line, the panelists tended to give somewhat lower scores to most departments than did the larger sample of raters.

Table 25 and Figure 13 compare the panelists and all participants on Question B, judging the effectiveness of doctoral programs. On this question, somewhat greater divergence of views is evident, particularly for Harvard, Wisconsin, Pennsylvania, Maryland, and Johns Hopkins. The panel particularly boosted Harvard and Michigan and downgraded Wisconsin and Maryland, by comparison with the 190 respondents. Although not shown in this and the preceding table, the small

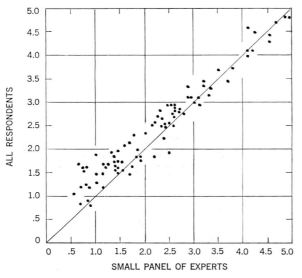

Fig. 12—Faculty quality ratings of 86 physics departments, as judged by all respondents and by a panel of experts.

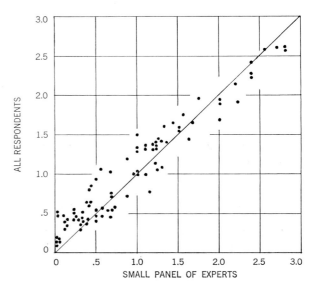

Fig. 13—Ratings of effectiveness of doctoral programs of 86 physics departments, as judged by all respondents and by a panel of experts.

TABLE 25: *Comparison of Ratings of Effectiveness of the Doctoral Program of High-ranking Physics Departments, by Rating Group*

INSTITUTION	All Respondents	Chairmen	Senior Scholars	Junior Scholars	Select Panel
Princeton	1	2*	4	1	3
Cal. Tech.	2	1	1	3*	1*
Stanford	3	2*	3	2	4
Harvard	4	4	2	3*	1*
California, Berkeley	5	5	5	5	5*
M.I.T.	6	8	6	6	5*
Cornell	7	6	7	7	5*
Illinois	8	7	8	8	9
Wisconsin	9	9	9	11	13
Chicago	10*	11	10	10	8
Yale	10*	12	12	9	10*
Columbia	12	10	11	12	10*
Rochester	13	16	13	13	16
Michigan	14	14*	14	14	10*
Washington (Seattle)	15	14*	16	18	14
Pennsylvania	16	13	18	16*	19
Maryland	17	22	15	15	21*
Minnesota	18	17	17	21*	17*
Johns Hopkins	19	18*	19	25	17*

* Rank shared with another department.

panel of experts rated Duke among the "Strong" and "Attractive" departments, assigning it a rank of nineteenth on Question A and fifteenth on Question B.

A few interesting differences appear between the ratings given to departments on the two different questions. For example, Princeton was placed fourth in quality of faculty but first in attractiveness to graduate students, while Berkeley dropped from first to fifth position. Columbia dropped from seventh on Question A to twelfth on Question B, a pattern common to many fields of study at Columbia and probably related to its size and urban location.

Institutional background

Institutional affiliations—where a professor received his highest degree and where he is currently employed—obviously have some effect on the scores given to various departments. To analyze this effect, the judgments which respondents made of their Ph.D. alma mater and the department where they were teaching at the time of the survey were individually scrutinized. Table 26 lists the departments which had four or more alumnus participants in the survey, and shows the difference between the mean score on quality of graduate faculty given by alumni to the department and that provided by the 190 total respondents. The alumni of Duke and Virginia differed most from the non-alumnus view, rating their doctoral departments about one-third higher than outsiders did. Yale was the only major institution to which the alumni did not give a more favorable rating, reflecting either a more objective view on the part of those who knew the department best or the presence of halo effect on the part of non-alumni. The average difference for all departments was

TABLE 26: *Difference between Mean Scores of All Respondents and Ratings by Alumni, Quality of Graduate Faculty, Physics Departments*

DEPARTMENTS WITH FOUR OR MORE ALUMNUS RATERS	NUMBER OF ALUMNUS RATERS	AVERAGE DIFFERENCE FROM MEAN SCORES OF 190 RESPONDENTS	
		Amount	Percent
Harvard	16	+.29	6.2
Chicago	15	+.33	8.3
California, Berkeley	13	+.22	4.6
Wisconsin	10	+.31	8.4
M.I.T.	9	+.11	2.5
Michigan	9	+.32	9.2
Princeton	9	+.18	3.9
Illinois	7	+.33	8.0
Cal. Tech.	6	+.06	1.3
Carnegie Tech.	6	+.58	18.7
Rice	6	+.46	16.0
Duke	5	+1.02	34.2
Columbia	4	+.68	15.7
Rochester	4	+.29	8.4
Virginia	4	+.76	30.5
Yale	4	−.02	.5
Average for 49 departments with alumni raters	177	.42	17.2

TABLE 27: *Ratings of Quality of Graduate Faculty, High-ranking Physics Departments, by All Respondents and by Those without Close Institutional Affiliation*

INSTITUTION	RATINGS BY:			
	All Respondents		Non-employee—Non-alumnus Respondents	
	Rank	Score	Rank	Score
California, Berkeley	1	4.78	2	4.76
Cal. Tech.	2	4.77	1	4.77
Harvard	3	4.71	3	4.68
Princeton	4	4.60	4	4.59
Stanford	5	4.47	5	4.46
M.I.T.	6	4.45	6	4.44
Columbia	7	4.32	7	4.30
Illinois	8	4.10	8	4.08
Cornell	9	4.07	9	4.06
Chicago	10	4.00	10	3.96
Yale	11	3.77	11	3.76
Wisconsin	12	3.69	12	3.67
Michigan	13*	3.46	14	3.42
Rochester	13*	3.46	13	3.45
Pennsylvania	15	3.37	16	3.34
Maryland	16	3.35	15	3.35
Minnesota	17	3.31	17	3.30
Washington (Seattle)	18	3.16	18	3.14
Johns Hopkins	19*	3.12	20	3.11
U.C.L.A.	19*	3.12	19	3.12
Carnegie Tech.	21	3.09	21	3.06

* Rank and score shared with another department.

.42, or approximately 17 percent higher than the over-all ratings provided by the universe of physics respondents. While this was slightly greater than the average difference in English, it was substantially below that for economics and political science. Table 11 (p. 81) compares the four disciplines.

A second step was taken, separating out the ratings which respondents gave to the departments where they were currently employed. Since the maximum number of raters from any one department was four, it would destroy the confidentiality of the responses to reveal the average difference in ratings by department. However, the average difference for the 86 departments between ratings provided by employees and the ratings given by outsiders was .81, about one-third higher than the score given to a department by non-employees. A comparison of the four disciplines is shown in Table 12 above. In physics, the bias in favor of one's own department tended to be about twice as great as the bias in favor of one's Ph.D. alma mater.

After separating out the scores representing departmental affiliation—whether through alumnus or employment affiliation—a new rating of departments was calculated. The new rank ordering, produced by respondents judging departments with which they did not have a personal attachment, hardly differed from the over-all ranking, as can be seen in Table 27. The outsiders reversed the order of Berkeley and Cal. Tech. in the first two spots and that of Pennsylvania and Maryland in the fifteenth and sixteenth positions. Out of the entire list of 86 departments, 57 retained their

TABLE 28: *Regional Ratings of Quality of Graduate Faculty of Leading Physics Departments*

| INSTITUTION | ALL RESPONDENTS | | RESPONDENTS, BY REGION | | | | | | | |
| | | | East | | Midwest | | South | | West | |
	Rank	Score	Rank	Score	Rank	Score	Rank	Score	Rank	Score
California, Berkeley..........	1	4.78	1	4.77	2	4.75	1	4.79	2	4.89
Cal. Tech...................	2	4.77	2	4.69	1	4.81	2*	4.76	1	4.94
Harvard....................	3	4.71	3	4.68	3	4.73	2*	4.76	3*	4.57
Princeton...................	4	4.60	4	4.65	4	4.57	5	4.56	5	4.55
Stanford....................	5	4.47	5*	4.43	6	4.36	4	4.59	3*	4.57
M.I.T......................	6	4.45	5*	4.40	5	4.54	6	4.44	7	4.26
Columbia...................	7	4.31	7	4.30	7	4.34	7	4.23	6	4.50
Illinois.....................	8	4.10	9	4.05	8	4.19	8	4.09	9	4.05
Cornell.....................	9	4.07	8	4.11	9	4.13	9	3.92	10	4.00
Chicago....................	10	4.00	10	3.97	10	4.11	11	3.83	8	4.15
Yale.......................	11	3.77	11	3.70	11	3.88	10	3.88	11*	3.47
Wisconsin..................	12	3.69	12	3.66	12	3.84	12	3.62	11*	3.47
Michigan...................	13*	3.46	15	3.42	13	3.61	15	3.37	13*	3.31
Rochester..................	13*	3.46	14	3.46	14	3.56	13	3.44	18	3.18
Pennsylvania...............	15	3.37	13	3.54	15	3.36	21	3.14	17	3.20
Maryland..................	16	3.35	16	3.38	17	3.33	16	3.33	13*	3.31
Minnesota..................	17	3.31	17	3.23	16	3.34	14	3.40	16	3.25
Washington (Seattle).........	18	3.16	19	3.21	20	3.09	19*	3.20	19	3.16
Johns Hopkins..............	19*	3.12	20	3.20	21	3.06	18	3.21	27	2.66
U.C.L.A...................	19*	3.12	21	3.10	18	3.12	24	3.03	15	3.27
Carnegie Tech..............	21	3.09	18	3.22	19	3.11	31	2.91	21	2.93

* Rank and score shared with another department.

positions, 16 changed by one rank position, and three changed by two positions. It can be concluded, therefore, that even though there appear to be fairly substantial differences between the ratings respondents gave to departments to which they had a personal attachment and the view of outsiders, the sample was sufficiently large that these disagreements had only a negligible effect on the relative standing of the various departments. A total of 86 raters were either alumni or current staff members of the nine departments rated as "Distinguished," but the more favorable ratings given by these respondents to their affiliated departments were sufficient to raise the average score of these departments by only .013 (that is, by only three-tenths of 1 percent). The 91 raters affiliated with the twelve "Strong" departments raised the average score of the "Strong" departments by only .018 (about one-half of 1 percent). At the other end of the scale, 38 respondents with institutional connections to the lowest rated 20 departments had the effect of raising the raw scores of these departments by an average of .028 (about 2 percent). Thus the distribution of the biases and the weighting of the sample were compensatory factors, preventing any significant distortion of quality rankings.

Regional variations

The regional location of respondents had some effect upon the way in which they rated departments in various parts of the country. Variations in ratings by region, however, are not quite as pronounced in physics as they are in the three other disciplines. Table 28 lists the "Distinguished" and "Strong" departments and indicates their rank and score by respondents in four sec-

tions of the country. For the "Distinguished" departments the differences are not very great—averaging only .19 between the highest and lowest regional rating. Substantial disagreements are evident among the next twelve, however, with the Westerners frequently at odds with their colleagues in the other sections of the country. For example, the scores for Yale range from a high of 3.88 in the Midwest and South to a low of 3.47 in the West; Johns Hopkins ranges from a high of 3.21 in the South to a low of 2.66 in the West; Rochester from 3.56 in the Midwest to 3.18 in the West. Pennsylvania, on the other hand, was rated lowest by the Southerners (3.14) and highest by its own region (3.54). On the whole the Easterners and the Midwesterners were fairly close to the over-all ranking of departments, while the Southerners and Westerners were frequently at odds on the departments ranking below thirteenth.

TABLE 29: *Ratings of Quality of Graduate Faculty, Physics Departments, by Raters' Current Region*

| RATERS' REGION OF EMPLOYMENT | DEPARTMENTS LOCATED IN: | | | | ALL DEPART-MENTS |
	East	Midwest	South	West	
	Average Rating				
East.......	2.71	2.47	1.67	2.91	2.44
Midwest...	2.58	2.54	1.69	2.74	2.39
South......	2.70	2.66	2.13	2.97	2.60
West......	2.50	2.43	1.67	2.86	2.35
All raters...	2.65	2.54	1.83	2.85	2.47
	Percentage Difference from Over-all Mean				
East.......	+2.3	−2.8	−8.7	+2.1	−1.2
Midwest...	−2.6	.....	−7.7	−3.9	−3.2
South......	+1.9	+4.7	+16.4	+4.2	+5.3
West......	−5.7	−4.3	−8.7	+ .4	−4.9

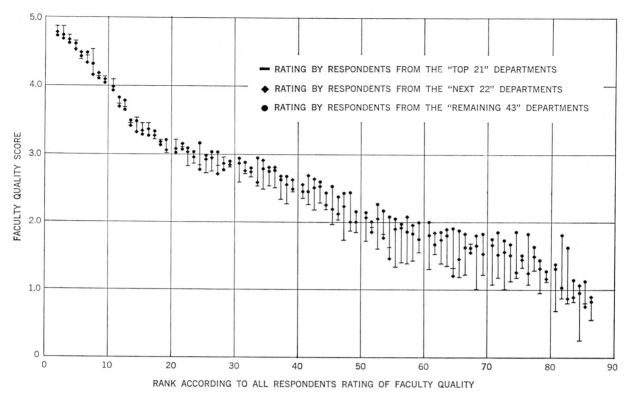

Fig. 14—Rated quality of faculty, as judged by respondents in physics departments in the first quarter, second quarter, and second half of rankings.

Table 29 provides a regional matrix showing the average ratings provided by respondents in the four regions to departments in those regions. The Southerners tended to give the highest scores, on the average, followed by raters in the East, Midwest, and West. This is at some variance with the other disciplines reviewed above, where the Westerners were frequently more generous in their ratings and the Easterners more chary.

Raters in all four regions agreed that the best departments of physics, averaging all departments in a region, were in the West, followed by those in the East, Midwest, and South. The Southerners were the only group of respondents who thought that their own departments were considerably better than raters outside the region did; the Midwesterners gave themselves the same average rating as the entire sample of respondents did, the Westerners rated themselves only .4 percent higher than all respondents, and the Easterners 2.3 percent higher.

Tables 28 and 29 indicate the necessity of achieving a reasonable regional balance in the sample of respondents for such a survey of opinions on quality of graduate faculty.

Departmental prestige

After the initial ranking of departments had been completed, a second run was done to separate out the scores given to the 86 departments by raters who were currently employed in the top quarter, second quarter, and lower half of departments as ranked by quality of graduate faculty. Figure 14 shows the results of this comparison. As with the other three disciplines, it can be generally concluded that the raters employed in the leading departments thought that the best departments were better, and the poorer departments worse, than did those employed in the less distinguished departments. For example, of the three subgroups, the raters from departments in the top quarter gave the highest score to 12 of the 20 leading departments, and they also gave the lowest rating of the three groups to 34 of the 40 lowest-rated departments.

For the upper 45–50 departments, there was surprisingly little disagreement among the three subgroups of respondents. The long bar for the seventh-ranked department, Columbia, stands out as the only case of major disagreement among the first 20. Generally, the spread between the highest and lowest score for these three groups of raters is quite small until one reaches the 50–86 range. Thus the left-hand side of Figure 14 looks more like the distribution of similar ratings in English, whereas the right-hand side is closer to the wide spread exhibited by the economists and political scientists. The fact that there is greater disagreement among the lower-ranked departments than among the higher is quite to be expected.

The less distinguished a department is, generally the less that is known about it; the less that is known about a department, the wider the disagreement among raters about its quality. While this is reflected in the disparity of judgments about the lower-ranking departments in Figure 14, it was also reflected in the extent to which respondents did not give any rating to a department. One of their alternatives in responding to the questionnaire was to check "insufficient information" in place of one of the subjective rating categories. Figure 15 shows a strong positive correlation between the average score of departments and the percentage of respondents who gave some substantive rating. All of the departments in the "Distinguished" category were rated by at least 95 percent of the respondents, while the "Strong" departments (with one exception) were rated by between 78 percent and 96 percent. The exception was the University of Washington (Seattle), which stands out in Figure 15 with a high-quality ranking but was rated by only 62 percent of respondents. The median department was rated by about 65 percent of the 190 respondents; two departments were rated by 25 percent or less. In general, faculty quality is closely associated with sufficient information to make a substantive judgment; this is not surprising, since by definition distinguished scholars are well known by their peers, and the absence of any knowledge about a department is usually interpreted as lack of distinction. Only rarely is a department well known for being poor!

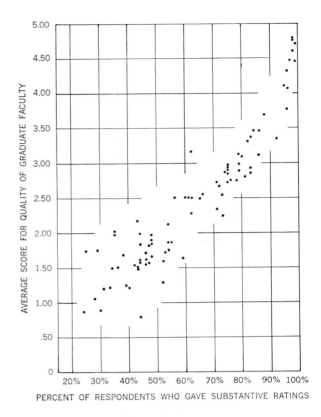

FIG. 15—Rated quality of physics faculty, by percent of respondents providing ratings.

POLITICAL SCIENCE

Select panel

A small panel of experts in political science was chosen with the advice of officers of the American Political Science Association. The panel of 12 included editors of leading political science journals, officers of professional societies, directors of special research projects, and other leading scholars. Several panelists had participated in the original survey; the others were polled in the fall of 1964.

Members of the panel had received their doctorates from universities in the East and Midwest, although the geographic distribution of their places of employment approximately duplicated the distribution of the over-all sample. Table 30 compares the rank order given to the "Distinguished" and "Strong" departments, based on quality of faculty, by the experts panel and by the larger sample reported in chapter 3. While the experts generally agreed with the over-all ranking assigned by the 165 scholars for the first five departments, some noticeable disagreements appear on the rest of the list. The small panel thought less highly of Princeton, Cornell, and Johns Hopkins, dropping them each by four ranks, and raised North Carolina by five. Two of the first eighteen departments

in over-all rank were dropped from the "Strong" category by the experts, and one (not shown in Table 30) was raised from twenty-first to seventeenth. The rank correlation with the over-all ratings was .903 for the experts panel, .974 for the chairmen, .981 for the senior scholars, and .989 for the junior scholars.

Figure 16 plots the raw scores assigned to the 64 departments by the small panel and by the over-all group. The panel assigned a lower rating to most departments, particularly in the lower categories, as evidenced by the drift of the scatter to the left of the diagonal line. Below the "Strong" category, the panel gave a higher raw score to only five departments, while the other 41 fared worse. As in the case of the other disciplines discussed in this chapter, however, the small size of the panel accounts for many of the irregularities in rank order; the over-all correlation is quite close.

Table 31 and Figure 17 contrast the experts' view of the effectiveness of doctoral program with that of the 165 raters. Again, considerable disagreement is evident between the experts and the larger sample. In only three cases are they in agreement on the over-all rank, and in several instances

TABLE 30: *Comparison of Faculty Quality Ratings of High-ranking Political Science Departments, by Rating Group*

INSTITUTION	RANK				
	All Respondents	Chairmen	Senior Scholars	Junior Scholars	Select Panel
Yale..................	1	1	3	1	1
Harvard...............	2	2	1	2	2
California, Berkeley......	3	3	2	3	3
Chicago...............	4	4	4	4	5
Columbia..............	5	5	5*	5	4
Princeton..............	6	6	5*	6	10*
M.I.T.................	7*	7	10	7	6
Wisconsin..............	7*	8*	7	9	8
Stanford...............	9	10	8	8	7
Michigan...............	10	11	9	10	9
Cornell................	11	12	11	11	15*
Northwestern...........	12	8*	12	12	10*
U.C.L.A...............	13	13*	13	13	13
Indiana................	14	13*	14	14	14
North Carolina..........	15	15	15*	15	10*
Minnesota..............	16	16	15*	17	18*
Illinois................	17	17*	17	18	15*
Johns Hopkins..........	18	20	18	16	22*

* Rank shared with another department.

the variation is four or more rank positions. M.I.T., Wisconsin, Michigan, and North Carolina were boosted by the panel, while Berkeley, Chicago, Princeton, and Columbia were dropped. Figure 17 shows that while the select panel's normal bent was toward lower scoring, in several instances high-ranking departments were rated considerably higher by the panel than by all respondents.

Comparison of the over-all rankings of faculty quality with those for effectiveness of doctoral program shows some marked differences. Of the

16 departments ranking highest for both quality of faculty and effectiveness of program, seven hold identical positions on both lists; only three change more than two positions. Columbia drops from fifth place on Question A to ninth place on Question B, while Stanford rises from ninth to sixth position and Johns Hopkins goes from eighteenth to a tie for fifteenth.

Comparison with Somit and Tanenhaus survey

A year prior to the A.C.E. survey, a study of the political science profession was conducted by

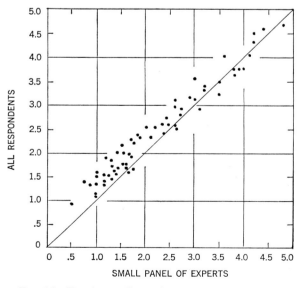

FIG. 16—Faculty quality ratings of 64 political science departments, as judged by all respondents and by a panel of experts.

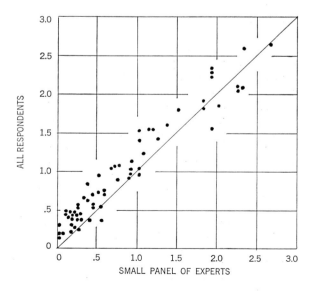

Fig. 17—Ratings of effectiveness of doctoral programs of 64 political science departments as judged by all respondents and by a panel of experts.

TABLE 31: *Comparison of Ratings of Effectiveness of the Doctoral Program of High-ranking Political Science Departments, by Rating Group*

| | RANK | | | | |
INSTITUTION	All Respondents	Chairmen	Senior Scholars	Junior Scholars	Select Panel
Yale...................	1	1	2	1	1
Harvard...............	2	2	1	2	2*
California, Berkeley......	3	3	3	4	7*
Chicago...............	4	4	4	3	7*
Princeton..............	5	5	5	5	7*
Stanford..............	6	6	6	6	4*
M.I.T.................	7	7	8	7	2*
Wisconsin.............	8	8	7	8	4*
Columbia..............	9	9	9	12	11*
Michigan..............	10	10	10	9	6
Northwestern..........	11	11	11	11	11*
Cornell...............	12	12	12	10	13
Indiana...............	13	14	13	13	14
North Carolina........	14	15	14	14*	7*
Johns Hopkins.........	15*	17	15	17	16*
U.C.L.A..............	15*	13	18	16	16*

* Rank shared with another department.

Somit and Tanenhaus.[8] They sent a questionnaire to 830 political scientists, and one of the items asked about the reputation of 33 university political science departments. About half of the recipients returned responses to this question, and the published scores and ranks turned out to be a preview of the A.C.E. survey.

The most interesting aspect of a comparison of the two sets of data is that they were based on two quite different sampling techniques. Somit and Tanenhaus used a random selection method, selecting every fifth name in the alphabetically arranged directory of A.P.S.A. members. By contrast, the A.C.E. study relied on the judgments of graduate deans and chairmen to identify the most knowledgeable scholars in their departments. Thus the former survey was broadly representative of political scientists in colleges, universities, and nonacademic employment, and the latter was representative of knowledgeable scholars in the major universities. Of the dozen highest-ranked institutions by quality of faculty in the 1964 A.C.E. survey, only one department (Michigan) was judged to be more than one rank higher or lower in the 1963 survey. Among the next ten, only Johns Hopkins produced a marked disagreement. This may be accounted for partly by the greater stress Somit and Tanenhaus placed on international relations—including the joint consideration of the School of Advanced International Studies in Washington with the Department of Political Science in Baltimore in the raters' judgments—and partly by the one-year difference in the period of evaluation.

Table 32 shows the rank given by the Somit and Tanenhaus respondents to the leading 18 departments in the A.C.E. survey. Figure 18 plots the

[8] Albert Somit and Joseph Tanenhaus, *Political Science: A Profile of a Discipline.*

1963 and 1964 ratings for 27 of the departments included in the Somit and Tanenhaus study. The high correlation between the two surveys is quite evident.

Publications index

To learn what relationship, if any, exists between the faculty quality ratings and some more "objective" or "quantitative" measure of scholarship, an article equivalent index was calculated and compared with the faculty quality scores. Five journals were reviewed, and the authorship of

TABLE 32: *Comparison of Ranks of Leading Political Science Departments as Rated by A.C.E. Study of Quality of Faculty and Somit and Tanenhaus Survey*

| | RANK | |
INSTITUTION	A.C.E.	Somit & Tanenhaus
Yale..........................	1	2
Harvard.......................	2	1
California, Berkeley............	3	3
Chicago.......................	4	4
Columbia......................	5	6
Princeton.....................	6	5
M.I.T.........................	7*	Not rated
Wisconsin.....................	7*	8*
Stanford......................	9	8*
Michigan......................	10	7
Cornell.......................	11	10*
Northwestern..................	12	13
U.C.L.A.......................	13	10*
Indiana.......................	14	14
North Carolina................	15	17
Minnesota.....................	16	16
Illinois.......................	17	15
Johns Hopkins.................	18	12

* Rank shared with another department.

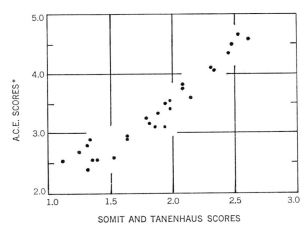

A.C.E. SCORES*

SOMIT AND TANENHAUS SCORES

Fig. 18—Comparison of the ratings by the 1964 A.C.E. study and by the 1963 Somit and Tanenhaus survey of 27 political science departments. The A.C.E. rating is based on rated quality of graduate faculty. Six institutions at the end of the Somit and Tanenhaus list have been omitted; they follow the pattern shown by the other 27.

articles, book reviews, and book notes over a period of four years was tallied and weighted.[9] Eight book reviews or 16 book notes were assumed to equal one article. The authorship of books reviewed in *Political Science Quarterly* was checked against the 1961–62 membership roster published by the American Political Science Association; authorship of a book was weighted as the equivalent of six articles and editorship as two, while joint authorship was divided equally among the collaborators.[10]

Figure 19 shows the 64 political science departments in the survey by their article equivalent index and their over-all faculty quality score. The eight departments with article equivalents of over six were among the top ten according to faculty quality ratings. Conversely, of the 21 departments showing less than one article equivalent, only three had faculty quality ratings above 2.00. Although there remains a sizable middle group whose faculty quality scores and publications ratings are scattered, the departments with high faculty quality scores tend to show high article equivalents and vice versa.

[9] Fall 1960 through summer 1964 issues of the following journals were checked: *American Political Science Review, World Politics, Political Science Quarterly, Journal of Politics, Midwest Journal of Political Science.*

[10] No brief is held for this system being either the most complete or discriminating method of evaluating published scholarship. The identification and weighting of books may be the least accurate and meaningful component of the index. Many authors could not be traced in the directory. Furthermore, the directory is in many cases now out of date, and scholars' mobility is such that a book researched and written at one institution may not be published until that author has moved. In using this index, it is assumed that errors of omission and misassignment tend to be evenly distributed among the departments in the survey and cancel out.

As in English and economics, publication is concentrated. The top ten departments according to either faculty quality or article equivalents account for slightly over 50 percent of the article equivalents produced by the 64 departments. Departments in the bottom half according to either measure account for less than one-eighth of the article equivalents. As might be expected, several highly reputed liberal arts colleges show higher publication production than some of the doctorate-granting institutions.

Institutional background

Of the political science respondents in the A.C.E. survey, 95 percent earned their doctorates at 37 major departments. Although this may seem to be a heavy concentration in a few departments, these same departments accounted for 84 percent of all earned doctorates in the field over the past ten years. The remaining 5 percent of respondents either did not have the doctorate or had received it from a foreign university. Thus 27 of the 64 departments surveyed did not have a single alumnus respondent in our sample.

The concentration of respondents at first suggests that this may be a source of biased rating in favor of the older prestige institutions. On the other hand, these are the departments which have long turned out the most distinguished scholars in the discipline, and thus their alumni are the individuals whose judgments should be particularly sound. In order to determine the degree and direction of possible bias resulting from high alumni representation from a few departments, a separate

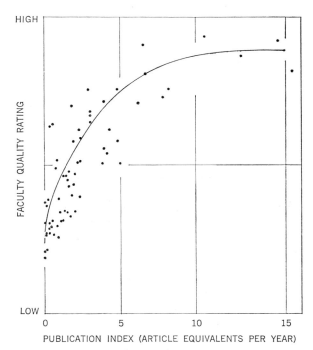

HIGH

FACULTY QUALITY RATING

LOW

0   5   10   15

PUBLICATION INDEX (ARTICLE EQUIVALENTS PER YEAR)

Fig. 19—Relationship of rated quality of graduate faculty to index of publications, 64 political science departments.

TABLE 33: *Difference between Mean Scores of All Respondents and Ratings by Alumni, Quality of Graduate Faculty, Political Science Departments*

DEPARTMENTS WITH FOUR OR MORE ALUMNUS RATERS	NUMBER OF ALUMNUS RATERS	AVERAGE DIFFERENCE FROM MEAN SCORES OF 165 RESPONDENTS	
		Amount	Percent
Harvard.............	23	+.27	5.9
Chicago.............	19	+.29	6.7
Princeton...........	10	−.04	1.0
Yale................	9	+.22	4.7
California, Berkeley...	9	+.38	8.4
Wisconsin...........	9	+.45	11.9
Columbia...........	8	+.67	16.4
U.C.L.A.............	6	+.45	13.3
Illinois.............	6	+.72	23.2
Minnesota..........	5	−.16	5.1
Johns Hopkins.......	5	+.70	22.6
Northwestern........	5	+.50	14.3
Michigan...........	4	−.13	3.6
Duke...............	4	+.29	9.8
Average for 35 departments with alumnus raters	155	.50	20.5

set of ratings was calculated for these departments using only the scores of their alumni. Table 33 shows the average difference from the over-all rating of the quality of graduate faculty by alumni of departments with four or more alumni among the 1964 respondents. Generally the average difference was inverse to the score a department received; "Distinguished" and "Strong" departments, on the average, received a rating .37 higher from alumni than from non-alumni, while the average for 37 departments was .50. Table 11 (p. 81) compares the political science figures with those of the other three fields discussed in this chapter.

A second source of possible bias in the ratings is the favored treatment which respondents gave to the institution at which they were employed. In this case there was no undue concentration, for no department was invited to have more than four scholars participate in the evaluation. Table 12 (p. 82) indicates the average difference from over-all score provided by persons of their own current departmental affiliation. The average difference is .82.

The alumni and current institutional biases appear fairly sizable when viewed in isolation; the important point, however, is to see what effect these institutional loyalty factors have on the over-all ratings. To assess this effect, the ratings for each department were recalculated after eliminating judgments of Ph.D. alma mater and current employer for each respondent. These "clean" ratings provide an unbiased view by outsiders, although they also represent the views of the least knowledgeable people. Table 34 gives the scores for the "Distinguished" and "Strong" departments as recorded by all respondents and by those who

had no alumnus or employee attachment to a department. As can be seen, the ratings by outsiders are slightly lower than the over-all ratings, but in no case is the difference greater than .07. Six departments change rank, but no major shifts are apparent. On reflection it will be seen that the few departments near the top of the ranking were the only ones with many alumni, and generally the bias in favor of the top departments was quite small. The large biases were evident for departments near the bottom of the list, but there were not more than two or three alumnus and employee ratings in the total of 165 for these departments. Thus, although these biases are significantly large in the case of some few individuals, the nature of the sample is such that the biases tend to cancel out.

TABLE 34: *Ratings of Quality of Graduate Faculty, High-ranking Political Science Departments, by All Respondents and by Those without Close Institutional Affiliation*

INSTITUTION	RATINGS BY:			
	All Respondents		Non-employee—Non-alumnus Respondents	
	Rank	Score	Rank	Score
Yale..............	1	4.67	1	4.65
Harvard...........	2	4.60	2	4.55
California, Berkeley.	3	4.51	3	4.47
Chicago...........	4	4.34	4	4.28
Columbia.........	5	4.08	6	4.01
Princeton.........	6	4.04	5	4.03
M.I.T.............	7*	3.77	7*	3.75
Wisconsin.........	7*	3.77	9	3.72
Stanford..........	9	3.76	7*	3.75
Michigan..........	10	3.63	10	3.63
Cornell...........	11	3.57	11	3.56
Northwestern.......	12	3.50	12	3.48
U.C.L.A...........	13	3.39	13	3.35
Indiana...........	14	3.34	14	3.32
North Carolina.....	15	3.23	15	3.22
Minnesota.........	16	3.16	16	3.16
Illinois...........	17	3.11	18	3.06
Johns Hopkins......	18	3.10	17	3.07

* Rank and score shared with another department.

Regional variations

Regional loyalty and variation in firsthand knowledge account for some of the differences in the way scholars in one region judge their colleagues in another. The pattern in political science is similar to, although in a few respects at some variance with, the regional pattern seen in other disciplines. Table 35 gives the faculty quality ratings of the "Distinguished" and "Strong" departments by respondents in four broad regions of the country.

While the ratings of faculty by respondents in the various regions are generally consistent, there are some differences. Among the top ten depart-

TABLE 35: *Regional Ratings of Quality of Graduate Faculty in Leading Political Science Departments*

INSTITUTION	ALL RESPONDENTS		RESPONDENTS, BY REGION							
			East		Midwest		South		West	
	Rank	Score	Rank	Score	Rank	Score	Rank	Score	Rank	Score
Yale	1	4.67	2	4.58	1	4.87	2	4.60	1	4.55
Harvard	2	4.60	1	4.65	3	4.50	1	4.70	2	4.53
California, Berkeley	3	4.51	3	4.41	2	4.59	3	4.56	3	4.46
Chicago	4	4.34	4	4.31	4	4.41	4*	4.31	4	4.34
Columbia	5	4.08	5	4.01	7	3.95	4*	4.31	5	4.16
Princeton	6	4.04	6	3.92	5	4.06	6	4.13	6	4.11
M.I.T.	7*	3.77	8	3.68	9	3.82	8	3.83	7	3.70
Wisconsin	7*	3.77	9	3.66	6	4.02	9	3.66	8	3.66
Stanford	9	3.76	7	3.73	8	3.85	7	3.93	11	3.48
Michigan	10	3.63	10	3.60	11	3.75	11	3.53	10	3.57
Cornell	11	3.57	11	3.54	12	3.60	10	3.57	9	3.58
Northwestern	12	3.50	13	3.40	10	3.76	15	3.22	13	3.38
U.C.L.A.	13	3.39	12	3.41	13	3.47	16*	3.20	12	3.40
Indiana	14	3.34	14	3.32	15	3.37	12	3.43	15	3.16
North Carolina	15	3.23	15	3.16	14	3.44	13	3.34	19	2.82
Minnesota	16	3.16	16	3.10	16	3.33	19	3.08	17	3.00
Illinois	17	3.11	17	2.98	17	3.21	16*	3.20	14	3.20
Johns Hopkins	18	3.10	19	2.96	18	3.17	14	3.33	16	3.04

*Rank and score shared with another department.

ments, only three show rank differences of more than two positions between the highest and lowest regional rating. Columbia is ranked fourth by Southerners but seventh by Midwest raters; Wisconsin is ranked sixth by its own region but ninth by the East and the South; Stanford is ranked lowest (eleventh) in its own region, but seventh in the East and South. There is least agreement on Johns Hopkins, Northwestern, and North Carolina. The Southerners give Johns Hopkins fourteenth position, the Easterners, nineteenth. The Midwesterners rate Northwestern tenth, the Southerners, fifteenth. The Southern raters rank North Carolina thirteenth, while the Western raters put it in nineteenth place.

The Southerners gave the lowest average scores in political science. This is in marked contrast to the results in economics, in which this geographic group was quite generous with its assessments. The Eastern political scientists were also "low graders" and, in fact, rated nearly two-thirds of the departments lower than the over-all average. The Midwesterners appeared most lenient, for they not only awarded higher regional scores but rated 70 percent of all the departments above the over-all average. They placed 17 of their own 19 departments well above the average score given by raters from other regions. The Westerners gave approximately one-half of all the departments above average scores, but were quite hard on the South, giving eight out of that region's 12 departments below average scores.

Table 36 shows the average ratings given by respondents living in the four regions to the departments located in these regions. Whereas in economics the Southerners rated their own depart-

TABLE 36: *Ratings of Quality of Graduate Faculty, Political Science Departments, by Raters' Current Region*

RATERS' REGION OF EMPLOYMENT	DEPARTMENTS LOCATED IN:				ALL DEPART- MENTS
	East	Midwest	South	West	
	Average Rating				
East	2.48	2.47	2.05	2.67	2.42
Midwest	2.52	2.64	2.07	2.74	2.50
South	2.49	2.38	2.05	2.63	2.39
West	2.56	2.57	1.87	2.71	2.45
All regions	2.51	2.53	2.03	2.70	2.45
	Percentage Difference from Over-all Mean				
East	−1.2	−2.4	+1.0	−1.1	−1.2
Midwest	+ .4	+4.4	+2.0	+1.5	+2.0
South	− .8	−5.9	+1.0	−2.6	−2.5
West	+2.0	+1.6	−7.9	+ .4	—

ments 16 percent above the ratings by all respondents, in political science this difference is only 1 percent.

Departmental prestige

Finally, the political science raters were regrouped according to the score given by all respondents to their employing departments. Responses from raters at departments with over-all scores on faculty quality placing them in the "top quarter," "second quarter," and "second half" were calculated separately and compared. While respondents from departments in the "top quarter" gave the highest ratings to eight of their own departments, they gave no such ratings to the departments in the second quarter and to only one in the

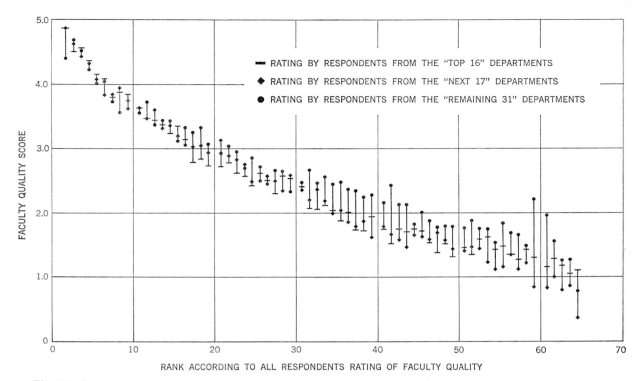

Fig. 20—Rated quality of faculty, as judged by respondents in political science departments in the first quarter, second quarter, and second half of rankings. (Two departments tied for thirty-second position; hence, both are included in the second quarter.)

second half. As in economics, they rated the upper ranks higher, and the lower ranks lower, than the over-all ratings provided by all respondents. Raters from the 17 departments in the second quarter were the highest rating group for only four departments in the top quarter, five in the second quarter, and none in the second half. They accounted for the largest number of the lowest ratings, 28 out of 64. Interestingly enough, raters from departments falling in the second half did not follow an obviously reverse pattern, for they rated five of the "top 16" departments and 12 of the "second 17" higher than did all respondents. Not surprisingly, these raters looked favorably upon their own departments, giving the highest rating to all but one department in the second half.

The exact rank order of the top 18 departments varies from group to group. When the over-all rankings are compared with those of raters from the top quarter, there are six changes in rank; when compared with those from the second quarter, ten changes. However, all except one of these are changes of only one rank position. On the other hand, when the over-all rankings are compared with those of raters from the second half, nearly all show some difference. Seven departments change by one position, five by two, and three by three. Yet the same nine institutions appear in the "top ten" listing of each group and the same 19 appear in the "top 20" of each group.

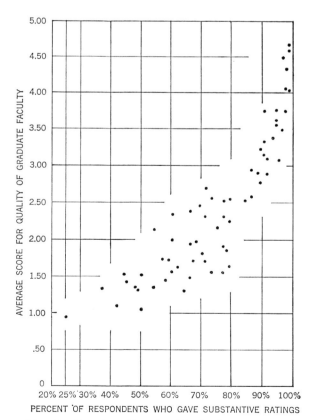

Fig. 21—Rated quality of political science faculty, by percent of respondents providing ratings.

Figure 20 graphically shows the considerable narrowness and consistency in the range of scores assigned by groups to each of the 64 institutions.

Figure 21 arrays the 64 departments by over-all score and the percent of respondents who gave the department a "substantive rating" on Question A, quality of graduate faculty, that is, who checked a block other than "insufficient information." The scatter shows that in general the score follows the percent of substantive ratings. The departments with high scores are those that respondents "knew" or at least were willing to rate. All the departments scoring 3.00 or better have response rates in excess of 85 percent. On the other hand, the departments with low scores have relatively low response rates. No institution with a score of 1.50 or below was rated by more than two-thirds of the raters. However, the narrow range above and the spread below 3.00 clearly indicate that the calculated scores and the response rate are not one and the same.

Summary

The detailed review of four disciplines yields a number of generalizations that are useful in interpreting the ratings of all fields. First, the device of small select panels, partly replicating the procedure of the first Hughes and the Keniston studies, was found to be less reliable as a guide to the ratings made by the entire sample of respondents than were any of the three subgroups (as determined by age and rank). This probably results from the small size of the panels, rather than the nature of their selection. We conclude that any future survey should use panels of 50 or more knowledgeable persons to ensure reliability.

Second, regional variations are about what one would have anticipated—propinquity seldom breeds contempt. However, the fairly substantial regional differences in ratings highlight the need for balanced regional representation on rating panels.

Third, although biases in favor of Ph.D. alma mater and current institution are quite marked, the manner in which the panels were selected for the A.C.E. study appears to have satisfactorily compensated for distortion resulting from affiliation biases.

Fourth, the better departments are by and large the more productive departments in terms of scholarly publications—although this correlation is by no means perfect. There appears to be a high degree of concentration of major publications among the leading departments at the one extreme, and a sizable number of doctorate-granting departments which made almost no contribution to the major national professional journals at the other extreme. Apparently the "publish or perish" dictum, insofar as it exists, is limited to a relatively small number of distinguished institutions.

In general, the detailed review of these four disciplines confirmed our original judgment of the most appropriate size and composition of rating panels. The findings of this chapter may also be useful to others making future subjective assessments.

V · *Patterns of Quality in Universities*

THE PRECEDING CHAPTERS have concentrated on individual departments in 29 academic fields; in this chapter some generalizations about quality programs will be drawn considering the university as a whole. At the outset of the study, it was decided not to aggregate scores to arrive at university-wide ratings for two primary reasons. First, any over-all rating would involve (implicitly or explicitly) some judgment about how the various fields of study should be weighted. Should classics and geography be weighted equally with English and history? Is bacteriology or pharmacology as important as biochemistry or zoology? Universities do not make equal commitments to all fields, and therefore they should not be judged on a simple average of their departmental ratings. A second reason for not summating scores is that many institutions do not offer work in all the fields under review. It seems unreasonable to penalize an institution for not having an engineering school, a classics department, or a doctoral program in astronomy.

A few examples from the most distinguished institutions will illustrate the difficulty of aggregation. If one merely averages the scores for the departments in which the Ph.D. is offered, ignoring fields where no graduate work is given, then the Rockefeller Institute would place among the top five institutions, even though it concentrates only on the biological sciences. Harvard and Yale, which rank near the top in most areas, are somewhat weaker in the engineering sciences: Harvard is rated as "Distinguished" in 23 arts and sciences fields, but its engineering departments are in the second or third categories. If engineering is weighted equally with the arts and sciences fields, Harvard would tie with M.I.T. and Berkeley for first position; if engineering is omitted, Harvard clearly emerges as first. Similarly, Yale is either third or sixth in the top group of universities depending upon the exclusion or inclusion of engineering.

Because there is no equitable way to aggregate the departmental ratings, and because it was felt that over-all ratings were less meaningful than departmental or divisional ratings, we leave to the reader the task of drawing generalizations from the detailed presentations in chapter 3. In some of the sections that follow, however, over-all averages have been used (without identifying institutions)

for correlations with other indices such as salary levels, library resources, and fellowships.

Concentrations of strength by divisions

General ratings for an academic division may be somewhat more meaningful than university-wide scoring, since most academicians feel that to maintain strength in one field of study requires the presence of strong departments in other closely allied disciplines.[1] For instance, it is difficult to have a distinguished physics department without also having a strong mathematics department, or to have a strong biochemistry department without good chemistry and biology departments.

The evidence of the 1964 study lends moderate support to the view that good departments in closely allied fields cluster together. For example, there is no university having a "Distinguished" economics department which does not also have a "Distinguished" or at least a "Strong" political science department, and vice versa. Nineteen institutions had "Strong" or "Distinguished" economics or political science departments; the difference between the scores of these two departments averaged only .34 on a five-point rating scale. Carnegie Tech. was the only high-scoring institution which granted the doctorate in only one of these fields, and its department is a peculiar hybrid which includes representatives from all the social science disciplines.

Similarly, chemistry, mathematics, and physics departments are closely allied, and in almost every case where one is strong the other two are, also. The single notable exception is N.Y.U., which has a "Distinguished" mathematics department without the support of strong departments in the allied fields. The tie between botany and zoology appears to be somewhat weaker, and perhaps the greatest variation in relative strengths is found among the humanities departments.

Mathematics at N.Y.U., German at Texas, biochemistry at M.I.T., chemical engineering at

[1] For a contrary view, see George Stigler's provocative essay, "Meager Means and Noble Ends," in *The Intellectual and the Market Place* (New York: Free Press of Glencoe, and London: Collier-Macmillan, Ltd.), pp. 33–42. Stigler advocates a policy of "selective eminence" for university administration, suggesting that a good library is a near substitute for stimulating colleagues in related disciplines. The fact that he considers his view radical lends support to the statement in the text.

Delaware, geography at Louisiana State, philosophy at Pittsburgh, and anthropology at Arizona—among the few marked exceptions where a single department achieves eminence without the support of strong allied fields—are an interesting study in themselves. In each case an unusual congeries of local and environmental factors, tempered occasionally by historical accident, seems to account for the situation. The question of interdependence among academic disciplines is analyzed further in Appendix C.

Table 37 lists the highest-rated universities on quality of graduate faculty in each of five general divisions: humanities, social sciences, biological sciences, physical sciences, and engineering. Those listed achieved the highest average scores within the respective divisions and had at least two "Distinguished" departments. California, Berkeley, appears in the leading group in all five divisions, a finding which supports the claim that it is the best balanced distinguished university in the country. Harvard and Stanford appear in four divisions; Columbia, Illinois, Yale, Princeton, Michigan, and Cal. Tech. in three; and M.I.T., Chicago, and Wisconsin in two.

A comparison of Table 37 with Keniston's divisional ratings suggests that the institutions in the lead have changed over a period of time. Princeton and Wisconsin have moved ahead since 1957 in the social sciences, replacing Minnesota and Cornell. In the biological sciences Stanford has taken a giant stride from thirteenth in 1957 (it probably would have ranked fifteenth then had the Rockefeller Institute and Cal. Tech. been included in Keniston's survey) to fifth position, while Illinois has displaced Indiana. Stanford has also moved ahead in the physical sciences, followed closely by Illinois, while Chicago and Columbia have slipped modestly. In the humanities the same six institutions lead in 1957 and 1964, although they have shifted positions slightly. Keniston did not study engineering, so that no comparisons can be made with earlier ratings.

A review of the field-by-field reports in chapter 3 indicates interesting concentrations. For example, of the eight departments at Chicago receiving "Distinguished" ratings, six are in the social sciences. M.I.T. has seven of its nine "Distinguished" ratings in engineering and the physical sciences; Cal. Tech. has six of its eight in those areas. Eight of Stanford's ten "Distinguished" departments are in the sciences and engineering, while seven of Yale's ten are in humanities and social sciences.

Concentrations of students with national fellowships

Concurrent with the subjective survey of graduate programs, a separate study was undertaken of students holding first-year graduate fellowships in the Woodrow Wilson, NSF Regular, NSF Cooperative, and National Defense Education Act title IV programs over a four-year period (1960–61 through 1963–64). The results provide some comparisons relevant to the present study.

Nearly 13,000 fellows during this four-year period were classified as Level I; that is, entering graduate students, or students who when awarded a fellowship had completed not more than half a year of advanced work. Table 38 shows the regional distribution of these fellows by school of baccalaureate origin and by graduate school attended. Forty-six percent of the fellows remained for graduate study in the region where they had attended undergraduate college; approximately 7,000 "migrated" to another part of the country. (It should be noted that the percentage of those remaining or migrating is largely a function of the size of the region; if the crossing of a state boundary is taken to constitute migration, then the percentage is about 75 percent; if the country is divided into quadrants and "migrating" is defined as moving from one to another of those quadrants, then the figure is only about 42 percent—not the 54 percent implied in Table 38.) Table 39, which shows the net flow of top graduate students, indicates that only New England and the Far West attracted more fellowship holders from other regions than they sent to those other regions.

TABLE 37: *The Leading Universities, by General Area of Study, as Measured by Quality of Faculty, 1964*

Humanities	Social Sciences	Biological Sciences	Physical Sciences	Engineering
Harvard..... 4.36	Harvard....... 4.66	Harvard....... 4.42	Harvard....... 4.60	M.I.T........... 4.48
California,	California,	California,	California,	California,
Berkeley... 4.27	Berkeley.... 4.48	Berkeley.... 4.33	Berkeley.... 4.55	Berkeley..... 4.23
Yale........ 4.17	Chicago....... 4.39	Rockefeller Inst. 3.97	Cal. Tech...... 4.46	Stanford........ 4.02
Princeton.... 3.91	Yale.......... 4.12	Cal. Tech...... 3.95	M.I.T......... 4.33	Cal. Tech....... 3.94
Columbia.... 3.79	Princeton...... 3.98	Stanford...... 3.92	Princeton...... 4.33	Illinois.......... 3.91
Michigan.... 3.69	Wisconsin..... 3.91	Michigan...... 3.85	Stanford...... 4.22	
	Columbia...... 3.77	Wisconsin..... 3.76	Chicago....... 3.98	
	Michigan...... 3.75	Illinois........ 3.73	Illinois........ 3.82	
	Stanford...... 3.75	Yale.......... 3.68	Columbia...... 3.78	

TABLE 38: *Regional[a] Distribution of National Fellows, 1960–63*

REGION OF BACCALAUREATE ORIGIN	REGION OF GRADUATE SCHOOL ATTENDED									
	New England	Mideast	Great Lakes	Plains	Southeast	Southwest	Rocky Mountains	Far West	Foreign	Total
New England.....	745	301	129	37	47	16	11	244	22	1,552
Mideast..........	653	1,295	285	79	117	33	20	283	15	2,780
Great Lakes.......	347	344	1,035	120	144	52	37	303	17	2,399
Plains............	110	149	201	489	84	50	47	162	11	1,303
Southeast........	179	213	217	43	1,042	76	14	142	9	1,935
Southwest........	54	56	68	32	93	330	18	94	6	751
Rocky Mountain...	30	47	43	28	24	45	180	89	—	486
Far West.........	187	183	105	45	34	36	34	678	13	1,315
Foreign..........	75	60	36	6	12	4	—	55	37	285
Total........	2,380	2,648	2,119	879	1,597	642	361	2,050	130	12,806

[a] The states included in the regions shown are as follows:
New England (6 states): Connecticut, Maine, Massachusetts, New Hampshire, Rhode Island, Vermont.
Mideast (5 states and the District of Columbia): Delaware, District of Columbia, Maryland, New Jersey, New York, Pennsylvania.
Great Lakes (5 states): Illinois, Indiana, Michigan, Ohio, Wisconsin.
Plains (7 states): Iowa, Kansas, Minnesota, Missouri, Nebraska, North Dakota, South Dakota.
Southeast (12 states): Alabama, Arkansas, Florida, Georgia, Kentucky, Louisiana, Mississippi, North Carolina, South Carolina, Tennessee, Virginia, West Virginia.
Southwest (4 states): Arizona, New Mexico, Oklahoma, Texas.
Rocky Mountain (6 states): Colorado, Idaho, Montana, Nevada, Utah, Wyoming.
Far West (5 states): Alaska, California, Hawaii, Oregon, Washington.

Two of the fellowship programs, the Woodrow Wilson and the NSF Regular, give the fellowship holder complete freedom in his choice of graduate school. As might be expected, fellows in these two programs tended to concentrate; about two-thirds of them went to the top ten universities on the faculty quality ratings. NSF Cooperative fellows are selected nationally, but nominations are based on a quota determined by the level of recent Ph.D. production. NDEA title IV fellowships are awarded to approved programs at the various universities; the institutions themselves make the selections. Table 40, which summarizes the distribution of these awards in 1960–63 for arts and sciences (omitting education and engineering), reveals clearly how selection procedures affect the distribution of top graduate student talent. About 86 percent of the NSF Regular and 82 percent of the Woodrow Wilson fellows were concentrated in the leading 25 universities as measured by quality

rating of graduate faculty. By contrast, more than half of the NSF Cooperative fellows and four-fifths of the NDEA title IV fellows attended universities ranked below the first 25. In short, the latter two programs have accomplished their aim of spreading the best talent among many institutions. The over-all distribution for the four programs combined seems a reasonable compromise; it not only supports graduate education at the distinguished universities but also encourages the strengthening and expansion of graduate programs in some of the younger and smaller universities. Some observers have felt that the middle group of universities, caught between these two aims, benefited less than might have been expected on the basis of the quality of their graduate programs. For example, the universities ranked from twenty-sixth to fiftieth awarded 23 percent of all Ph.D.'s over the last decade and received 17 percent of the students with national fellowships, while the next 55 uni-

TABLE 39: *The "Balance of Trade" of Students Holding Major National Fellowships, 1960–63*

REGION	NET GAIN OR LOSS IN EXCHANGE WITH REGIONS										NET GAIN (LOSS) AS % OF FELLOWS ORIGINATING IN OWN REGION
	NE	ME	GL	P	SE	SW	RM	FW	Foreign	Total	
New England.........		+352	+218	+ 73	+132	+ 38	+ 19	− 57	+ 53	+828	+53.4
Mideast..............	−352		+ 59	+ 70	+ 96	+ 23	+ 27	−100	+ 45	−132	− 4.7
Great Lakes..........	−218	− 59		+ 81	+ 73	+ 16	+ 6	−198	+ 19	−280	−11.7
Plains...............	− 73	− 70	− 81		− 41	− 18	− 19	−117	− 5	−424	−32.5
Southeast............	−132	− 96	− 73	+ 41		+ 17	+ 10	−108	+ 3	−338	−17.5
Southwest............	− 38	− 23	− 16	+ 18	− 17		+ 27	− 58	− 2	−109	−14.5
Rocky Mountain......	− 19	− 27	− 6	+ 19	− 10	− 27		− 55	0	−125	−25.7
Far West.............	+ 57	+100	+198	+117	+108	+ 58	+ 55		+ 42	+735	+55.9
Foreign..............	− 53	− 45	− 19	+ 5	− 3	+ 2	0	− 42		−155	
Total.............	−828	+132	+280	+424	+338	+109	+125	−735	+155		

TABLE 40: *Distribution of National Fellowships by Program, Academic Area, and University Grouping* [a]

AREA OF STUDY AND FELLOWSHIP PROGRAM	NUMBER OF FELLOWS ATTENDING UNIVERSITIES GROUPED IN:					
	Top 10 [b]	Next 15	Next 25	Next 55	All Other [c]	Total
PHYSICAL SCIENCES	1,390	430	419	520	400	3,159
NSF	981	160	61	44	25	1,271
NSF Cooperative	133	102	110	117	76	538
Woodrow Wilson	255	66	38	20	10	389
NDEA IV	21	102	210	339	289	961
BIOLOGICAL SCIENCES	439	198	202	388	369	1,596
NSF	263	80	35	23	38	439
NSF Cooperative	33	19	20	37	43	152
Woodrow Wilson	125	50	23	10	15	223
NDEA IV	18	49	124	318	273	782
SOCIAL SCIENCES	1,084	647	543	525	169	2,968
NSF	61	20	1	1	13	96
NSF Cooperative	11	14	2	4	2	33
Woodrow Wilson	813	340	113	68	28	1,362
NDEA IV	199	273	427	452	126	1,477
HUMANITIES	1,052	733	647	583	176	3,191
NSF	2	—	—	—	—	2
NSF Cooperative	—	—	1	—	—	1
Woodrow Wilson	961	554	201	100	73	1,889
NDEA IV	89	179	445	483	103	1,299
Total in four fields	3,965	2,008	1,811	2,016	1,114	10,914

PROGRAMS	TOTAL BY PROGRAM											
	No.	%	No.	%	No.	%	No.	%	No.	%	No.	%[d]
NSF	1,307	72	260	14	97	5	68	4	76	4	1,808	99
NSF Cooperative	177	24	135	19	133	18	158	22	121	17	724	100
Woodrow Wilson	2,154	56	1,010	26	375	10	198	5	126	3	3,863	100
NDEA IV	327	7	603	13	1,206	27	1,592	35	791	18	4,519	100
Total	3,965	36	2,008	18	1,811	17	2,016	18	1,114	10	10,914	99

[a] Grouped by over-all rank as measured by quality of graduate faculty (Question A).
[b] One high-ranking institution with low enrollment and doctorate production has been excluded from the top ten group in this table.
[c] Includes foreign institutions.
[d] May not total 100 percent because of rounding.

versities awarded fewer degrees (20 percent of the total) and actually received a larger number of the fellowships. The National Science Foundation's current expansion of its Cooperative program into a much more extensive traineeship program and the Office of Education's policy of freeing an increasing number of its awards from the "new and expanding program" rubric promise to give greater emphasis to the aspiring second echelon of universities (barring political pressures to distribute funds more nearly on a geographic basis).

Figures 22–25 correlate quality of graduate programs as measured by Question B (the effectiveness of doctoral program) with the number of fellows entering graduate school whose awards are from the two major "free choice" programs (NSF Regular and Woodrow Wilson). Fitted curves illustrate the close relationship between the subjective assessments and the distribution of fellows.

Geographical distribution

In policy statements during recent years, government agencies or national commissions have frequently advocated an improved geographic distribution of major graduate centers. The 1964 survey would seem to justify their concern. It found that "Distinguished" departments were concentrated in 13 states; 80 percent of them were in only five states. Institutions in the Southeast and Rocky Mountain states could not claim a single department in the highest category in any of the 29 fields studied; the Southwest and Plains could point to only one each.

However, in judging graduate centers of high quality, we should look also at the second-highest category—the departments ranked as "Strong"— since these departments may be equally good educationally even though they lack the bright luster of the departments at Harvard and Berkeley.

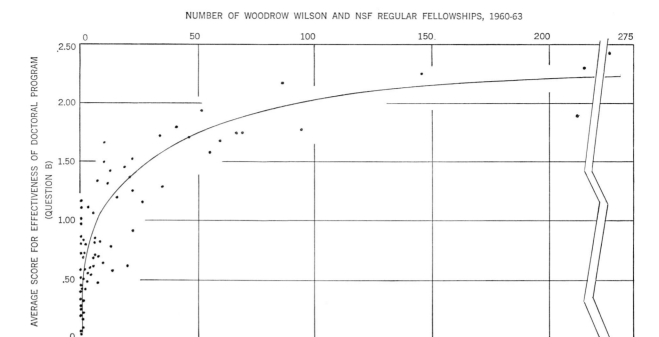

Fig. 22—Relationship between location of "free choice" fellowship holders and rated quality of effectiveness of doctoral programs in the humanities.

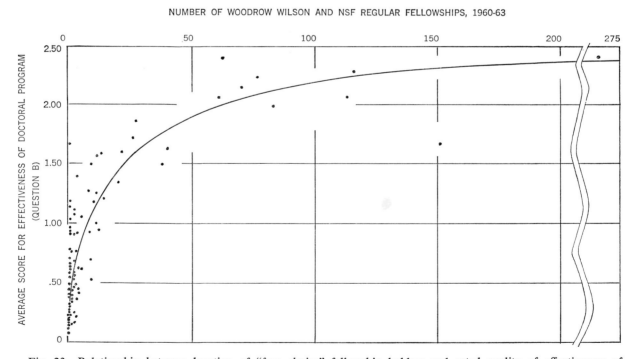

Fig. 23—Relationship between location of "free choice" fellowship holders and rated quality of effectiveness of doctoral programs in the social sciences.

TABLE 41: *Geographical Distribution of "Strong" and "Distinguished" Departments, by Academic Division, 1964*

Region	Humanities	Social Sciences	Biological Sciences	Physical Sciences	Engineering	Total
New England	16	12	20	17	7	72
Mideast	32	21	46	25	19	143
Southeast	5	5	9	2	—	21
Southwest	3	1	3	4	3	14
Great Lakes	29	28	48	27	20	152
Plains	2	6	16	5	4	33
Rocky Mountain	—	—	1	—	—	1
Far West	16	20	36	21	16	109
Total	103	93	179	101	69	545

Table 41 gives a breakdown of leading departments by region and academic division.

The 545 departments shown in Table 41 were spread over 63 different universities, geographically distributed as follows:

New England	6
Mideast	20
Southeast	7
Southwest	3
Great Lakes	12
Plains	6
Rocky Mountains	1
Far West	8
Total	63

It is evident that the Rocky Mountain, Plains, Southwest, and Southeast regions are generally underrepresented in proportion to their popula-

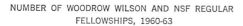
NUMBER OF WOODROW WILSON AND NSF REGULAR FELLOWSHIPS, 1960-63

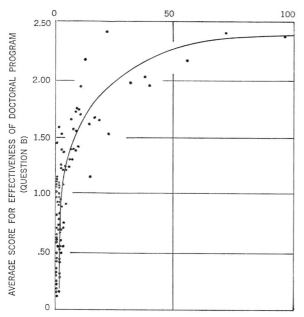

Fig. 24—Relationship between location of "free choice" fellowship holders and rated quality of effectiveness of doctoral programs in the biological sciences.

tions and college enrollments. The Northeast (New England and Mideast), because of its historic leadership in higher education and the strength of its private institutions, is most overrepresented. This is particularly evident in the humanities, a reflection of the long literary tradition of the region.

One might hazard the guess that, of the underrepresented areas, the South could make the greatest advances in institutional quality during the next decade or two. Although no Southern university ranked among the top 22 institutions in Berelson's study five years ago, ten of the next 27 were Southern. The leaders in the South, as indicated by the 1964 survey of graduate education, include Duke, Texas, North Carolina, Rice, Tulane, and Vanderbilt, followed closely by seven public universities and one private university. Each of these 14 institutions would seem to have the potential for achieving major national status in the years ahead; particularly encouraging are the vitality and leadership exhibited by the private universities in the region.

One discouraging feature of our regional review, however, is that the nation's capital stands out as one of the few major cities in the United States which do not have one or more universities of notable strength. (If international relations had been included in our survey, the Johns Hopkins School of Advanced International Studies and Georgetown University might have made a strong showing in that field.) In the 29 disciplines under review, a total of 56 departments in the four universities of the District of Columbia were included in the study, and only two managed to achieve ratings above "Adequate plus." It is to be hoped that the recent consortium agreement among the universities in the capital will bring about some improvement in the years immediately ahead.

The cost of quality

Few persons would deny that good education is costly education, and the evidence of our survey indicates a close relationship between faculty salaries and quality of graduate faculty. Figure 26 plots the average over-all rating for each uni-

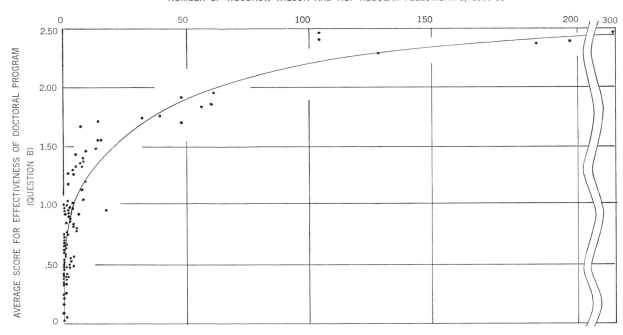

Fig. 25—Relationship between location of "free choice" fellowship holders and rated quality of effectiveness of doctoral programs in the physical sciences.

versity against average faculty compensation as reported by the American Association of University Professors. The regression line suggests the relationship between these variables, and the correlation is significantly high ($r=.873$). Table 42 summarizes the data on quality and faculty salary.

TABLE 42: *Average Faculty Compensation in Universities, by Rated Quality of Graduate Faculty*

Universities, by Average Over-all Rating	No. of Universities	Average Faculty Compensation
4.01 and above.........	4	$14,700
3.51–4.00..............	8	13,400
3.01–3.50..............	9	12,600
2.51–3.00..............	16	12,100
2.01–2.50..............	21	10,900
1.51–2.00..............	25	10,300
1.50 and below.........	12	9,500

As indicated in the detailed survey of economics in the preceding chapter, the correlation between salaries and quality probably would have been even greater had salary data for only the two highest ranks been used. Even the poorer institutions tend to be competitive in the salaries of instructors and assistant professors. Therefore, as the economics data indicated, the quality of graduate education has a high positive correlation with salaries for the two upper professional ranks and no significant correlation with the salaries for the two lower ranks.

In the investigation of the relations among quality, cost per student, and size of institution, it

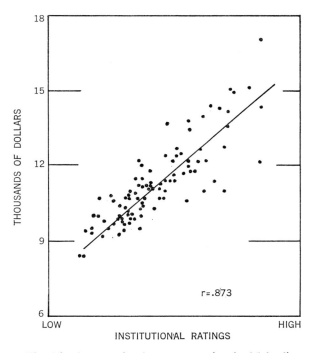

Fig. 26—Average faculty compensation in 95 leading graduate institutions, 1964–65, by rated quality of graduate faculty.

was found that the collected sources of data on university expenditure were of little use because of their inconsistency. Finding some reliable measure for converting part-time students into full-time equivalents—a necessary step in making accurate comparisons between some of the smaller residential universities such as Princeton and Duke with the large urban institutions such as N.Y.U. and the University of Southern California—was also difficult. A third problem is the difference in enrollment "mix" at various institutions, not only in the proportions of undergraduate and graduate populations, but also in the proportions of students in arts and sciences and in the professional schools of medicine, law, public health, nursing, and architecture.

Given these difficulties, Figure 27 can present only a rough and imperfect picture of the relationship between size and cost for institutions classified as of high or medium quality. Since only a long and detailed study would provide comparable cost data, the study used "educational and general income" per student (omitting grants and contracts for research) as a comparative measure. Included in this figure are income from tuition and fees and endowment income, plus, for private institutions, unrestricted current gifts or, for public universities, state appropriations for current operating expenses. In estimating full-time undergraduate student equivalents, the study deflated part-time enrollments by three-fifths; further, each graduate and advanced professional student was counted as the equivalent of three undergraduates in order to cover the expected difference in resources devoted to their education.

The 103 universities for which the study could obtain roughly comparable information on income ranged from about 2,500 to 48,000 undergraduate student equivalents. The average income per student unit was approximately $1,460, the private universities being about $100 above this average and the public universities an equal distance below. The average income per student for the 25 institutions which led in over-all quality in the 1964 study was about $1,900; it was $1,200 for the remaining universities. Perhaps the most striking feature of Figure 27 is the indication that there are fairly marked economies of scale for the highest-quality institutions, whereas only insignificant economies of scale are evident among the other 78 universities. Stated another way, large universities with 30,000 or more students appear to be better able to achieve distinction with only average per-student income, whereas the income needed to attain high quality for lesser enrollments was substantially greater than the average. It should be remembered, however, that the few high-quality *small* universities are private, while the larger ones are predominantly public; thus only part of the apparent reduction in income (and presumably in cost) per student associated with larger enrollments in the top-quality universities is a reflection of size.

The question of optimal university size in terms of both quality and cost is of such importance that more research should be undertaken in this area. The general impression one gets from imperfect

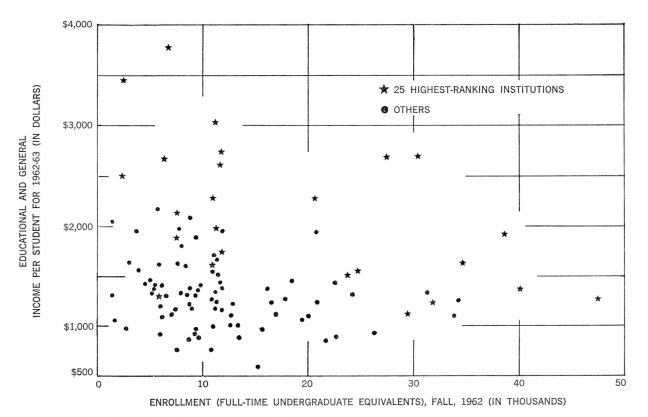

Fig. 27—Relationship between enrollment and educational and general income per student.

data is that for high-quality universities there are fairly marked economies of scale up to an enrollment of approximately 20,000 student units (counting each graduate and advanced professional student as three "units"). Beyond 20,000, there is less evidence that large size is accompanied by cost reductions per student.

The concept of optimal size, however, should be applied to departments rather than to the university as a whole, since the major economies lie in the areas of distinguished faculty and library and laboratory resources. An outstanding physics department of relatively small size may require the presence of six or eight distinguished senior physicists, an excellent research library, and expensive laboratory equipment. An outstanding department with five times as many graduate students need not multiply these resources by five, however; additional junior staff and modest increases in library and laboratory facilities may be sufficient to handle a considerably larger number of students. Unfortunately, few universities collect cost data on a departmental basis, and no one publishes such information; it is therefore difficult to document the relationship between cost and scale in quality education.

The Commission on Plans and Objectives for Higher Education hopes to make further studies of departmental size and quality to throw additional light on the important question of "critical mass." However, major obstacles lie in the path of the researcher who attempts to gather truly comparable financial data from institutions. Perhaps the present study, by its isolation of one variable—quality—may be a helpful first step in learning more about the interrelationship of size, quality, and cost of education.

Quality and library resources

The library is the heart of the university; no other single nonhuman factor is as closely related to the quality of graduate education. A few universities with poor library resources have achieved considerable strength in several departments, in some cases because laboratory facilities may be more important in a particular field than the library, and in other cases because the universities are located close to other great library collections such as the Library of Congress and the New York Public Library. But institutions that are strong in all areas invariably have major national research libraries. The 17 universities among the first 20 institutions in our study (omitting the three leading institutions of science or technology) had total library holdings ranging from 1.3 million to nearly 8 million volumes; the average holding was 2.7 million volumes. The bottom 20 institutions among the 106 in the survey had libraries ranging from 125,000 to 1 million volumes, averaging 465,000.

The total number of volumes, however, tells us little about the adequacy of a library for scholarly use. Old libraries, though usually larger than those in the newer universities, may have poorer modern collections. Some fields of study require much larger library resources than others; for example, the libraries of Rice and M.I.T. cannot be judged on the same scale with those of Texas and Harvard. Accordingly, an index which may be a more appropriate measure of relative library strength is suggested in Table 43.

Three items were taken into account in constructing this "library resources index": Column 1 is an index of total volumes held; column 2, an index of volumes added annually; and column 3, an index of current periodicals. In each case the average number of volumes or periodicals for all universities in the survey is taken as 1.00. The inclusion of current additions minimizes the advantages of the older libraries and improves the showing of the newer universities such as Maryland, Rochester, and Brandeis. By including periodicals, we make some allowance that in certain fields of study—particularly in science—the most valuable research tool is the periodical rather than the book.

The figures in the fourth column of Table 43 are for an over-all resources index, obtained by averaging the three separate indices. This over-all index is probably a more sensitive indicator of a library's strength than the index of total volumes alone. Some of the older eminent universities with large collections do not look so markedly superior; universities such as Louisiana State, Missouri, Utah, and Colorado make a somewhat better showing. The research libraries that would be generally accepted as outstanding score about 2 or above on the over-all index. All the universities with over-all faculty quality ratings of 3.0 and above ("Strong" and "Distinguished") scored above 1.4 on the library resources index. Those libraries

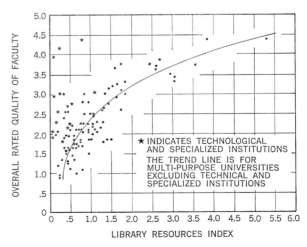

Fig. 28—Relationship of library resources index to over-all rating of quality of graduate faculty.

which fall below .5 are probably too weak to support quality graduate programs in a wide range of fields, although they may be adequate for an institution that specializes in technology or in advanced work in a very limited number of areas.

Figure 28 shows the relation between the library resources index and the over-all quality of graduate faculty (as measured by Question A). A line of best fit is drawn without regard to the specialized institutions (marked with a different symbol), where library resources are a less important factor in quality of advanced education. The correlation coefficient ($r=.794$), although not as high as in the case of faculty quality and salaries, indicates a significant relationship.

Faculty and student honors and awards

In his presidential address before the American Statistical Association in 1964, Albert Bowker, chancellor of the City University of New York,

TABLE 43: *Library Resources of 106 Universities, 1963–64, by Library Resources Index Ranges (100=average for 106 universities)*

Institution	Total Volume Index	Volumes Added Index	Periodicals Index	Over-all Library Resources Index
Harvard	7.32	5.06	3.51	5.29
California, Berkeley	2.99	3.19	5.34	3.84
Yale	4.75	3.08	2.73	3.52
U.C.L.A.	2.03	3.14	4.05	3.07
Cornell	2.60	3.52	2.96	3.03
Illinois	3.79	2.48	2.53	2.93
Stanford	2.44	2.13	3.57	2.71
Michigan	3.26	2.85	1.65	2.58
Columbia	3.49	2.16	2.11	2.58
Chicago	2.36	1.99	2.96	2.44

Over-all library index of 1.50–1.99 (9 institutions arranged alphabetically):

Johns Hopkins	Ohio State	Princeton	Washington (Seattle)
Minnesota	Pennsylvania	Texas	Wisconsin
Northwestern			

Over-all library index of 1.00–1.49 (21 institutions arranged alphabetically):

Colorado	Louisiana State	North Carolina	Rutgers
Duke	Michigan State	Oregon	Southern California
Florida	Missouri	Penn State	Utah
Indiana	N.Y.U.	Pittsburgh	Virginia
Iowa (Iowa City)	New Mexico	Purdue	Wayne State
Kansas			

Over-all library index of .75–.99 (18 institutions arranged alphabetically):

Arizona	Kentucky	Oklahoma	Tulane
Brown	M.I.T.	Rochester	Vanderbilt [a]
California, Davis	Maryland	Syracuse	Washington (St. Louis)
Connecticut	Nebraska	Tennessee	Washington State
George Peabody [a]	Notre Dame		

Over-all library index of .50–.74 (17 institutions arranged alphabetically):

Alabama [b]	Emory	Kansas State	St. Louis
Arkansas	Florida State	Oklahoma State	Temple
Boston U.	Fordham	Oregon State	West Virginia
Catholic	Georgetown	Rice	Western Reserve [b]
Cincinnati			

Over-all library index of less than .50 (31 institutions arranged alphabetically):

American	Claremont	Iowa State (Ames)	Rensselaer
Brandeis	Clark	Lehigh	Rockefeller
Brooklyn Polytech. [b]	Delaware	Loyola (Chicago)	St. John's [b]
Bryn Mawr	Denver	Massachusetts	Texas A&M
Buffalo [b]	George Washington	New School	Tufts
Cal. Tech.	Georgia Tech.	No. Carolina State	Virginia Polytech.
Carnegie Tech.	Houston	North Dakota	Wyoming
Case	Ill. Inst. of Tech. [b]		Yeshiva [b]

[a] George Peabody and Vanderbilt share the Joint University Library.

[b] Institution does not appear in Samore and Holladay (see "Source" below). Data are from institutional exhibits in Allan M. Cartter (ed.), *American Universities and Colleges* (9th ed.; Washington: American Council on Education, 1964).

Source: Theodore Samore and Doris C. Holladay, *Library Statistics of Colleges and Universities, 1963–64: Institutional Data,* U.S. Office of Education Circular No. 769 (Washington: Government Printing Office, 1965). The source indicates that not all institutions reported data on periodicals in the same way. Some included duplicates (U.C.L.A., Harvard, Oklahoma, Stanford); others, non-periodical serials (California—Davis, Princeton, Washington [Seattle], Chicago); still others reported data for 1962–63 (Yale, Northwestern, Chicago, Massachusetts). No attempt has been made to adjust the reported data.

ranked universities on the basis of a number of "indices of faculty quality and indices of attractiveness." He provided two separate rankings, one for humanities–social sciences, and one for sciences. The former was based on four factors: the number of Woodrow Wilson fellows attending an institution and the number of former Woodrow Wilson fellows, Guggenheim fellows, and American Council of Learned Societies awardees on the faculty. The science index was based on the number of National Science Foundation fellows attending an institution and the number of Nobel Prize winners and members of the National Academy of Sciences on the faculty.[2]

For purposes of comparison, Bowker's data are not ideal, since they cover a period of years preceding the American Council on Education survey. He included the numbers of Guggenheim fellows for 1961–63, A.C.L.S. awardees for 1958–63, and Woodrow Wilson fellows and former fellows as of 1961–62 in constructing his humanities–social sciences index. The science index included Nobel Prize winners in the sciences from 1940 through 1963, National Academy members in 1963, and National Science Foundation graduate fellows in 1962–63. Despite these limitations, if there have not been major shifts in the relative strength and reputation of universities over the last years (and the comparisons between the 1957 and 1964 surveys in chapter 3 did indicate some noteworthy changes), there ought to be a fairly good correlation between Bowker's indices and the A.C.E. survey scores.

Figures 29 and 30 correlate the rank order of universities in the Bowker and A.C.E. studies for the sciences and the humanities–social sciences. In general, the correlation is quite close, although in a few instances there are some fairly sizable differences. Quite apart from the accuracy of the two types of assessments, there are a number of procedural factors that account for much of the difference. First, below the top 20–30 institutions on either list, Bowker's indices are not sensitive enough to reflect quality adequately. For example, in his science list only 39 out of 48 institutions ranked had more than four NSF fellows in attendance (five was the cut-off point), only 33 had two or more members of the National Academy, and only 16 had Nobel Prize winners. Thus, below the first 25–30 institutions, the graduate schools are ranked in the sciences only on the basis of one or two of the three Bowker indices. Second, Bowker's indices favor the large institution as against the small, in that a University of California, a Columbia, or an N.Y.U., just by pure size, has a much greater chance of having more faculty

[2] See Bowker, "Rankings of Graduate Schools in the United States" (Unpublished MS, February 1964), and Bowker, "Quality and Quantity in Higher Education," *Journal of the American Statistical Association*, March 1965, pp. 1–15.

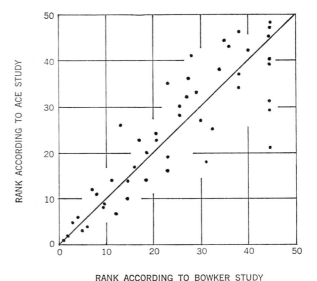

Fig. 29—Comparative ranks of universities for the sciences, 1964 A.C.E. study and the Bowker study.

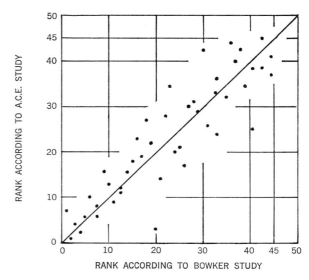

Fig. 30—Comparative ranks of universities for the social sciences—humanities, 1964 A.C.E. study and the Bowker study.

honors. The rankings used for the A.C.E. index, by contrast, are a simple average of individual departmental ratings in the sciences areas. Third, Bowker's honors in sciences include the field of medicine, and not all of the institutions among his 48 had medical schools. Fourth, the inclusion of the institutions where former Woodrow Wilson fellows now teach may be of questionable value in assessing the strength of graduate schools, for the nomination procedures in the early years of that program favored the able undergraduate who was attractive and poised and interested in a teaching career, but not necessarily the most promising scholar. In addition, most of these former fellows were too young in 1963 to be teaching graduate work, and therefore this index may reveal more about the attractiveness of the undergraduate college of the university than about its graduate school. The fact that more than 60 percent of the former Woodrow Wilson fellows were not teaching in universities on Bowker's list tends to confirm this point.

Allowing for the differences noted above and for the two- or three-year time difference between the Bowker indices and the A.C.E. survey, the two types of qualitative assessments roughly corroborate each other. Bowker's approach tends to favor the larger institutions and those situated in major urban centers such as New York and Chicago, while the 1964 A.C.E. survey gives a better ranking to the smaller and rapidly improving graduate schools. It seems likely that had Bowker included scholars noted in biographical dictionaries, volume of research grants, size of libraries, and publications records, such a combined index from many sources would have nearly duplicated the subjective appraisals provided by our questionnaire.

A speculation concerning the improvement of quality reputation

A review of the comparisons between subjective quality ratings and other variables leads to a recurring question: Is there any way to identify the universities that seem to hold the most promise of improving their relative positions in the years immediately ahead? One is tempted to make such judgments on the basis of scattered bits of information: a university's administrative leadership, its present or probable future endowment, its location in a developing region or a thriving metropolis, the state legislature's attitudes toward education. In reviewing some of the measures in this and the preceding chapters, we have searched for other common signs less impressionistic in nature. Four items emerge as possible indications of change.

First, a careful review of the detailed data in chapter 3 suggests that there is a close correlation between the rating a department receives and the degree to which it is sufficiently well known to have been judged by most respondents. In a number of cases where these two factors markedly diverge, it appears that departments which are rapidly improving were rated relatively high on reputation by those who knew the department sufficiently well to judge it, but relatively few respondents in fact judged it. The reverse (most respondents agreed a department was relatively weak) seemed common for departments widely known to have declined in quality in recent years. Thus one might postulate that where reputation for quality outstrips notoriety (using that word in its general sense of "being well known" rather than as a term of condemnation) an institution is rising in prestige, and where the reverse is true it is likely to be falling.

A second measure that may be useful in identifying improvement is the degree to which a department was rated much higher by judges from its own region than by those from other regions. Presumably those in close proximity are better informed and more immediately aware of changes in quality.

Third, it is a reasonable assumption that institutions having salary levels considerably higher than one might expect, judging from their current reputation for quality, are likely to improve their position in the near future. Thus the institutions lying far above the regression line in Figure 26, whatever their present quality position, seem likely to improve their departmental ratings and those lying far below the regression line seem likely to have their departmental ratings deteriorate.

Finally, universities having libraries superior to what might be expected on the basis of their quality reputation also seem in a good position to improve their relative standing. Thus the universities lying considerably above the fitted curve in Figure 28 seem to have better potential for improvement than those below.

The advantage of each of these four measures is that they rely not on absolute levels or scores but on an institution's showing in comparison with other institutions of about the same quality reputation. More important, because deviations from the norms are most clearly evident for institutions that are presently ranked rather low in quality, these measures may help to identify change where it is usually most difficult to observe. Perhaps these four factors are the shadows which cast themselves ahead of events. They are certainly not infallible indicators, for abrupt changes in leadership or material resources can quickly alter the path an institution will follow. But it seems reasonable that when most or all of these factors are favorable, a university's quality reputation will rise.

A few of the clearest cases could be used over a period of time as test cases to examine these conjectures. If the speculations are correct, then the institutions favorably identified will improve their relative standing by the time of the next evaluation study. It is intended that another assessment of graduate programs will be undertaken by the A.C.E. within five years; this hypothesis is bequeathed to our successors for empirical testing.

VI · *Conclusion*

THE ANALYSIS OF OBJECTIVE MEASURES given in chapters 4 and 5 tends to corroborate the findings of the subjective assessments reported in chapter 3. Departmental strength is directly associated with quantity of publication performance and with academic salaries in the upper two professional ranks. Divisional strength, as measured by the divisional averages of departments from chapter 3, correlates closely with Bowker's "objective" indices. Over-all university strength, as represented by average scores on the 1964 A.C.E. survey, is closely associated with university salary levels and library resources. If these measures reflect the constituent elements that make up the quality of an institution, it is not surprising that they support one another. It seems likely that if one were to include enough factors in constructing a so-called objective index —allowing for variations in institutional size and a university's commitments to certain fields of study —the results of our subjective assessment would be almost exactly duplicated.

The type of study reported in these pages has two or three particular advantages. First, the study is based on departmental units rather than on university-wide assessments. While the former, when aggregated, may give approximately the same results for the university as a whole, the latter conceal the considerable diversity within an institution. For example, it may be useful to know that engineering at New Hope U. and classics at the University of Massissota are not up to the high level of quality of the institution as a whole. Information on salaries, library resources, research grants, fellowship funds, and so on are seldom available for individual departments, and thus a survey such as the present one is the only means of assessing departmental strength. In the case of the less well-known, newer, or smaller university, a measure based on departmental units also permits an outstanding department in such a university to receive the attention and acclaim that it deserves. University-wide measures always penalize the good department in the medium-quality institution; our survey has attempted to highlight its achievements.

Second, a well-designed opinion survey, although it may be subject to some time lag, is likely to be much more up to date than the traditional objective measures. Universities can live on their reputations much more successfully and for longer periods than can most business firms. A university may continue to attract Woodrow Wilson fellows, to retain a Nobel laureate or two, to expand its library, and to raise faculty salaries, and yet be declining in quality either relatively or absolutely. The reverse is also true: a university which is making rapid strides may find its reputation lagging by a decade or two. As nearly as one can tell from the few notable instances where departments have markedly improved or declined in recent years, the present study seems to be subject to a lag of only one to three years.

Finally, a qualitative study based on departmental rather than on university-wide reputation serves many practical purposes. It little helps presidents, deans, and department chairmen to be told that their university ranks seventh, or seventeenth, or fifty-seventh in over-all standing; it may help them a great deal to have a rough indication of how the outside world views their relative strength in each of several disciplines. Department chairmen are fond of telling deans, deans of telling presidents, and presidents of telling trustees, how eminent or how much in need of additional support they are in certain areas. The present study does not pretend to reflect all aspects of eminence or its absence, but it provides an approximate view by one hundred or more dispassionate judges who are not on the university's own payroll. The first step in the improvement of an institution is self-knowledge; such knowledge can be extremely useful even though it may not be flattering. Each president and graduate dean of the 106 institutions included in the survey has received a confidential report about his university; it is hoped that this information will be useful in strengthening graduate education across the country.

The expansion of graduate education

Graduate education in the arts and sciences has expanded during every decade since the granting of the first earned doctorate in the United States in 1861. Although the pace has been uneven, three periods of rapid growth stand out. The first was roughly from 1921 to 1931, when the number of doctorates granted annually rose dramatically from 650 to 2,500. At the beginning of the decade fewer than 60 universities were awarding the highest degree; by 1931 another 18 universities had become major contributors.

The second period of rapid expansion followed World War II. Earned doctorates fell from an annual pre-war level of slightly over 3,000 to less than 2,000 in 1946; by 1954 this number soared to 9,000. Nearly two dozen newcomers were added to the doctorate-granting ranks, although the major expansion occurred within older universities.

The third period of rapid growth is today, and we shall probably look back in a few years and identify 1962–72 as a decade of great vigor. At the beginning of this period the annual rate of earned doctorates was 11,500 ; at the conclusion it should be 25,000–30,000. Nearly 50 universities which offered their first doctorate in the last ten years promise to become major producers, and approximately ten additions to the list of doctorate-granting institutions are being made each year.

As was indicated in chapter 1, studies by the Commission on Plans and Objectives which project the demand for doctorates on college and university faculties indicate that if the quality of faculty is simply maintained (that is, if the ratio of college teachers with the doctorate to total college teachers remains constant), the peak demand is likely to be in 1966–67 when about 13,000 new doctorates will be required.[1] After 1967, however, the annual additions required are likely to diminish as the rate of increase in total enrollment declines. Continuing the "constant quality" assumption, annual requirements would drop to less than 10,000 per year during 1980-85. Thus, with a continued rise in the number of doctorates awarded annually, the quality of college faculties will, in all likelihood, show a rapid improvement during the decade of the 1970's.

The expansion in doctorate production that has occurred in the last few years can be attributed to a considerable extent to the expansion of fellowship aid in the late 1950's—the enlargement of the National Science Foundation and Woodrow Wilson programs and the inauguration of the NDEA titles IV and VI programs. Today's doctorates, however, are from the baccalaureate classes of the late 1950's, which were relatively constant in size. The rapid rise in baccalaureate degrees that started around 1962 is now beginning to show itself in graduate enrollment figures, and the present flood of undergraduates will hit the graduate and professional schools by 1970. Enrollment estimates for graduate schools predict an expansion from 315,000 students in 1960 to approximately 1 million by 1975.[2] If these trends continue, there will be as many students in graduate school by the end of the century as there were undergraduates in college in the 1940's. Assuredly

the world of higher education will be much altered by the end of the century as a result of these dramatic increases in enrollments. One can face the future with something approaching equanimity only if one has a firm belief in Say's Law.[3]

Until World War II graduate education was dominated by a few large universities. The leading 15 universities in Keniston's survey in 1957 awarded 75 percent of all the doctorates in 1925, 59 percent in 1934, and 49 percent in 1950; they award less than 40 percent today. If these universities double the number of degrees awarded over the next fifteen years (and they have expanded less than one-third over the past fifteen years), they will account for less than 20 percent in 1980. Thus, the old prestigious universities are rapidly losing their dominant numerical position, and in many areas they are being challenged qualitatively as well. Table 44 groups 105 universities in the 1964 survey (omitting the Rockefeller Institute) according to present over-all quality and traces their degree history back four decades. The top ten now award little more than a quarter of the doctorates, as opposed to nearly 45 percent forty years ago. The share of the next 15 (only 12 of which were awarding the doctorate in the 1920's) has declined from 32 percent to 26 percent. The 25 in the third group have increased their share of the total from one-eighth to one-fifth, and the bottom group, enlarged from 26 to 55 universities over forty-three years, has expanded particularly rapidly since 1950.

Table 45 presents the same information in absolute numbers, showing the average number of doctorates awarded annually. The giants among the Ph.D. producers award several hundred degrees each year (the largest in 1962–63 were Columbia [517], Illinois [450], Harvard [446], Wisconsin [428], and Berkeley [418]), but these figures are only a small fraction of the number of baccalaureate degrees most of these institutions award. To maintain an internal balance of interests, most universities will not permit graduate enrollment to make up more than one-third to one-half of total enrollment; thus, unless a group of purely graduate universities is developed, on the model of the early Johns Hopkins and Chicago experiments, the greatest expansion in future years will have to come from the smaller and newer graduate schools.

The 106 universities in our survey awarded well over 90 percent of the doctorates in the arts and

---

[1] See A. M. Cartter, "The Supply and Demand of College Teachers," *Proceedings,* American Statistical Association, September 1965, pp. 70–80.

[2] See A. M. Cartter and R. Farrell, "Higher Education in the Last Third of the Century," *Educational Record,* Spring 1965, pp. 119–28.

[3] Jean Baptiste Say, the eighteenth-century French political economist, argued that supply creates its own demand. It is some comfort to recall that fifty years ago, when free education was extended to the twelfth grade, the nation was worrying about where all the jobs would come from to employ high school graduates. And less than twenty years ago many observers were gravely concerned about the nation's capacity to absorb the graduates of a collegiate system that attempted to educate 20 percent of its youth beyond the high school.

TABLE 44: *Earned Doctorates*[a] *Awarded by Institutions, Grouped by 1964 Faculty Quality Rating, Percentage Distribution, 1920–62*

INSTITUTIONS, BY FACULTY QUALITY GROUP	PERCENT DISTRIBUTION				
	1960–62	1950–59	1940–49	1930–39	1920–29
"Top 10"..	27	29	35	38	44
"Next 15"..	26	28	29	30	32
Number of institutions awarding Ph.D. in period indicated....	*15*	*15*	*14*	*13*	*12*
"Next 25"..	21	22	20	19	13
Number of institutions awarding Ph.D. in period indicated....	*25*	*25*	*24*	*21*	*20*
"Next 55"..	21	19	14	12	10
Number of institutions awarding Ph.D. in period indicated....	*55*	*54*	*49*	*39*	*26*
All institutions in 1964 survey............................	95	98	98	99	99
Number of institutions awarding Ph.D. in period indicated....	*105*	*104*	*97*	*83*	*68*
Total number of earned doctorates...........................	*26,793*	*68,813*	*25,817*	*22,482*	*10,743*

[a] Doctorates in education have been excluded.

Source: Percentages for 1960–62 calculated from data in Allan M. Cartter (ed.), *American Universities and Colleges* (9th ed.; Washington: American Council on Education, 1964), and Wayne E. Tolliver, *Earned Degrees Conferred, 1959–60, 1960–61, 1961–62*, U.S. Office of Education Circulars 687 721, and 719 respectively (Washington: Government Printing Office, 1962, 1963).

Percentages for 1920–59 calculated from data in Lindsey R. Harmon and Herbert Soldz (compilers), *Doctorate Production in United States Universities, 1920–62*, NAS–NRC Publication No. 1142 (Washington: National Academy of Sciences—National Research Council, 1963).

sciences over the last decade, but they are likely to account for not much more than half by 1980. By that year, if present trends continue, probably another two hundred institutions will have joined the class awarding an average of ten per year, and another hundred will grant some doctorates in selected fields. Some of these institutions already have small programs, and many more that do not now offer work beyond the master's degree level will aspire to full university status in the years immediately ahead. Some observers have noted that the range of quality from the best to the poorest graduate schools is widening and that the gap is likely to become greater with each passing year. Studies such as the present one, perhaps superfluous a generation ago when the world of higher education was relatively small and most scholars knew their colleagues at other institutions, may therefore become increasingly useful in the future.

Even ten years ago the Association of American Universities, then 39 strong, and its Association of Graduate Schools, could claim to represent the largest and strongest universities in the country. Today, with 40 member institutions in the United States, A.A.U.-A.G.S. encompasses universities which today produce two-thirds of the doctoral degrees, but it cannot be said to include all of the strongest universities. Nine of the first 40 universities in over-all reputation, as judged by average faculty quality ratings in the 1964 study, are not members of the A.A.U.-A.G.S. and several current members were not judged to be among the top half (53) of the universities in the A.C.E study sample.

Partly as a result of the restricted membership of A.A.U.-A.G.S., the Council of Graduate Schools in the United States was formed in 1961. Beginning with 100 major doctorate producers (all included in this study), it has now expanded to include nearly 250 institutions, some of which do not grant the doctorate. While the A.G.S. may be too restricted to be as influential in setting standards as it once was, C.G.S. faces the danger of being too large. It has made an admirable start, but it

TABLE 45: *Average Annual Doctorate*[a] *Production by Universities, Grouped by 1964 Faculty Quality Rating, 1920–62*

INSTITUTIONS, BY FACULTY QUALITY GROUP	ANNUAL AVERAGE NUMBER OF DOCTORATES AWARDED PER INSTITUTION				
	1960–62	1950–59	1940–49	1930–39	1920–29
"Top 10".................	237	199	90	85	48
"Next 15".................	154	126	54	51	29
"Next 25".................	76	62	21	20	7
"Next 55".................	34	25	8	7	4
All institutions in 1964 survey.	80	65	26	27	16

[a] Doctorates in education have been excluded.

Source: Same as for Table 44.

may run the risk of losing its effectiveness if it speaks only for its most "representative" members.

Evaluative information, such as that presented in this study, will be little more than a curiosity unless the stronger graduate schools and the associations representing university presidents and deans take the initiative both in setting standards and in helping the smaller and weaker institutions to live up to those standards. It is hoped that this and successive surveys to be undertaken at approximately five-year intervals will be of value to these groups in their attempts to strengthen graduate education, and thereby to invigorate all of American higher education.

Appendix A · *Doctoral Programs in Linguistics*

THE DEVELOPMENT OF LINGUISTICS as a formal degree program at the doctorate level is relatively recent. In the 1957–63 period only 268 doctorates were awarded—an average of less than 40 per year. However, when small panels were being created for the four disciplines reviewed in chapter 4, it was decided to assemble a similar panel in linguistics. With the advice of the Center for Applied Linguistics and the Conference Board of the Associated Research Councils, a panel of 13 experts was invited to rate doctorate programs.

The panel, consisting of distinguished members of this new discipline, included past and present officers of related professional associations, journal editors, distinguished academic scholars, and one research consultant to industry. Five were from the East, five from the Midwest, two from the West Coast, and one from the South.

The panel received the same form of questionnaire distributed to respondents for the other 30 disciplines, and 26 institutions were listed. This list included all of the doctorate-granting departments of linguistics, three formal programs offered by departments other than linguistics,[1] and two programs offered by a formal interdepartmental committee.[2] Excluded were eight institutions reporting dissertations written on a linguistic topic in the 1957–63 period but supervised by some other department,[3] and six institutions where programs in linguistics were in the early development stage.[4]

Table 46 summarizes the ratings shown by the panel of 13 experts. Column 1 shows the rank of the

[1] At M.I.T. (Department of Modern Languages), State University of New York at Buffalo (Department of Modern Languages and Literature), and at the Hartford Seminary Foundation (Department of Cultural Disciplines).

[2] At U.C.L.A. and at Princeton.

[3] Bryn Mawr, Catholic, Florida State, George Peabody, Michigan State, Tulane, Vanderbilt, and Western Reserve. See *Dissertations in Linguistics, 1957–64* (Washington: Center for Applied Linguistics, November 1965).

[4] Hawaii, Minnesota, Pittsburgh, Rochester, Southern California, and Stanford.

"Distinguished" and "Strong" programs on Question A (quality of graduate faculty); column 2, the rank on Question B (effectiveness of doctoral program); and column 3 indicates the number of doctorates awarded in the 1960–64 period.[5]

The review in chapter 4 of the ratings by experts panels in four disciplines indicated some significant differences between the ratings by small panels and larger sample universes. Accordingly, the ratings in linguistics should be judged with some caution.

[5] See institutional exhibits in Jane Graham (ed.), *A Guide to Graduate Study: Programs Leading to the Ph.D. Degree* (3d.; Washington: American Council on Education, 1965).

TABLE 46: *Rankings of Programs in Linguistics*

Institution	Quality of Faculty	Effectiveness of Program	Doctorates Awarded, 1960–64
"Distinguished" and "Strong"			
M.I.T.	1	2*	2
Yale	2	2*	9
Cornell	3	1	21
California, Berkeley	4	9*	11
Chicago	5	4	4
Indiana	6	6	28
Harvard	7	9*	15
Pennsylvania	8	7*	6
U.C.L.A.	9	7*	(a)
Michigan	10	5	27
Texas	11	11*	27
Columbia	12	13*	11
"Adequate plus" (alphabetical order):			
Brown			1
Buffalo			(a)
Hartford Seminary Foundation			(a)
Illinois			(a)
Princeton		11*	(a)
Washington (Seattle)		13*	1
Wisconsin			3

* Rank shared with another department.
a None reported in Jane Graham (ed.), *A Guide to Graduate Study* (3d.; Washington: American Council on Education, 1965).

Appendix B · *Note on Departments of Russian*

THE ORIGINAL PLAN of this survey included coverage of Russian language and literature programs, and a questionnaire was prepared and mailed to selected respondents. However, upon review, it appeared that the results were too incomplete to include in the main body of the survey report.

The list of doctorate-granting departments was prepared in the same manner used for other fields of study. However, only nine separately identifiable departments appeared in the Office of Education reports of doctoral degrees granted in the 1953–62 period. Ratings were obtained of these nine departments from 43 respondents, but it appeared that a number of major graduate programs had been omitted. Degrees in Russian language and literature are frequently awarded in departments of modern languages, Slavic languages, in combination with various languages, or in foreign area study programs, and are not properly reported in annual degree reports. Some respondents wrote in additional programs, but because the coverage was clearly incomplete, it was decided to omit these ratings.

Among those departments listed on our questionnaire form, Harvard, California (Berkeley), and Columbia were rated highly by the 43 respondents (only 60 percent usable responses), and Michigan and Indiana were indicated as strong departments. In a number of cases, omission from this listing reflects the failure to include the institution on the questionnaire.

Appendix C · Reliability of Departmental Ratings

By ALEXANDER W. ASTIN

Director, Office of Research, American Council on Education

AN IMPORTANT CONSIDERATION in utilizing ratings of the kind presented in the foregoing chapters is the extent to which obtained differences between mean ratings of departments in a given field can be relied upon. (In psychological test theory, this is the problem of "reliability" of the measuring instrument.) In order to estimate the reliability of mean ratings of the departments, raters in each of the 30 fields [1] were divided into two groups ("odds" and

[1] For the purposes of this appendix, Russian was included, making a total of 30 fields of study. See Appendix B, "Note on Departments of Russian."

TABLE 47: *Split-Half Reliability of Departmental Ratings*

Field	Split-Half Reliability (uncorrected) r	Split-Half Reliability (corrected) $\dfrac{2r}{1+r}$
Classics	.98	.99
English	.99	.99
French	.98	.99
German	.99	.99
Philosophy	.99	.99
Russian ($N=8$)	.96	.98
Spanish	.98	.99
Anthropology	.99	.99
Economics	.99	.99
Geography	.99	.99
History	.99	.99
Political science	.99	.99
Sociology	.99	.99
Bacteriology	.97	.98
Biochemistry	.98	.99
Botany	.97	.98
Entomology	.98	.99
Pharmocology	.94	.97
Physiology	.95	.97
Psychology	.99	.99
Zoology	.98	.99
Astronomy	.97	.98
Chemistry	.99	.99
Geology	.99	.99
Mathematics	.99	.99
Physics	.99	.99
Chemical engineering	.98	.99
Civil engineering	.96	.98
Electrical engineering	.96	.98
Mechanical engineering	.97	.98
Median	.98	.99

"evens"), using the unit position of an arbitrary identification number that had been assigned earlier to each rater. Mean ratings were then computed separately for the odds and evens. The independent pairs of ratings for each field were then correlated with each other.

The resulting correlations ("split-half" estimates of reliability) are shown in the first column of Table 47. The second column shows the same coefficients corrected by means of the Spearman-Brown formula. This correction yields estimates of the reliability of the mean ratings based on all, rather than half, of the judges. Without exception, the mean ratings of departments in each field show an extraordinarily high degree of reliability. The uncorrected estimates for the 30 fields range from .94 to .99, with a median uncorrected reliability of .98. The median corrected reliability estimate is .99. Clearly, even very small differences between mean ratings of departments are

TABLE 48: *Correlation Among Quality Ratings in Different Fields*

Field	Number of Correlations with Other 29 Fields Greater Than .70	Number of Correlations with Other 29 Fields Greater Than .80
Zoology	24	12
History	24	12
Political science	23	11
Chemistry	23	11
Economics	22	14
English	21	15
Mathematics	21	9
Physics	21	10
Psychology	20	10
Entomology	19	6
Bacteriology	18	5
Sociology	18	7
Geology	17	2
Philosophy	17	11
French	16	8
German	16	7
Biochemistry	16	5
Electrical engineering	15	3
Mechanical engineering	14	3
Russian	12	3
Spanish	12	4
Astronomy	11	1
Physiology	10	3
Chemical engineering	8	—
Botany	8	1
Classics	4	1
Civil engineering	3	1
Anthropology	1	—
Pharmocology	—	—
Geography	—	—

meaningful. Although the standard error of measurement varies slightly from field to field, these results suggest the following general rule of thumb for interpreting any department's mean rating: the chances that a new mean rating obtained from an independent set of judges would fall within 0.4 points of the current rating are better than 99 in 100. More conservatively, the chances are better than 4 in 5 that the new mean rating will be within 0.2 points of the current rating. The reliability of differences among top-ranked institutions would tend to be even higher, since there was relatively more disagreement among the judges on the comparative quality of the lowest-ranked institutions.

Currently in progress by the Office of Research of the American Council on Education are several studies based on the intercorrelations of the mean ratings of the 30 fields. Although the preliminary results from these analyses suggest the existence of an over-all "graduate quality" factor, there are distinct differences among some of the fields in terms of their relative rankings from one institution to another. Table 48 lists the 30 fields in order of the number of correlations with the other 29 fields that exceeded .70. The last column of the table shows the number of correlations with the other 29 fields that exceeded .80. These results indicate that the mean rating for any one of at least six of the fields—zoology, history, political science, chemistry, economics, or English— would provide a relatively accurate estimate of the over-all quality of an institution's graduate programs. However, several of the fields—notably geography, pharmacology, and anthropology—share relatively little in common with the other fields. In general, the quality ratings for these fields would not be accurately reflected in any single measure of over-all quality.

Appendix D · *The Questionnaire*

ON THE FOLLOWING pages are reproduced the questionnaire shells and the survey description which was furnished all participants. All questionnaires had the same first page, which gathered biographic and academic information concerning the respondents. Page two carried the three questions and listed the departments to be rated. Questionnaires for all fields in which 33 or fewer departments were to be rated consisted of just these two pages. Questionnaires for fields with more than 33 departments included a third page on which the remaining departments were shown. The third page displayed the same columnar arrangement as page two but had abbreviated column headings.

Questionnaires for the biological sciences carried a note apprising participants of the problem of identifying all the departments and requesting the addition of any unlisted departments that awarded the doctorate in the field.

RETURN BY APRIL 25, 1964 TO:
SURVEY OF GRADUATE EDUCATION
American Council on Education
1785 Massachusetts Ave., N.W.
Washington, D.C. 20036

Commission on Plans and Objectives for Higher Education
SURVEY OF GRADUATE EDUCATION

PART I – ACADEMIC AND BIOGRAPHIC DATA

ALL RESPONDENTS: Please complete each item in this part.

1. Year and institution of each earned degree.				2. Present academic rank and title.		
Degree	Year of award	Awarding institution				
BA or BS						
MA or MS				3. Age at last birthday_____		4. Sex _____
PhD				5. Have you ever served as department chairman for over one year?		
Other				_____Yes		_____No

6. How many professional meetings in your field have you attended in the last 4 years? _____National meetings _____Regional meetings	7. How many articles and books have you published since the award of your highest degree? (Exclude book reviews.) _____Articles _____Books

8. In the blocks below, show: (A) the actual division of the time you spend on professional activities during the academic year, and (B) what you consider to be the ideal division of your time as a university professor.

Type of Activity	A	B
	Actual percent of time	Ideal percent of time
1. Undergraduate instruction and classroom preparation.		
2. Graduate instruction and preparation (including directing research of advance degree students).		
3. Research and writing.		
4. Academic administration.		
5. Professional activities outside the university (e.g., consulting, speaking, attending conferences, etc.)		
6. Other. Specify.		
Total	100%	100%

UPON COMPLETION OF EACH OF THE ABOVE ITEMS, CONTINUE ON PAGE 2.

SURVEY OF GRADUATE EDUCATION

PART II – INSTITUTIONAL EVALUATION

Please check the relevant boxes in each section below to indicate:
- A. Your judgment of the quality of the graduate faculty in your field in each institution,
- B. Your rating of the doctoral training program in your field at each institution,
- C. Your estimate of the changes in the relative standing of departments in your field likely to take place in the near future.

A	B	C
Which of the terms below best describe your judgment of the quality of the graduate faculty in your field at each institution listed? Consider only the scholarly competence and achievements of the present faculty. Limit the number of "Distinguished" ratings to no more than 5.	How would you rate the institutions below if you were selecting a graduate school to work for a doctorate in your field today? Take into account the accessibility of faculty and their scholarly competence, curricula, educational & research facilities, the quality of graduate students and other factors which contribute to the effectiveness of the doctoral program.	What change in relative positions of dep'ts in your field do you anticipate in the next 5-10 years? Base your judgment on administrative leadership, quality of younger staff, and the general environment at each institution. Assume continuation of present trends in financial support.

Distinguished	Strong	Good	Adequate	Marginal	Not sufficient to provide acceptable doctoral training	Insufficient information	Extremely attractive	Attractive	Acceptable	Not attractive	Insufficient information	FIELD OF STUDY: INSTITUTIONS: By State & alphabetically within each State.	Relative IMPROVEMENT	SAME relative position	Relative DECLINE	Insufficient information
1	2	3	4	5	6	7	1	2	3	4	5		1	2	3	4

SURVEY OF GRADUATE EDUCATION
by the
Commission on Plans and Objectives for Higher Education
American Council on Education

The Commission is undertaking a study of the evolving character, structure, and functions of American universities, concentrating on developments over the last twenty-five years and likely future growth. The initial stage of the study will be focussed on graduate education; later stages will be devoted to the impact of the expanding research function, the relationship of the professional schools to the arts and sciences, the role of the undergraduate college in the large multipurpose university, growing international commitments, and internal aspects of administration, organization, and finance.

The first phase of the study of graduate education is concentrating on graduate fellowship patterns, and on qualitative aspects of doctoral programs. The attached questionnaire deals with the last-named, and the nature of the questionnaire sample is briefly summarized below for your information.

Institutions: Included in the study are the original 100 charter institutions of the Council of Graduate Schools in the United States, plus 6 additional institutions which granted more than 100 doctorates during the 1953-62 decade.

Academic Fields: Included are thirty major academic disciplines, in which doctorates are commonly awarded in American universities. The fields account for approximately three-quarters of all doctorates awarded, and have been selected to provide comparisons with earlier studies in 1925, 1934, and 1957. The number of institutions granting the doctorate varies from a low of 9 in Russian to a high of 96 in Chemistry.

Questionnaire Respondents: Graduate Deans were requested to suggest names of knowledgeable respondents in the various academic fields at each institution. Four respondents have been selected in departments which accounted for more than 2% of the doctorates in that field over the past decade; three respondents in departments which accounted for .5% to 1.9% of doctorates; two respondents in departments granting fewer than .5% of doctorates; and one respondent in departments offering graduate work but not granting the doctorate. The total number of questionnaires being sent out is approximately 5,000, about 30% going to department chairmen, 40% to other senior scholars, and 30% to junior scholars not more than 10 years past the completion of their doctoral studies.

Analysis of Returns: Questionnaire returns will be analyzed so as to determine how age, rank, administrative responsibility, institution where doctorate obtained, and present employment affects evaluations. Comparisons of the large sample will be made with smaller samples in some fields— e.g. smaller samples drawn from officers of professional associations, editors of major professional journals, members of advisory panels for foundation and government agencies, chairmen of departments in outstanding liberal arts colleges, etc. Particular attention will be given to regional returns, comparing regional views with those of the rest of the country. Summary results, grouping the leading institutions in three or four broad categories, will be published at a later date. More detailed information concerning their own institution will be made available to Deans and Department Chairmen on a confidential basis at their request.

Direction of the Study: The study is under the staff direction of Allan Cartter, Vice-President of the American Council on Education. The Commission Chairman is President O. Meredith Wilson, University of Minnesota. Serving on the Advisory Committee for the study are:

BERNARD BERELSON, Vice-President, The Population Council
BRYCE CRAWFORD, JR., Dean of the Graduate School, University of Minnesota
JOSEPH MCCARTHY, Dean of the Graduate School, University of Washington
GORDON N. RAY, President, John Simon Guggenheim Memorial Foundation
W. CLARKE WESCOE, Chancellor, University of Kansas

Appendix E · *Institutions Included in 1964 Survey*

FOR CONVENIENCE, in both the text and tables of this report, the names of institutions have been used in abbreviated form. Also a number of the analyses have been based on regional groupings. In the list below, the abbreviated name and regional symbol (E, East; S, South; M, Midwest; W, West) are given for each institution included in the survey.

Abbreviated Name	*Region*	*Full Name and State*
Alabama	S	University of Alabama
American	E	American University (D.C.)
Arizona	W	University of Arizona
Arkansas	S	University of Arkansas
Boston U.	E	Boston University (Mass.)
Brandeis	E	Brandeis University (Mass.)
Brooklyn Polytech.	E	Polytechnic Institute of Brooklyn (N.Y.)
Brown	E	Brown University (R.I.)
Bryn Mawr	E	Bryn Mawr College (Pa.)
Buffalo	E	State University of New York at Buffalo
California, Berkeley	W	University of California, Berkeley
California, Davis	W	University of California, Davis
Cal. Tech.	W	California Institute of Technology
Carnegie Tech.	E	Carnegie Institute of Technology (Pa.)
Case	M	Case Institute of Technology (Ohio)
Catholic	E	Catholic University of America (D.C.)
Chicago	M	University of Chicago (Ill.)
Cincinnati	M	University of Cincinnati (Ohio)
Claremont	W	Claremont Graduate School and University Center (Calif.)
Clark	E	Clark University (Mass.)
Colorado	W	University of Colorado
Columbia	E	Columbia University (N.Y.)
Connecticut	E	University of Connecticut
Cornell	E	Cornell University (N.Y.)
Delaware	E	University of Delaware
Denver	W	University of Denver (Colo.)
Duke	S	Duke University (N.C.)
Emory	S	Emory University (Ga.)
Florida	S	University of Florida
Florida State	S	Florida State University
Fordham	E	Fordham University (N.Y.)
George Peabody	S	George Peabody College for Teachers (Tenn.)
George Washington	E	George Washington University (D.C.)
Georgetown	E	Georgetown University (D.C.)
Georgia Tech.	S	Georgia Institute of Technology
Harvard	E	Harvard University (Mass.)
Houston	S	University of Houston (Texas)
Illinois	M	University of Illinois
Ill. Inst. of Tech.	M	Illinois Institute of Technology
Indiana	M	Indiana University
Iowa (Iowa City)	M	University of Iowa
Iowa State (Ames)	M	Iowa State University

Abbreviated Name	Region	*Full Name and State*
Johns Hopkins	E	Johns Hopkins University (Md.)
Kansas	M	University of Kansas
Kansas State	M	Kansas State University
Kentucky	S	University of Kentucky
Lehigh	E	Lehigh University (Pa.)
Louisiana State	S	Louisiana State University
Loyola (Chicago)	M	Loyola University (Ill.)
M.I.T.	E	Massachusetts Institute of Technology
Maryland	E	University of Maryland
Massachusetts	E	University of Massachusetts
Michigan	M	University of Michigan
Michigan State	M	Michigan State University
Minnesota	M	University of Minnesota
Missouri	M	University of Missouri
N.Y.U.	E	New York University
Nebraska	M	University of Nebraska
New Mexico	W	University of New Mexico
New School	E	New School for Social Research (N.Y.)
North Carolina	S	University of North Carolina at Chapel Hill
No. Carolina State	S	North Carolina State University at Raleigh
North Dakota	M	University of North Dakota
Northwestern	M	Northwestern University (Ill.)
Notre Dame	M	University of Notre Dame (Ind.)
Ohio State	M	Ohio State University
Oklahoma	S	University of Oklahoma
Oklahoma State	S	Oklahoma State University
Oregon	W	University of Oregon
Oregon State	W	Oregon State University
Pennsylvania	E	University of Pennsylvania
Penn. State	E	Pennsylvania State University
Pittsburgh	E	University of Pittsburgh (Pa.)
Princeton	E	Princeton University (N.J.)
Purdue	M	Purdue University (Ind.)
Rensselaer	E	Rensselaer Polytechnic Institute (N.Y.)
Rice	S	Rice University (Texas)
Rochester	E	University of Rochester (N.Y.)
Rockefeller Inst.	E	Rockefeller Institute (N.Y.) [1]
Rutgers	E	Rutgers—The State University (N.J.)
St. John's	E	St. John's University (N.Y.)
St. Louis	M	Saint Louis University (Mo.)
Southern California	W	University of Southern California
Stanford	W	Stanford University (Calif.)
Syracuse	E	Syracuse University (N.Y.)
Temple	E	Temple University (Pa.)
Tennessee	S	University of Tennessee
Texas	S	University of Texas
Texas A&M	S	Texas A&M University
Tufts	E	Tufts University (Mass.)
Tulane	S	Tulane University (La.)
U.C.L.A.	W	University of California, Los Angeles
Utah	W	University of Utah
Vanderbilt	S	Vanderbilt University (Tenn.)
Virginia	S	University of Virginia
Virginia Polytech.	S	Virginia Polytechnic Institute
Washington (St. Louis)	M	Washington University (Mo.)
Washington (Seattle)	W	University of Washington
Washington State	W	Washington State University
Wayne State	M	Wayne State University (Mich.)

[1] Name changed to Rockefeller University in the spring of 1965.

Abbreviated Name	*Region*	*Full Name and State*
West Virginia	S	West Virginia University
Western Reserve	M	Western Reserve University (Ohio)
Wisconsin	M	University of Wisconsin
Wyoming	W	University of Wyoming
Yale	E	Yale University (Conn.)
Yeshiva	E	Yeshiva University (N.Y.)

AMERICAN COUNCIL ON EDUCATION

LOGAN WILSON, *President*

The American Council on Education, founded in 1918, is a *council* of educational organizations and institutions. Its purpose is to advance education and educational methods through comprehensive voluntary and cooperative action on the part of American educational associations, organizations, and institutions.